In *The Spectator and the City in Nineteenth-Century American Literature*, Dana Brand traces the development of the English language tradition of the *flâneur*, a detached, casual, yet powerful urban spectator who regards the metropolis as an entertaining spectacle and text. Brand refutes the common assumption that the *flâneur* originated in Paris in the early nineteenth century and shows how the development of this quintessentially modern figure began in London at least as early as the seventeenth century. After discussing the evolution of the *flâneur* in relation to its social, cultural, and historical contexts, he goes on to suggest that the English tradition of the *flâneur* had a significant influence on American literature and urban culture in the nineteenth century. Examining the encounter between spectators and city life in the works of Poe, Hawthorne, and Whitman, Brand offers new readings of their work, as well as a new perspective on such issues as Poe's invention of the detective story, Hawthorne's complex fascination with cities and modern life, and Whitman's effort to develop a new kind of urban poetry. Brand considers and compares the efforts of these authors to engage modernity and to develop new literary forms adequate to the representation of urban life. He suggests that, contrary to what is often assumed, American writers in the middle years of the nineteenth century were as concerned as their European contemporaries with the question of what the modern city might do to the imagination and what the imagination might in turn do with the modern city.

The Spectator and the City in
Nineteenth-Century American Literature

For Sheila

The Spectator and the City in Nineteenth-Century American Literature

DANA BRAND

Hofstra University

The right of the
University of Cambridge
to print and sell
all manner of books
was granted by
Henry VIII in 1534.
The University has printed
and published continuously
since 1584.

CAMBRIDGE UNIVERSITY PRESS

Cambridge

New York   Port Chester   Melbourne   Sydney

Published by the Press Syndicate of the University of Cambridge
The Pitt Building, Trumpington Street, Cambridge CB2 1RP
40 West 20th Street, New York, NY 10011, USA
10 Stamford Road, Oakleigh, Melbourne 3166, Australia

First published 1991

Printed in the United States of America

Library of Congress Cataloging-in-Publication Data
Brand, Dana.
The spectator and the city in nineteenth-century American literature /
Dana Brand
p.   cm.
Includes bibliographical references (p.   ).
ISBN 0-521-36207-5 (hardcover)
1. American literature – 19th century – History and criticism.
2. City and town life in literature.   3. Cities and towns in
literature.   4. Flaneurs in literature.   I. Title.
PS217.C57B73   1991
810.9'321732'09034 – dc20   91-9991
                                                                     CIP

British Library Cataloguing in Publication Data
Brand, Dana
The spectator and the city in nineteenth-century American
literature.
1. United States. English literature, 1830–1900.
Hawthorne, Nathaniel, 1804–1864.   Poe, Edgar Allan, 1809–
1849.   Whitman, Walt, 1819–1892
I. Title
810.9003

ISBN 0-521-36207-5 hardback

Contents

Acknowledgments

For reading all or part of this manuscript at various stages, I wish to thank Wai-Chee Dimock, J. Hillis Miller, Geoffrey Sill, David Weimer, and Allon White. For useful suggestions and references, I am grateful to Richard Brodhead, Charles Feidelson, Carl Freedman, Jonathan Freedman, John McClure, Deborah Nord, Fred Pfeil, Bruce Robbins, and William Sharpe. I am extremely grateful to my readers at Cambridge University Press, as well as to those who were involved in editing this manuscript: Liz McGuire, Julie Greenblatt, Melinda Mousouris, and Brian MacDonald. I wish to thank the Metropolitan Museum of Art for granting permission to use the print that appears on the cover of this volume.

I owe a great debt to my parents, Leonard and Helen Brand, who first introduced me to the paradoxical pleasures of exploring cities. My greatest debt is to my wife, Sheila Fisher, to whom this book is dedicated. Her intellectual companionship, editorial acumen, and brilliance as an urban spectator have been vital to this book. Without her love and support, it would not have been written.

Chapter 1

The Flaneur and Modernity

Any discussion of modernity depends upon arbitrary definitions, arbitrary distinctions, and highly tentative and qualified generalizations. Any definition of modernity implies controversial assumptions about historical development and consistency. It implies that there are "characteristic" features that distinguish an arbitrarily designated time frame from earlier ones. This act of distinction and definition involves an impressive array of epistemological problems. It is impossible to establish, first of all, whether any experience is characteristically modern. How is it possible to study the "modern" experience of the crowd, if we have no clear understanding of the way in which crowds were experienced in earlier centuries? The use of the word *modernity* may also distort and confuse cultural inquiry by implying connections, which may not exist and may not be demonstrable, between all of the cultural phenomena that are peculiar to the modern period. The development of the railroad and the decline of the influence of religion may both be considered part of modernity, but does this then mean that they are related and if so, how is it possible to formulate the relation? By reifying the distinction between modern and premodern experience, the idea of modernity also tends to simplify and distort the character of complex and gradual processes of development. It tempts those who study modernity to divide history by such an event as the invention of photography, in this way causing them to ignore the degree to which aspects of a photographic relation to reality may have been present in older forms of image culture. In addition to being attended by these problems, the idea of modernity is dangerously universalizing. Although it may seem obvious that the experience of modernity must differ depending upon such factors as class, gender, race, nationality, religion and degree of religious involvement, place of residence, and temperament, this awareness is not always evident in the existing discourse about "modern life" or "the experience of modern man."

As I begin what purports to be a study of the phenomenon of modernity, I want to acknowledge these problems and show some respect for them. I want to resist the temptation to simply invoke the term, in a blaze of distinguished French and German names, leaving its meaning open, compromising none of its dialectical richness, so that it can be redefined at various points according to context. It is impossible to use the word *modernity* with the kind of clarity or consistency I would like. The most I can do is promise to be as attentive as I can be to the problems I have just cited, and to be as clear as I can be given the slipperiness of what I am dealing with. In the following discussion, I will use the word *modernity* to refer to a relatively limited yet, as I hope to demonstrate, extremely important and pervasive historical phenomenon. My understanding of modernity derives from a consensual understanding of the term within a recent tradition of discourse about modernity.[1] This tradition has its roots in some of the writings of Charles Baudelaire and in Walter Benjamin's incomplete and therefore infinitely suggestive interpretation of Baudelaire.[2] What distinguishes the conception of modernity within this tradition is its emphasis on the social and historical meanings of what are understood to be "modern" changes in the phenomenological character of experience.

As such recent scholars of modernity as Habermas, Berman, and Frisby have noted, definitions of modernity, written from widely varying ideological perspectives, are nevertheless often similar in their basic elements. Theoreticians of modernity as diverse as Wordsworth, Marx, Nietzsche, Benjamin, Foucault, Lefebvre, and de Man have all observed that, in the modern world, the phenomenological character of experience is less unified, coherent, or continuous than it was in earlier historical periods. As the social and philosophical structures associated with earlier forms of political and economic organization have weakened, it has become harder to assign a stable meaning or value to individual things and experiences. It has become harder to connect the individual components of experience with each other. Yet as older forms of organizing experience have weakened, new forms of producing experience have developed. Capitalism and modern industrial technology produce an immense and perpetually renewing spectacle of commodities and images. Experience has, as a result, become more various and more immediately stimulating, at the same time as it appears to be less substantial and meaningful. There is a surplus of signifiers and a dearth of signification. It is possible to bathe in such a world, to collect images, or to enjoy the way in which they rapidly succeed each other. It is harder to be oriented, rooted, or convinced of the solidity or permanence of anything one believes or observes.

The paradoxical nature of modern experience, understood in this way, has had an inevitable impact on the way in which art is produced and perceived. One of the earliest self-conscious efforts to describe the effect of this change on the artistic imagination is Charles Baudelaire's "The Painter of Modern Life." This essay, in which Baudelaire offered a description of a consciousness capable of representing what he himself called "modernity," is the theoretical work in which, according to Jurgen Habermas, artistic modernity first assumed "clear contours" ("Modernity vs. Postmodernity," 4). No other nineteenth-century text figures as prominently in twentieth-century discussions of the development of the idea of artistic modernity. In order to understand the context of Baudelaire's pioneering description, however, it is useful to recognize that much of what Baudelaire observes was also observed, from a radically different perspective, by William Wordsworth in a preface written half a century before.

In the preface to the second edition of *Lyrical Ballads* (1800), Wordsworth describes the effect upon the imagination of what he perceives to be "modern" changes in the character of experience. He complains that the "invaluable works of our elder writers" are being "driven into neglect by frantic novels, sickly and stupid German tragedies, and deluges of idle and extravagant stories in verse." Declaring himself and Coleridge to be in opposition to this modern thirst for the sensational, Wordsworth offers an account of the "causes unknown to former times" that have created such an aesthetic climate.

> The human mind is capable of excitement without the application of gross and violent stimulants; and he must have a very faint perception of its beauty and dignity who does not know this, and who does not further know that one being is elevated above another in proportion as he possesses this capability. It has therefore appeared to me that to endeavor to produce or enlarge this capability is one of the best services in which, at any period, a Writer can be engaged, but this service, excellent at all times, is especially so at the present day. For a multitude of causes unknown to former times are now acting with a combined force to blunt the discriminating powers of the mind, and unfitting it for all voluntary exertion to reduce it to a state of savage torpor. The most effective of these causes are the great national events which are daily taking place, and the encreasing accumulation of men in cities, where the uniformity of their occupations produces a craving for extraordinary incident which the rapid communication of intelligence hourly gratifies. (*The Prose Works*, 128–30)

In his preface, Wordsworth identifies modern life with the "accumulation of men in cities" and the concomitant development of a culture in which all events and all information have the status of spectacle, consumed by those who "crave" it. Such a culture, according to Wordsworth, weakens the "discriminating powers of the mind . . . unfitting it for all voluntary exertion." The new consciousness, Wordsworth implies, is passive. Reduced to a "savage torpor," it finds no pleasure in such traditional "exertions" as the perception of meaning, likeness, and continuity within the flux of experience. It can only find interest in the way in which each moment differs, grossly and violently, from previous moments. It can only find pleasure in the perpetual liberation from context and continuity that "extraordinary incident" provides.

Wordsworth's analysis provides a model for what was to become a classic criticism of the effects of modernity. The objects of his criticism are big cities, newspapers, and popular fiction, but very similar arguments have been made, over the past two centuries, for the deleterious effects of television, popular music, cinema, and MTV. At the same time, these arguments continue to be made with respect to urbanization, journalism, and popular fiction, often as if these were very recent cultural developments. In his analysis, Wordsworth makes an association that Baudelaire would also make, and that would, through Baudelaire, become central to much of the subsequent discourse about modernity. The lazy, passive modern imagination, Wordsworth suggests, is quintessentially urban. Although it may spread, and although, in the nineteenth as well as the twentieth century, it certainly has spread beyond the physical boundaries of cities, the changes in the nature of experience designated by the term *modern* were identified throughout the nineteenth century and are still to some degree identified with what Wordsworth calls "the increasing accumulation of men in cities." As Asa Briggs points out in his history of nineteenth-century Britain, a history he entitled *The Age of Great Cities*, the physical and social fact that seemed, to nineteenth-century observers, to distinguish their century from all previous centuries, was the growth of great cities (57). If the fundamental cultural fact of the nineteenth century was understood to be the development of great cities, the representative modern subjectivity was understood to be that of the city dweller, the passive yet compulsive consumer of a rapidly and perpetually changing spectacle.

In "The Painter of Modern Life," Baudelaire offered a more detailed and more sympathetic description of the modern urban consciousness that Wordsworth found so threatening to the popularity of older literature. Accepting the fact that such a consciousness would find it difficult to respond to certain older forms of art, Baudelaire suggested that it could produce new, identifiably modern forms of imaginative expression. Introducing the word *modernity*, and defining it as "the ephemeral, the fugitive, the contingent, the half of art whose other half is the eternal

and the immutable" (13), Baudelaire proceeds, in his essay, to describe
an artist who would be capable of representing these qualities. He suggests that "the painter of modern life" must have a consciousness that
is open to the ephemeral, fugitive, and contingent. He must adapt, in
other words, to the features of urban modernity and not, as Wordsworth
would advise, resist them. In the following passage, Baudelaire presented
his conception of the ideal imaginative posture of an artist of modern
life:

> The crowd is his element, as the air is that of birds and water of
> fishes. His passion and his profession are to become one flesh with
> the crowd. For the perfect *flâneur*, for the passionate spectator, it
> is an immense joy to set up house in the heart of the multitude,
> amid the ebb and flow of movement, in the midst of the fugitive
> and infinite. To be away from home and yet to feel oneself every-
> where at home; to see the world, to be at the centre of the world,
> and yet to remain hidden from the world – such are a few of the
> slightest pleasures of those independent, passionate, impartial na-
> tures which the tongue can but clumsily define. The spectator is a
> prince who everywhere rejoices in his incognito. The lover of life
> makes the whole world his family, just like the lover of the fair
> sex who builds up his family from all the beautiful women that he
> has ever found, or that are – or are not, to be found; or the lover
> of pictures who lives in a magical society of dreams painted on
> canvas. Thus the lover of universal life enters into a crowd as though
> it were an immense reservoir of electrical energy. Or we might
> liken him to a mirror as vast as the crowd itself; or to a kaleidoscope
> gifted with consciousness, responding to each one of its movements
> and reproducing the multiplicity of life and the flickering grace of
> all the elements of life. (9)

In this definition, Baudelaire embraces the very features of modern
subjective experience that Wordsworth felt were most threatening to the
health of the poetic imagination. For Baudelaire, the passivity induced
by urban life is not a "savage torpor" so much as the basis for a new
form of creativity. As a "mirror," or a "kaleidoscope," the imagination
of the ideal "painter of modern life" is indeed passive and undiscriminating. Yet for these reasons, it can capture the ephemeral and the random. It does not resist change because it does not demand continuity.
It is not confused by multiplicity because it has no predisposition in favor
of unity. It becomes as unstructured as the modern metropolitan environment through which it moves.

    To characterize the posture toward experience that a "painter of mod-
ern life" must assume, Baudelaire uses a French word for which there

is no exact English equivalent. In common French usage, a *flâneur*[3] is someone who, without any set purpose, strolls through and observes the life of a city or town. As Walter Benjamin has observed,[4] the word was commonly used in Baudelaire's time, to refer to members of a class of writers and journalists who, in the *feuilletons*, the serial feature sections of the Paris newspapers, and in books called *physiologies*, wrote sketches of urban life from the perspective of a strolling or panoramically situated observer. According to Benjamin, the flaneur, as a journalistic and literary type, originated in the 1830s, when the writers of the *feuilletons* began to represent city life with the same elegant, detached, and leisurely tone they used in their theatrical and literary reviews. At all times insisting upon the randomness with which they encountered what they described, the flaneurs, in their city sketches, would "watch" and present the crowds on the boulevards, and in the arcades, as if they were watching a performance. They would present themselves as reading these crowds as if they were reading the most innocuous and diverting texts. In order to produce this effect, they would claim to possess extraordinary powers of interpretation. The flaneur, Benjamin writes, typically presented himself[5] as a "botanist on asphalt" (36), in possession of special languages and keys that made it possible to identify and classify the components of the crowd. He would also often claim to be able to gain access to the history and consciousness of others. He made it appear as if it were possible, "unencumbered by any factual knowledge, . . . to make out the profession, the character, the background, and the life-style of passers-by" (39). Such powers of interpretation, combined with his invisible detachment, would have enabled the flaneur to experience the crowd as if he were, in Baudelaire's words, a "prince who everywhere rejoices in his incognito" (9).

In the completed portions of the "Paris Arcades" project, Benjamin dismisses the flaneur as a fairly transparent social fantasy. According to Benjamin, such a fantastically gifted urban interpreter existed to assure a literate bourgeois audience that urban crowds were not as illegible as they appeared to be, that social life was not as incoherent as it appeared to be, and that the masses were not as politically threatening as they appeared to be. By assuring his audience that the urban crowd existed for their delectation, and that one's fellow city-dwellers were all "harmless and of perfect bonhomie," the flaneur obscured the nature of social relationships within the city. Benjamin writes that "the political secret," on which this literature was based, is "that life in all its variety and inexhaustible wealth of variations can thrive only among the grey cobblestones and against the grey background of despotism" (37), the reign of Louis-Phillipe. The extreme implausibility of this approach to urban life accounted for the fact that it had, according to Benjamin, virtually disappeared by the middle of the 1840s. He explains: "People knew one another as debtors and creditors, salesmen and customers, employers and employees, and above all as competitors. In the long run it did not seem very likely that they could be made to believe that their associates were harmless oddballs" (39).

Although Benjamin, in the completed portions of the "Paris Arcades" project, did not go far beyond this fascinatingly suggestive and yet reductive and even dismissive conception of the flaneur's importance, it appears, from the notes that remain, that Benjamin intended to do more with the figure of the flaneur in the larger work that was to have grown out of the material he collected. The flaneur, as Benjamin appears to conceive of him in these notes, and in his correspondence with Adorno,[6] was a "dialectical image,"[7] an archetype in which an aspect of historical reality was made manifest. As Susan Buck-Morss has formulated it, Benjamin seems to have seen the flaneur as offering, "philosophical insight into the nature of modern subjectivity – that to which Heidegger referred abstractly as the 'throwness' of the subject – by placing it within specific historical experience. In the *flaneur*, concretely, we recognize our own consumerist mode of being in the world" ("The *Flâneur*, the Sandwichman, and the Whore," 104–5).

From Benjamin's notes, and from the correspondence with Adorno, it also appears that Benjamin perceived a significant analogy between the flaneur's "consumerist mode of being in the world" and the new public spaces that were creating that mode of being. The flaneur, as Baudelaire had described him, was a great container, a vast mirror and kaleidoscope. Yet although he presents himself as randomly open to everything, he actually, as Benjamin describes, saves himself from chaos and indeterminacy through his improbable pretensions to epistemological control. Producing his benign readings, the flaneur reduces the city to a panorama or diorama, a scale model, in which everything is, in effect, brought indoors,[8] transformed into a legible, accessible, and nonthreatening version of itself, encompassed by the comforting arc of the flaneur's sensibility. As a *grand magasin* of all experience, the flaneur is analogous to the arcades, department stores, grand boulevards, and world expositions that were his natural and contemporary habitat. Just as these new environments of consumer capitalism could contain an encyclopedia of objects, controlling their potentially disorienting diversity in order to make everything accessible to a consuming spectator, so the flaneur, through the medium of journalism, could impose order upon the potentially disorienting diversity of the city, by reducing it to accessible images that could be collected and consumed.

As a dialectical image, the flaneur was understood by Benjamin to provide a model for the general relationship between consciousness and experience that became dominant in metropolitan centers in what he considered to be the era of high capitalism. In his completed essay "Some Motifs in Baudelaire" and in a section of the notes for the "Paris Arcades" project labeled with the small letter "m" and entitled *"Mussigang"* (idleness), Benjamin associates the experience of the flaneur with the German word *Erlebnis*, which designates experience as, in essence, a collecting of lived moments. *Erlebnis* is distinguished from *Erfahrung*, another German word for experience which etymologically preserves the sense of experience as the journeying through life that is characteristic of premodern societies. As Benjamin defined the distinction in his notes: *"Erfahrung* is the harvest from work, while *Erlebnis* is the phantasmagoria of the idler."[9] As Benjamin appears to have understood him, the purpose of the flaneur was to produce *Erlebnis*, to serve as its advocate and exemplar, to suggest that all experience may be collected in the form of images, from which one may always be safely detached. Making the rich diversity of modern urban experience accessible to his audience, through the production of images in the context of journalism, the flaneur suggests the possibility of an accommodation to modern life. He suggests that it is possible to be at home in modernity, to wander through the arcades, the department stores, the grand commercial boulevards, the world's fairs, attentive to photographs and panoramas, surrendering to the fecundity of it all, marveling at the ability of the commercial metropolis to produce impermanent images that do not become part of lived experience but may instead be collected and stored in a great warehouse of memory.

By approaching experience in this way, the flaneur provides a model for the creative and consuming consciousness implicit in much of the art of the bourgeois nineteenth century. His panoramic interest in the everyday life of the metropolis is part of the premise of both realist and naturalist fiction. His consuming and collecting detachment anticipates aestheticism. His acceptance of the possibilities of discontinuity make him a predecessor of much twentieth-century art and his reduction of the world to a series of consumable images associates him with a nineteenth-century culture of images that would, in the twentieth century, grow into the all-encompassing envelope of the electronic media. To a large extent the flaneur is that in the nineteenth century which most anticipates the habits of image consumption of the twentieth century. As a dialectical image, he exemplifies the way in which, as Benjamin observed, "every epoch dreams its successor" (159). The idea of the flaneur presents, as Benjamin seems to have recognized, an extraordinarily broad range of possible references and connections. He is, in the "Paris Arcades" project, a kind of capital of nineteenth-century consciousness just as Paris can be understood to have been "the capital of the nineteenth century." Although I am not entirely comfortable with the Hegelianism of believing that there is such a thing as a historical reality that can be made manifest in an image, I do think that, by studying the flaneur as a concrete historical phenomenon, and as an image within the culture of the nineteenth century, it is possible to study the effect of urban culture on mental life, and on cultural products produced in this period. Yet many who may find this a plausible approach will be surprised by the literature I have chosen as the basis of such a study. I intend to show that the flaneur, understood by Benjamin and others as an exclusively and quintessentially Continental phenomenon, was in fact a significant presence in the culture of the United States in the three decades before the Civil War.

The prevailing assumptions about the origins of the flaneur, as well as the prevailing assumptions about the provincial, antiurban character of American antebellum culture, are such that we would not expect to find the flaneur in America at this time. Part of what I hope to establish in this study is that these assumptions have prevented us from encountering the urbanity and the modernity, such as they were, of the American literature written before the Civil War. The existence of these qualities in some of this literature should not be surprising. Few societies in history had ever urbanized as rapidly as America did in the first half of the nineteenth century. And if, as Paul de Man has written, modernity "exists in the form of a desire to wipe out whatever came earlier, in the hope of reaching at last a point that could be called a true present, a point of origin that marks a true departure" (148), then few cultures in history have been more self-consciously "modern" than the United States in the first half of the nineteenth century. Despite a strong native tradition of antiurbanism and despite the widespead perception of the inferiority of American cities as compared with those of Europe, many Americans, as I will consider in a later chapter, were fascinated by the cosmopolitan mode of being exemplified by the flaneur. The flaneur may even have had a particular suitability to American culture. To many Americans, he may have represented an aspiration, a desire for the subjective benefits of the metropolitan civilization that at that time existed most visibly in London and Paris but that was even more consonant with the avowed ideals of America's capitalist, democratic, bourgeois-dominated society than it was consonant with the values of the older European societies, in which pre- or antibourgeois values may have had a greater amount of influence than they did in the United States. America did not invent the department store, the panorama, or the industrial exposition, but it embraced them in the nineteenth century with a passion that suggests that the consciousness with which they can be associated is likely to have had a similar affinity with American culture. For these reasons, we should expect that American writers like Poe, Hawthorne, and Whitman would be as interested as their European contemporaries in the potential effect of urban life and, in the broadest sense, of modernity upon the creative imagination. As I will argue, their consideration of this issue, through their own engagement with urban modernity, would have important consequences for their creativity. In this context, it is significant that the early efforts of these authors to represent "the crowded life of cities" all involve the representation of a consciousness that incorporates many of the features of the flaneur, as Baudelaire and Benjamin have understood him.

Edgar Allan Poe's "The Man of the Crowd,"[10] for example, begins with a narrator describing his vantage "at the large bow window" (2:510) of a coffeehouse in London. Recovering from a serious illness, he is in a mood that he characterizes as "the converse of ennui." His intellect is "electrified" and he feels "a calm but inquisitive interest in everything." Turning his attention from his newspaper to the crowd that passes by his window, the narrator discovers that, in his special mood, he can read the passing crowd as easily as he had read the newspaper. "At first," he writes, "my observations took an abstract and generalizing turn. I looked at the passengers in masses, and thought of them in their aggregate relations. Soon, however, I descended to details, and regarded with minute interest the innumerable varieties of figure, dress, air, gait, visage, and expressions of countenance." Observing these details, he divides the crowd into abstract and general classes. Physiognomy and clothing enable him to "identify" men of leisure, men of business, clerks, pickpockets, gamblers, "modest young girls," and prostitutes. Equally legible signs permit him to distinguish the subclasses of status and temperament within the larger classes.

Throughout his description of the crowd, Poe's urban spectator maintains an affectation of interpretive ease. "It was not possible to mistake . . . the upper clerks of staunch firms" because, he insists, they all dressed identically and "they had all slightly bald heads, from which the right ears, long used to penholding, had an odd habit of standing out on end." Gamblers also were "easily recognizable." "All were distinguished by a certain swarthiness of complexion, a filmy dimness of eye, and pallor and compression of lip." "The tribe of clerks," likewise, "was an obvious one," with its own set of identifying features, and "many individuals of dashing appearance" were "easily understood as belonging to the race of swell pick-pockets." Poe's narrator is so certain of his power to read the crowd that he claims that, in addition to being able to identify types, he can "frequently read, even in that brief interval of a glance, the history of long years"(2:511). Nothing in his text, however corrupt or criminal, is able to disturb his composure. Before he encounters an old man, whose illegibility threatens to unravel his entire system, Poe's narrator is at home in the crowd he watches.

In another significant work of American literature, published twelve years after "The Man of the Crowd," another narrator looks out a window at a city with a similar faith in his ability to read and be at home in it. Comfortably smoking a cigar at the back window of a Boston hotel, Miles Coverdale, the narrator of Hawthorne's *The Blithedale Romance*, describes a mood of calm yet omnivorous curiosity very much like that of Poe's narrator.[11] Having recently left the rural isolation of Blithedale, Coverdale observes that: "Whatever had been my taste for solitude and natural scenery, yet the thick, foggy, stifled element of cities, the entangled life of many men together, sordid as it was, and empty of the beautiful, took quite as strenuous a hold upon my mind. I felt as if there could never be enough of it. Each characteristic sound was too suggestive to be passed over unnoticed" (3:146).

Like Poe's narrator in the window of his coffee shop, Coverdale feels "a hesitation about plunging into this muddy tide of human activity," preferring "to linger on the brink, or hover in the air above it" (3:147). Like Poe's narrator as well, the bustle of the city distracts Coverdale from an uncommitted act of reading. When he abandons his cheap novel to look out his window, he too decides that his special mood and vantage make his new act of reading scarcely more problematic than his earlier one. Looking at the back of houses, Coverdale is convinced that "realities keep in the rear" and that there is "vastly greater suggestiveness, in the back view of a residence . . . than in its front" (3:149). In this privileged moment of spectatorial dominion, Coverdale is so certain of the advantages of his position, and the power of his faculties of interpretation, that the people he watches from his window seem to him to be as comprehensible as "toy-people of German manufacture."

In nineteenth-century American literature, there is no better example of delighted urban spectatorship than the poetry of Walt Whitman.[12] From the pilothouses of ferryboats and from the top of Broadway omnibuses, Whitman represents the city in panoramic "full sweeps," filled with assertions of awakened, curious delight in urban ephemera, and comfortable intimacy not only with the urban scene, but with the faces and minds of the crowds themselves. As he writes in "Broadway" and as he repeats in similar terms in other poems, he delights to move through the "parti-colored world" of Manhattan, to see its "infinite, teeming, mocking life!" its "vast, unspeakable show and lesson!" (521). In this world, he finds "frequent and swift flash of eyes offering me love" (126). He sees entire crowds, of the present and future, "face to face" (159), and he experiences a profound intimacy with them. In his urban poems, if not always in his prose, Whitman maintains a posture of detached and delighted omniscience as complete as anything expressed by Coverdale or the narrator of "The Man of the Crowd."

In each of the texts cited, an individual abandons himself, with an indolent excitement, to the random observation of a rapidly changing urban scene. Strolling, or panoramically situated, each figure is at home in the city and each claims to have an extraordinary ability to read, empathize with, or gain access to the crowd that passes. These spectators are comfortable where, according to the antiurban orthodoxies of the period, they should be uncomfortable. They read what was assumed to be illegible. They express an interest in everyday urban life that is difficult to discuss in terms of the prevalent assumptions about American writing before the Civil War. Because they seem to be so anomolous, the texts in which these spectators appear have not received the attention they deserve as representations of urban life. Poe's encounter with the city in "The Man of the Crowd" and in his detective stories has received surprisingly little critical attention.[13] Hawthorne's interest in urban spectators has been virtually ignored, and his representation of the nature and consequences of an urban civilization in *The Blithedale Romance* has merely been noted, not extensively explored.[14] Although the idea that Whitman introduced the city as subject matter to American literature is one of the unquestioned commonplaces of Whitman criticism, the effort to define the nature of Whitman's representation of the city has rarely been attempted by critics, and when it has, it has proved particularly daunting.[15]

These and other American texts have been difficult to interpret in part because a context for interpreting them has been lacking. It has been assumed for far too long that America before the Civil War was not "modern," that it had no flaneurs just as it had no arcades, that the metropolitan features of modern experience that Benjamin finds in Paris, the "capital of the nineteenth century," have little relevance to the way in which life was lived in the provincial United States. Although Benjamin did not by any means create this misconception, he has contributed to it by offering an account of the development of modernity that suggests that it develops suddenly, and in response to specific material innovations of the nineteenth century that altered, and expressed invisible alterations in, the nature of commercial and social life. He has also contributed to this misconception by treating the flaneur as a local and historically limited phenomenon, a type adapted to the particular conditions of Paris in the 1830s. Although I find a great deal of value in Benjamin's analysis, and although I will essentially be using his conception of modernity, I will nevertheless attempt to show, in the next several chapters, that his historical account of the development of the flaneur and the concept of modernity associated with him are incorrect. In order to understand and interpret the appearance, in American literature, of figures who closely resemble the figure described by Benjamin, it is necessary to consider how he could have appeared in America when he did, what he would have meant, how he would have been perceived, and how the encounter with his mode of viewing modern cities may have affected the work of writers like Poe, Hawthorne, and Whitman.

The figure that Benjamin discovered in the *feuilletons* of the 1830s was not a new form of consciousness that had sprung into being in conjunction with the development of enclosed shopping spaces that facilitated strolling. He was the culmination of a long tradition, just as the Parisian arcades themselves represented the culmination of a long process of development of traffic-free spaces designed to facilitate shopping, strolling, and personal display. The development of what I am designating as the consciousness of modernity, like the development of consumer culture and the modern culture of images, is a much more gradual process than it is represented to be by Benjamin, and by others who have accepted his account of the origins of modernity understood in this way.[16] By the early nineteenth century, this process was far more advanced, as well as far more geographically widespread than Benjamin represents. The manners and strategies Benjamin associates with the flaneur may be found throughout the literature of Europe long before the late 1830s. Despite the lack of a widely current English word for him, the flaneur is as English a phenomenon as he is a French one, and it was primarily from England that he was imported to America. By the time Poe, Hawthorne, and Whitman encountered and represented this sort of urban spectator, he was an exceptionally widespread, familiar, and even somewhat old-fashioned figure in the English-speaking world. His development in England begins at least as early as the turn of the seventeenth century in cultural circumstances that have some similarity to those Benjamin has associated with the origins of the flaneur in France.

Chapter 2

The Development of the Flaneur in England

If modernity is identified with the rapidly changing, discontinuous, yet spectacular experience characteristic of life in modern cities, then aspects of modernity certainly had to have come into being before the early nineteenth century. Long before the nineteenth century, London and Paris were rapidly changing metropolises, filled with crowds, in which traditional social forms were being called into question, and in which modern forms of production were producing a society of spectacle. The flaneur, the inhabitant of modernity as Benjamin describes him, can be found fully developed in England at least as early as the beginning of the eighteenth century. His characteristic mental processes and strategies, however, begin to develop even earlier than that.

The culture of the flaneur has its origins, I believe, in the culture of spectacle that developed in London during its first period of extraordinary growth, in the sixteenth century.[1] During the sixteenth century, London quadrupled in size, having become not only the political center of England, but one of the main commercial centers of Europe. The accumulation of capital in London, as a result of centuries of profitable trading in cloth, and the investment of that capital in highly successful maritime expeditions and commercial ventures turned, as Steen Rasmussen has written, this "town on the edge of the large net of European trade" into the "centre of the still larger one which was to spread over continents" (51). London's prosperity not only fueled its incredible growth, it also greatly diversified its population. As a consequence of its new economic importance and because it was insulated from the political and religious turmoil of the Continent, London had attracted so many foreigners that, by the end of the sixteenth century, they may have accounted for as much as one-third of the population of the English capital. Furthermore, the centralization of British economic and political life in London, as well as upheavals in the nation's provincial and agrarian economies, encouraged migration to London of individuals of all classes from all parts of the British Isles.

14

In this bustling, thriving, and increasingly diverse metropolis, ongoing economic changes created an economic and cultural environment favorable for the development of a culture of urban spectacle. As such historians of English commerce as Beier, Finlay, and Adburgham have suggested, the beginnings of what can legitimately be called an English consumer society may be found in sixteenth-century London. The growth of international trade, the relative lack of restrictions on the market, and the relative social fluidity of Britain encouraged the development of an economy and a culture geared toward the manufacture, display, and purchase of new and nonessential commodities that, in addition to whatever other appeal they may have had, could signify social status.[2] The consumers of these products were aristocrats and wealthy commoners, who, because of the increasing importance of the court, and because of the city's development into an increasingly active and dominant social, commercial, and cultural center, were more and more likely as the century went on to spend all or part of the year in London. In the sixteenth century, life in London became more opulent, more ostentatious, and anyone observing the life of the city toward the end of the century would have noticed a greater variety not merely in the human spectacle but also in the spectacle of commodities. The representative environment of this commercial culture was the Royal Exchange, a new kind of commercial space that was in many respects the ancestor of similar spaces in which urban spectators, in later centuries, would find themselves at home.

The Royal Exchange, which opened in 1568, was planned and built by Sir Thomas Gresham on the model of a trading center at Antwerp.[3] It consisted, on the ground story, of an arcaded courtyard where international traders could do business with their English counterparts. Above the arcades were about 160 small shops, most of which were devoted to the sale of imported luxury goods. Soon after it opened, the Royal Exchange became a fashionable meeting place where wealthy Londoners, dressed in the latest fashions, could observe each other, gossip, exchange news, and purchase goods designed to demonstrate their wealth, much as they would in the Burlington Arcade two centuries later. The success of the Royal Exchange led to the opening, under the auspices of James I, of the New Exchange in 1608, which was constructed according to the same principles.[4] The degree to which these enclosed spaces for shopping, strolling, and display may have provided experiences usually associated with later centuries is evident in an account of the Royal Exchange written by a Reverend Samuel Rolle immediately after the destruction of the first exchange in the Great Fire of 1666. Rolle wrote:

What a princely foundation was the Royal Exchange! And of how great use! Was not that the centre in which those lines met, which were drawn from all parts of Europe? . . . Was not the place a little epitome, or rather representative, of all Europe? . . . As London was the glory of England, so was the Royal Exchange one of the greatest glories and ornaments of London. . . . As for the upper part, was it not the great storehouse whence the nobility and gentry of England were furnished with most of the costly things wherewith they did adorn themselves? Here, if anywhere, might a man have seen the glory of the world in a moment. What artificial thing could entertain the senses and fantasies of men that was not there to be had? Such was the delight that many gallants took in the magazine of all curious varieties, that they could almost have dwelt there; going from shop to shop, like bees from flower to flower, – if they had had but a fountain of money, that could not have been drawn dry! I doubt not but a Mahometan, who never expects more than sensual delights, would gladly have accepted of that place and the treasures of it, for his heaven. (Cited in Grant, 2:60–1)

Rolle's language in this passage suggests several things about the process by which, in the three-quarters of a century before it was written, London was understood to have become suitable, in itself, as a subject for representation. London, in this period, had become and was recognized to have become a metropolis, in the sense in which Mumford and other historians of urbanism have used the term. Drawing commerce and population to itself, it had become an immense human and material spectacle, a series of interlocking and analogous showplaces, a display of things and signs. An inevitable product of all of this watching, looking, showing, and signifying was a self-consciousness, a sense that London existed as something to be looked at and represented in and of itself, as something whose image would have meaning. That this is so is evident in the fact that, in the late sixteenth century, a specifically urban literature developed to provide images of London. Although London had been mentioned and briefly described in literary texts before this point, the late sixteenth and early seventeenth centuries saw the origin of a series of urban genres, whose express purpose was to provide images of London. In a historical period fascinated by the concept of the epitome or the microcosm, it is not surprising that one of these genres offered the possibility of grasping London much as the entire world might be grasped, according to Rolle, in the galleries of the Royal Exchange.

John Stow's *Survey of London*, published in 1597, was the first of several books in this period that seemed to offer the possibility, to adapt Rolle's phrase, of seeing all of the glory of London, and in this way all of the glory of the world in a moment. Stow's survey is a self-conscious effort to describe the physical, institutional, and to a lesser extent social and cultural composition of a city in its entirety. The survey begins with a brief discussion of London's "Mythical Origins." Stow then provides an account of the "Building of the Wall and description and statistics." After describing the physical encompassment of the city, Stow proceeds, in the remainder of the book, to offer a mental encompassment of it. His chapters are orderly and encyclopedic catalog descriptions, in succession, of London's "Fresh water supply," followed by its "Bridges; Gates; Towers and Castles (History being told in connection with the physical origins and encompassments); Schools, houses of learning; Guilds; Alms given in old times; Sports and Pastimes; Watches and Festivals; Honorable Things Done by Citizens; Then the Division of the City." Implicit in Stow's description is a conception of the primacy of the city, as a feature of society subordinate to nothing else. In Stow's panorama, the church and the crown are treated exclusively as institutions that create buildings that are part of the glories of London, and the buildings are given no more than the admiration that is due to them as buildings. Guildhalls are treated with the same reverence as churches, mansions are treated with the same reverence as palaces.

Representing the city as an independent and indeed primary entity, Stow goes to great lengths, in an appendix that was published with the *Survey* from 1603 on, to describe the ethos of the city, to represent it as an independent source of values, separate from the values of church and crown. Providing what is literally a description of the ideals of the increasingly ascendant *bourg*oisie, Stow explains that he has chosen to present London's greatness in the form of, as he writes in the title of the appendix, "an Apology (or Defence) Against the Opinion of Some Men, Which Think that the Greatness of That City Standeth Not with the Profit and Security of This Realm." London is valuable, he argues, because as a great city, it makes it possible for men to be "withdrawn from barbarous feritie and force to a certain mildness of manners, and to humanity and justice; whereby they are contented to give and take right, to and from their equals and inferiors, and to hear and obey their heads and superiors" (483). In this way they learn the "good behaviour [that] is yet called urbanitas, because it is rather found in cities than elsewhere" (483–4).

Stow's *Survey of London* spawned a genre of urban panorama books in the early seventeenth century.[5] All of the surveys seem to share an encyclopedic intention, a bourgeois urbanism that celebrates the city's magnificence and vitality, and a tendency to divide the city into separate spaces so as to give the reader the sense of looking at a coherent map or model of the metropolis. In its ability to produce these effects, this genre anticipates the flaneur's presentation of the city as divisible into legible types, as something that can be read and grasped in its entirety.

For all that they may have provided an accessible image of the city to residents of the increasingly self-conscious metropolis, the survey books shared, however, a predictable weakness. By presenting the city as it would exist at a hypothetical single moment in time, the genre created the effect of a static and specious completeness that would have been at odds with the visible dynamism of seventeenth-century London. Whether or not this static completeness would have seemed convincing or appealing, it would not have allowed for the exploitation of those aspects of the city's appeal that would have derived from its ability to move and change. Around the turn of the seventeenth century, other urban genres came into being that had different strengths and different weaknesses.

One new genre that developed to satisfy London's hunger for images of itself was what literary historians have designated as the "coney-catching" book. Coney-catching was a contemporary slang term, frequently used in the books, for swindling. The coney-catching books, though quite different in style and content from the survey books, often shared their encyclopedic intention. Rather than providing an encyclopedia of legitimate commercial activity, or of the architectural magnificence of the metropolis, the coney-catching books cataloged the various forms of deception and fraud that could be encountered in London. On the title page of one of the best and most popular of these books, Thomas Dekker's *The Bell-Man's Second Nights-Walke*, the complexity of the genre's intention is evident. The motto on the title page advertises the volume as "A Booke to make Gentlemen Merry, Citizens Warie, Countreymen Carefull." Although the book might conceivably have served all three of these purposes, its continued popularity presumably depended on whether or not it effectively accomplished the first of these tasks. Dekker's book is an entertaining survey of London places and fashions, as well as a diverting account of the various scams practiced by its beggars, thieves, con men, and prostitutes. A similar reflection of the fact that such books were read primarily for entertainment is the advertisement on the title page of another representative of the genre, a book attributed to Samuel Rowlands and entitled *Greenes ghost haunting conie-catchers*. The advertisement reads: "With the merry Conceits of Doctor Pinch-backe a notable Makeshift. Ten times more pleasant than anything yet published of this matter." Although this title page is followed by a ponderous moral introduction inveighing against coney-catchers, the text that follows is an entertaining and slightly racy series of stories about successful cons practiced upon people in London by coney-catchers and whores. Like Dekker's books, it is clearly a "pleasant" commodity intended to make "gentlemen merrie."

Dekker's division of his hypothetical audience into three sociological groups, each with different needs, is significant for understanding the social dimension of this genre, as well as other urban spectatorial genres that were to follow. Dekker's distinctions suggest that for a gentleman, and virtually everyone who could afford to buy a book at this point was a gentleman, a great city is a spectacle. It is preeminently a source of entertainment in which it only behooves others to be "warie" or "carefull." As H. V. Routh observes, the readers of this genre were most likely to be "gilded vagabonds" (316), the class of idle, wealthy, and ostentatious young men who were particularly important in sustaining the theaters, amusements, and luxury trades of the metropolis. This model of consumption anticipates much in the urban culture that would develop later. In every century in England, the market for images of the city seems to have consisted to a large degree of wealthy young men residing in the metropolis before the assumption of adult responsibilities. For this protobohemian subculture, as it is represented within a tradition extending from the coney-catching books to Pierce Egan's *Life in London*, a metropolis is not a community or a place to do business so much as it is a spectacle to be consumed, a carnival of glamorous freedom where gentlemen can test the limits of experience before accepting those limits as the contours of their identity as gentlemen.[6]

Unlike the survey books, the coney-catching books, because of their subject matter, offered a sense of the city not as complete and comprehensible at a glance, but as rapidly changing and randomly encountered. Most of them are narrated by peripatetic figures like Dekker's "Bell-Man," who presents himself as a night watchman, walking through the streets with his bell and lantern, observing what he sees in the same spirit as Diogenes with his oil lamp, a comparison the Bell-Man makes several times. Thus equipped, he assumes the role of a guide to the reader, writing in the epistle dedicatory: "Give mee leave to lead you by the hand into a Wildernesse whose crueltie you need not feare, because I teach the way to tame them: ugly they are in shape and divelish in conditions yet to behold them a far off, may delight you, and to know their qualities if ever you should come neere them may save you from much danger" (A4).

Although the Bell-Man is a peripatetic spectator, with allegedly expert skills of urban interpretation, Dekker, like his colleagues in this genre, does not take advantage of this premise to introduce the technical innovations that would have brought him closer to the nineteenth-century flaneur. The Bell-Man does not pretend to randomly encounter anything. His description of the varieties of London con games is not significantly different in structure from the panoramic description of London spaces one finds in Stow. Rather than encountering a truly random or discontinuous street scene, Dekker's Bell-Man organizes his account of urban vice through a careful regimentation of his material. Throughout *The Bell-Man's Second Nights-Walke*, one of Dekker's favorite metaphors is that of military rank. His catalog of the various forms of urban wild men a visitor or inhabitant is likely to encounter is presented as a survey of "ranks," "regiments," and "squadrons" (B4). The various scams practiced by this "divelish" army are made comprehensible by metaphoric comparisons to the hunting habits of predatory birds (thus various kinds of card cheats are compared to eagles, woodpeckers, and gulls) or the activity of ferreting out rabbits. In his chapter "Of Ferreting: The Manner of undooing Gentlemen, by taking up of commodities" the Bell-Man sets up the rules of a metaphor that structures not only his sketch but the genre in which he is participating: "1) He that hunts up and downe to find game, is called the Tombler. 2) The commodities that are taken up are cald Pursenets. 3) The Cittizen that selles them is the Ferret. 4) They that take up are the Rabbet-suckers. 5) He, upon whose credit these Rabbet-suckers runne is called the Warren" (E). The elaborate epistemological structure of these and other metaphors and ranking systems enable the Bell-Man to offer as much of a sense of control over his material as the writers of the urban surveys can offer. The same can be said of Robert Greene's *A Notable Discovery of Coosnage* and its sequel, *The Second Part of Conny-Catching*, which rigidly classify the various types of coney-catchers and outline what Greene calls the "laws" of their villainy. In spite of the apparent opacity and uncontrollable nature of their subject matter, the coney-catching books represent the city as legible, accessible, and so coherently divided into distinct categories that it can be taken in at a glance by an observer privileged to have access to the key the book provides.

Accomplishing this, the coney-catching books, like the survey books, present the city as a static, relatively complete entity. Unlike the survey books, they offer the possibility of consuming the spectacle of urban vice. They are introduced as the work of peripatetic spectators, but they do not show these spectators in action. Though they provide an extensive catalog of the kinds of scams practiced in the city, and though they claim to present this catalog for the purpose of making "Citizens warie" and "Countreymen Carefull," they nevertheless do not offer the fantasy that a spectator can recognize the practitioners of these scams before the scam has begun. The notion, so important to the development of the flaneur, that it is possible to determine the character and history of a stranger on the basis of nothing more than what can be observed during a typically brief and silent urban encounter is introduced into the literature of London by a different genre, the Theophrastian character book, a genre based upon the *Characters* of Theophrastus. It is in the English Theophrastian character, I believe, that the origins of the flaneur's conception of the urban crowd, if not the origins of the flaneur himself, are to be found.

Theophrastus, a pupil of both Plato and Aristotle, wrote his *Characters* around 319 B.C. Better known as the first to develop a systematic method of botanical classification, the career of this Greek polymath sheds an interesting light on Benjamin's description of the flaneur as a "botanist on asphalt." For having ordered the multiplicity of plant life with an Aristotelian taxonomy, Theophrastus then attempted to do the same with the even more complex and diverse substrata of human personality. His "characters," brief essays that rarely occupy more than a page in English translation, all have the same structure. Each begins with the definition of a word designating a character trait (e.g., arrogance, cowardice, officiousness, recklessness). The definition is then followed by an enumeration of the characteristic actions of an individual who exemplifies this trait and no others. Invariably adhering to this structure, the *Characters* of Theophrastus are deductive and linguistic. In each of them, an individual is derived from the definition of a word.

The English Theophrastian character differs significantly from its Greek model, in part because it was revived in a period in which the coney-catching books were popular, and in which such older genres as physiognomical treatises, estates satire, and typologies based upon the doctrine of humours, were also enjoying a new popularity.[7] The English Theophrastians, writing between 1614 and 1642, appear to have created a hybrid of the Greek character and these other genres. The typology of the English character, for example, is as likely to be sociological as it is to be moral. Following the tradition of Estates satire, there are numerous English characters of professional and class types. In Sir Thomas Overbury's collection, probably the best and certainly the most influential of the English Theophrastian character books, there are such characters as "a Serving Man," "A Noble," "A Saylor," "A Soldier," "A Taylor," "A Whoore," "An Innes of Court Man," "A Reverend Judge," and "A French Cooke." Related to this deviation from the Theophrastian tradition is the tendency of English writers to characterize types, not only according to behavioral patterns but also according to external appearance and appurtenances. In the English character, types can be identified by manner of dress, characteristic facial expressions, and locale. Thus Overbury writes that we can find "A Courtier" in Paul's Walk, "With a picke tooth in his hat, a capecloak, and a long stocking" (52). An "Affectate Traveller" is recognized by the fact that "His attire speaks French or Italian and his gate cries Behold me. He censures all things by countenances, and shrugs and speakes his own language with shame and lisping" (58). The *Characters* of Theophrastus, although they contain some striking behavioral particularities, never involve such explicit physical details.

As these examples demonstrate, the English character is more empirical than its Greek model. Defining a type, it goes beyond the definition to outline the external signs by which a representative of a type may be known. This makes it theoretically suitable for actual use on the streets of London. Unlike the Greek character, the English character suggests that if you see someone dressed in a certain way, frequenting a certain place, and exhibiting certain recognizable facial expressions and gestures, then you can expect that person to behave in a certain way. They turn the deductive process of Theophrastus into a form of induction. There is an immense logical leap here that is extremely significant for the development of the flaneur. The writers of the English character "leap" from the notion that it is possible to define pure characterological forms with identifiable secondary characteristics to the notion that it is possible to encounter such forms on a London street.[8] The faith in the possibility of this is the origin of the assertion of Poe's narrator in "The Man of the Crowd," that the upper clerks of staunch firms all have slightly bald heads and bent ears.

In an effort to define the theory of the English character, Sir Thomas Overbury, one of its most distinguished practitioners, observed that the word *character* derives from a Greek word meaning "to ingrave, or make a deepe impression" and that it is therefore suited to refer to "those elements which wee learne first, leaving a strong seale in our memories." The word *character* can also be used, Overbury writes, to refer to "an Aegyptian hieroglyphicke, for an impresse, or short embleme; in little comprehending much" (168). Overbury's definition, and the genre he is defining, focus on the process of making brief and immediate impressions into fixed "emblems," "in little comprehending much." This definition reflects a concept of personal identity implicit in the Theophrastian character and, as Georg Simmel has observed, particularly characteristic of urban life. In his essay on "The Metropolis and Mental Life," Simmel observes that "The temptation to appear 'to the point,' to appear concentrated and strikingly characteristic, lies much closer to the individual in brief metropolitan contacts than in an atmosphere in which frequent and prolonged association assures the personality of an unambiguous image of himself in the eyes of the other" (421). If Overbury's definition refers to this metropolitan tendency to be a "character," it also, however, may be understood to refer to a metropolitan tendency to see others as "characters." Overbury's theory of the character, like the genre of the English character in general, suggests that an urban crowd may be read as a text, that a characteristically brief and random urban encounter could provide enough information for a trained observer to identify the "character" of the individual he encounters.

If the English characters are understood as signs, in this sense, then it is significant that during the period of their greatest vogue, they were almost never published in isolation. Characters almost always appeared in large collections, the universally comprehensive intention of which is evident in many of their titles. Two of the most popular were the "Microcosmography" of John Earle and the "Micrologia" of R.M. The fact that the English characters almost always appeared in collections of this sort suggests how, as signs, the characters only have meaning within the context of a collection of signs. Within these comprehensive collections, as in an ideal language, every set of physical and behavioral details can stand for only one character type and it is always the only set of physical and behavioral details that can designate the character type. There is, for example, never more than one possible set of identifying marks for a "Soldier" or "A country gentleman" even though a great variety of physical and behavioral attributes may be observed among soldiers and country gentlemen. This insistence, in all of the character books, on the difference of each sign from every other, and on the absoluteness of what is actually an arbitrary relation between signifier and signified, is analogous to that which can be found in any comprehensive representational system structured as a language. The Theophrastian character books offered themselves as languages for interpreting the urban crowd. For an audience that could accept them as languages or as dictionaries, London would appear to be a text.[9]

As keys to and models of the urban crowd, the English character books were related to the survey literature that began with Stow. Throughout the seventeenth century, there were a number of character books that explicitly combined the techniques of the Theophrastian character with that of the London survey, to provide a coherent model of the city. A particularly interesting and self-conscious example of an effort of this sort is Donald Lupton's *London and the Countrey Carbonadoed and Quartred into Severall Characters* (1634). Lupton introduces the first half of this book by observing that "London is growne so Great that I am almost afraid to meddle with her. She's certainly a great World, there are so many little worlds in Her" (59). He then attempts to encompass this "great World" by offering a panoramic survey of the "little worlds" and to achieve this, he makes use of the techniques of the character book. The characteristic physical and "behavioral" features of specific places (e.g., St. Paul's, Smithfield, Newgate), generic places (e.g., playhouses, dancing schools), and human types (e.g., fisherwomen, scavengers) are enumerated as in any character book. Lupton focuses upon the isolation and definition of little worlds and by collecting them together, attempts to convey an impression of totalizing mastery. His self-consciousness about the nature of his enterprise is evident in the extraordinary violence of his title. Having grown so great that the mind can hardly meddle with her, London can only be subdued by an act of figurative violence against her complex totality. She must be carbonadoed, sliced, and skewered. She must be "quartered" into the discrete and comprehensible diversity of the character book. That the aim of Lupton's violence is to reduce London to a text is clearly evident in his description of his accomplishment in the introduction to the second half of the volume. Lupton writes: "This is the Circumference of London: It is the Embleme of the City in Folio, and the City of it in Decimo Sexto" (84).

In the naked authoritarian violence of Lupton's statements of intention, and in the self-conscious struggle for indelibility in Overbury's discussion of the character, it is possible to observe the social and epistemological tension that must have been involved in the creation of these early genres of urban legibility. To turn London into a text or a series of collectible images was certainly, as Benjamin has written of comparable efforts by the flaneur, an effort to establish some form of social control. Like the survey books, the character books offered their readers a sense of surveying an orderly and comprehensible world. The structure of the urban experience promised by this literature resembles that of a paradigm that Michel Foucault has found within other systems of social control that come into being at about the same time as the Theophrastian character book. Describing the seventeenth-century plague precautions that anticipated the structure of Jeremy Bentham's Panopticon, Foucault offers what could also serve as a succinct description of the order imposed upon the crowd by the typologies of the Theophrastian character. Foucault writes: "This enclosed, segmented space, observed at every point, in which the individuals are inserted in a fixed place, in which the slightest movements are supervised, in which all events are recorded, in which an uninterrupted work of writing links the centre and the periphery, in which power is exercised without division, according to a continuous hierarchical figure, in which each individual is constantly located, examined, and distributed . . . all this constitutes a compact model of the disciplinary mechanism" (197).

Bentham's Panopticon is a structural model for institutional buildings in which control is established through perpetual and universal surveillance. In a prison, school, or hospital designed according to its principles, inmates, students, or patients are housed in cubicles from which they cannot see each other but in which they are always visible to an invisible spectator in a central tower, which is the sole source of illumination. The Panopticon, Foucault observes, provides "the perfect disciplinary apparatus" because it "would make it possible for a single gaze to see everything constantly. A central point would be both the source of light illuminating everything and a locus of convergence for everything that must be known" (173). The systems of social control that evolve in the seventeenth and eighteenth centuries resemble this paradigm because they involve the division of society into legible types, into figurative cubicles to which a privileged observer may be imagined to have visual access. Those systems of social control that can be said to resemble the paradigm of the Panopticon divide into classes and religious, national, and professional groups. They distribute individuals into such categories as the sick, the insane, the respectable, the criminal, and the politically dangerous, and they depend upon establishing the legitimacy of systems, however specious, for this distribution.[10] The Theophrastian character book may have offered legitimacy to all such acts of distribution. The ease with which everyone could be placed in one's proper cubicle may also have contributed to a sense of the fixed and absolute nature of social categories. Such a book would offer the illusion that the organization of society is natural and visible and that it does not need to be maintained by the exercise of coercive power.

As a dream of social control and legibility through the reduction of human diversity to a system of signs structured like a language, the genre of the Theophrastian character book had an explicitly utopian implication. This utopia is, significantly, nonhierarchial. Its dynamic of power and coherence resembles that which Foucault and others have associated with the culture of capitalism and the dominance of the bourgeoisie. Its order does not derive from an identifiable source so much as it is diffused throughout the entire social mass and is constituted by the interplay of acts of observation. Each observing individual can identify with the order and, in the act of observing, can enjoy a sense that the order exists naturally and does not have to be imposed. The character books suggest that this order can simply be seen, that it could be randomly encountered, since everyone can be read and put in the proper slot. Such a structure implies a spectator, just as the Panopticon does. The Theophrastian character books did not, however, offer a portrait of the implied spectator, nor did they show him at work. Like the narrator of the *Characters* of Theophrastus, about whom one knows nothing other than that he claims to be ninety-nine years old, the writers or putative writers of the English characters are invisible and unobtrusive. Yet since, in their hands, the enterprise of character writing becomes more empirical and inductive, the English character writers prepare the way for a subjectivity that can see and can gather together what he has seen into a characterological reading.

The rudiments of such a subjectivity can be found in the narrative voice of the *Charactères* (1688) of Jean de La Bruyère, a text that was very much indebted to the English Theophrastians[11] and which accomplishes, as Roland Barthes has observed in an essay on La Bruyère, the process of epistemological division that I find in the Theophrastian character books.[12] By combining the empirical and inductive qualities of the English character with the subjective focus characteristic of the essays of Montaigne, La Bruyère represents the life of the Parisian upper classes through the medium of a narrator who addresses his readers familiarly, relating what he has seen people do and heard people say. He also expresses some personal likes and dislikes. Yet the subjectivity of La Bruyère's caricaturist is not articulated in great detail, and La Bruyère's narrative persona is only an explorer of "high society," not the city in the broad panoramic sense in which it is understood in the Theophrastian character books.

Influenced by the English Theophrastians, La Bruyère in turn influenced the periodical essayists of early eighteenth-century London, whose work then became influential in eighteenth-century Paris (Nicklaus, 104). As this illustrates, the development of the literature of urban spectatorship was an international process. Although my concern in this discussion is with the development of the flaneur within the English-speaking world, it is important to acknowledge that the development of the literature of urban spectatorship must have involved this kind of cultural cross-fertilization between Europe's two preeminent metropolises. In England and America, in fact, the most commonly invoked literary example of privileged and panoramic urban spectatorship was a French text influenced by La Bruyère (Yarrow, 387) and contemporary with Addison and Steele, a text that offers perhaps the clearest image of the conception of urban social life that was coming into being in conjunction with the genre of the character book and that would later form the basis of the assumptions of the flaneur. In the frame story of *Le diable boiteux* ("The Limping Devil" or "The Devil Upon Two Sticks") by Alain René Le Sage – a work published in Paris in 1707, translated into English shortly thereafter, and cited by numerous English and American flaneurs in the nineteenth century – a Spanish student nobleman named Don Cleofas frees a crippled devil named Asmodeus from a bottle and is rewarded by being brought to the top of the highest steeple in Madrid. There Asmodeus extends his hand "and in an instant all the roofs of the houses seemed removed: and the student saw the insides of them as plainly as if it had been noon day" (Le Sage, 22). Don Cleofas is fascinated by what he sees: "His eyes ran through all parts of the city, and the variety which surrounded him was sufficient to engage his curiosity for a long time." The devil perceives that the young man watches the "confusion of objects" with "much pleasure" but little understanding. In order to give Don Cleofas "a perfect knowledge of human life," Asmodeus undertakes to "explain . . . what all those people which you see are doing," and he promises to "disclose . . . the springs of their actions, and their most secret thoughts." Like the writer of a character book, Asmodeus shows Don Cleofas a series of what he calls "pictures" (22) of the inhabitants of Madrid, bereft not only of the covering of their roofs, but of the covering provided by their elaborate wigs, clothing, and makeup.[13]

In the last two decades of the seventeenth century, the expansion of periodical publication[14] led to the development of a new urban spectatorial genre, consisting of panoramic tours of London, presented in installments by a detached wanderer. Although the narrators of the coney-catching books had generally represented themselves as wanderers, this posture had little effect on the actual form of their representation of London. Yet in these periodical series, the wandering spectator actually offered an episodic presentation of the city, a sense that each installment was devoted to what the spectator had randomly encountered in the time since the last installment. This crucially important innovation illustrates, of course, the way in which the material nature of a text can affect the process of representation. As their own metaphors often suggest, the writers of character books and survey books turn a city into a volume: legible, complete, and static. Periodical publication, on the other hand, emphasizes the novelty and ephemerality of its content and in this respect, periodicals have undoubtedly played a significant role in creating the experience of modernity, the sense of reality as a perpetually new and discontinuous spectacle that can be consumed by a spectator unable to influence what he or she observes.

To unify their periodical series, authors of this new genre of urban spectatorial literature made use of several different yet related devices. Some of them – notably, in England, Tom Brown's *London Amusements* (1700), a part of his *Amusements Serious and Comical* – were presented as guided tours of Paris and London offered to intelligent and inquisitive aliens, such as Turks, Siamese, and American Indians.[15] Others used the seventeenth-century stock figure of the Cynic philosopher as an urban observer. Both of these devices enabled an author to write about a city with an unusual degree of detachment and curiosity. In the period immediately preceding the appearance of the *Tatler* (1709–11) and the *Spectator* (1711–12), the most popular works of "London" literature structured according to these principles were, in addition to Brown's work, Ned Ward's the *London Spy* (1698–1700), and an essay series entitled the *English Lucian* (1698). The latter two serials begin in the same way, with the introduction of a Cynic philosopher. The English Lucian describes himself as having been let out of hell and set down on Highgate Hill. The London Spy introduces himself as a rural philosopher who "after a tedious confinement to a country hut, where I dwelt like Diogenes in his tub" (1), has decided to go off to London. In these prominent essay serials, Ward and the authors of the *English Lucian* establish what was to become a pattern in urban spectatorial pieces of all kinds over the next two centuries. These urban spectators are detached from ordinary social, familial, or economic obligations. They present themselves as philosophers and therefore claim to have such a degree of control over their appetites that they may be sanctioned to look at and comment upon the various forms of London vice. Finally, both of these spectators promise their readers a "safe" imaginative exposure to urban curiosities without the necessity of exposure to the dangers and difficulties normally involved in observing them.

Having established their legitimacy and having set up the model of a subjectivity suited to the episodic presentation of a randomly encountered urban scene, the early English periodical essayists then proceeded to provide a kind of entertainment that has resulted in their general neglect. As Walter Graham wrote, in his 1930 history of English literary periodicals, the genre that was dominant in the periodical precursors of Addison and Steele is "valuable for its employment of 'character' and for the light it throws on taverns and coffee houses and social life of the period, yet may be given scant consideration in literature because of its obsession with filth and obscenity" (48).

Graham's characterization is entirely accurate. These crucially important immediate ancestors of the flaneur fill their explorations of London with stories so filthy, bizarre, and offensive or outlandish to the tastes of later periods that few have ever been reprinted and the few that have, have generally been reprinted in bowdlerized editions. Essay serials like the *English Lucian*, *London Amusements*, and the *London Spy* demonstrate beyond any doubt that the confident sense of encyclopedic encompassment offered by the survey books and the Theophrastian character books is only one of many possible pleasures that can be provided by a fictional urban spectator.[16]

The *English Lucian*, one of the most popular and durable of these essay series, begins with the predictable raptures of its narrator as he observes the panorama of London from Highgate Hill. After admiring the prospect of the city laid out before him, Lucian descends into the bustle of the city itself, still impressed by its beauty and, as he makes a special point of noting, the "Comeliness" of "those of the most Engaging Sex" (1). At first, Lucian decides that he must have landed in a version of the Golden Age, but he quickly discovers his mistake. The first place he visits, which is represented as the most notable and characteristic site in London, is the Royal Exchange. The subsequent numbers of the *English Lucian* bring Lucian to many of the other important places in London.

His description of such standard stops on the tourist's itinerary as West-minster Hall and Lincoln's Inn Fields are interspersed with obscene stories presented with the avowed – yet, as in the case of the coney-catching books, unconvincing – intention of exposing vice. Most of the stories involve people being conned because of the excessive size of their sexual or gustatory appetites. Drunkenness is pervasive and it is represented as a state in which all inhibitions are nonexistent and sexual desire is out-rageously intensified. In the English Lucian's world, all identity is fluid. There is a great deal of cross-dressing, mistaking the gender of one's bedfellows, or confusing the sexual organs with other parts of the body. There are also numerous practical jokes, nearly all of an erotic or sca-tological nature. In all of these ways, the world of the English Lucian is carnivalesque in the specific sense in which Mikhail Bakhtin uses the term in the third chapter of his book *Rabelais and His World*.

In addition to representing what Bakhtin identifies as characteristically carnivalesque subject matter, the texts of these early urban spectators are carnivalesque in the way they use these elements to parody and subvert traditional power relations. As absolute inversions of Stow, who de-mands respect for everything in London as part of its great whole, noth-ing is treated with respect in these London surveys. The London Spy makes the particular point of observing over and over again that all of London's public spaces, whatever their supposed dignity or importance in the economy or politics of the kingdom, are places where lustful and illicit activities, all categorized in prurient detail, go on. As he observes, after taking in the show of madmen in their cages at Bedlam, the crowd that comes to observe the insane is scarcely more of a civil body politic. Of Bedlam, he writes: "'Tis an alms-house for madmen, a showing room for whores, a sure market for lechers, a dry walk for loiterers" (52). The Royal Exchange is featured in Ward as a place where young women are kidnapped and sold into slavery by West Indian traders. In Brown, it is referred to as a place for the "exchange" of "male and female commodities" (23). The subversive nature of this carnivalesque genre is particularly evident in the cynical view each of them presents of com-mercial activity in London. Describing what goes on at the Royal Ex-change, Brown writes:

> Some call trade honest gain, and to make it more palatable have lacquered it with the name of godliness, and hence it comes to pass, that the generality of Londoners are counted such eminent profes-sors. But of all guessers, he came nearest the mark that said, Trade was playing a game at dropping fools' pence into knaves' pockets, 'til the sellers were rich, and the buyers were bankrupts.
>
> That magnificent building there [the Royal Exchange], which

stands in the middle of London, is for the accommodation of Lady
Trade and her heirs and successors for ever, and is so full of amusements about twelve o'clock every day, that one would think all the
world was converted into newsmongers and intelligencers; for such
is the first salutation among all mankind that frequent that place.
"What news from Scandaroon and Aleppo?" says the Turkey Mer-
chant. "What price bear currants at Zante? Apes at Tunis? Religion
at Rome? Cutting a throat at Naples? The cure of a clap at Padua?
. . . Hark you, Mr. Broker, I have a parcel of excellent logwood,
block-tin, spider's-brains, philosopher's-guts, Don Quixote's
windmills, hens-teeth, ell-broad pack-thread, and the quintessence
of the blue of plums."(21–2)

This cynicism about respectable trade, this contemptuous dismissal of
all efforts to represent it as honest and godly, is succeeded by a list out
of Rabelais, a satire of commodification that presents the Royal Exchange
as a carnival of grotesque exaggeration whose main source of interest is
that it is so "full of amusements."

Viewing London as a series of sensations, having so much less of an
interest in the city's order and coherence, the carnivalesque urban spectators are able to represent the features of London experience that would,
in the nineteenth and twentieth centuries, be associated with its modernity. Both Ward and the so-called Lucian revel in the manic vitality of
the urban scene, in the ability of the city to produce disorientation and
sensory overload. Ward describes the streets of London in the following
way:

My Ears were so Serenaded on every side, with the Grave Musick
of sundry Passing Bells, the rattling of Coaches, and the Melancholy
Ditties of Hot Baked Wardens and Pippins, that had I had as many
Eyes as Argos, and as many Ears as Fame, they would have been
all Confounded, for nothing could I see but Light, and nothing
hear but Noise. (The Casanova Society, 26)

In his description of the Royal Exchange, Ward offers what may be
one of the earliest detailed accounts of the unruly density of the modern
commercial environment. He writes: "Advertisements hung as thick
around the pillars of each walk as bells about the legs of a morris dancer,
and an incessant buzz, like the murmurs of the distant ocean, made a
diapason to our talk, like a drone to a bagpipe" (The Folio Society, 53).
The constant exposure to sensation causes Ward to observe, more than
a century before Wordsworth or Baudelaire, that Londoners develop an
insatiable appetite for newspapers that contain nothing but titillating
accounts of "Things Terrible and Prodigious."

Representing the city in this way, the carnivalesque urban spectators emphasize the intractability of a human reality that cannot be encompassed by the obsessive demand for order that motivated the Theophrastian character book. There is typology in this genre, but for the most part it is the typology of carnival, the grotesque exaggeration of human types appreciated for their grotesquerie, rather than the orderly types of the Theophrastian character books. London is presented as, and enjoyed for the fact that it is, a place where the most bizarre, unruly, and uncontained provinces of human experience may be encountered and observed. The carnivalesque urban spectator offers access to all of this, but despite his frequent claim in the introduction to the serial to be a reborn Diogenes, he neither judges nor interprets what he sees. The city, like the carnival, is a place where the uncanny may be encountered, and where random, discontinuous, passing people and forms may assume a fleeting symbolic significance, interacting unexpectedly with the unconscious. This feature of the urban, exemplified for modern readers by the "Ulysses in Nighttown" section of *Ulysses*, is evident in the scattered remnants that have survived of the seventeenth-century urban spectator. There too, the portions of the mind that carnival lets loose and that bourgeois culture aims to suppress are figured back to the mind by the experience of the geography of the city, and particularly those specific and forbidden parts of the city that are associated with the extremes of behavior and with sex. By exploiting the possibility of encountering the city in this way, these virtually forgotten writers were raising profoundly important cultural possibilities to which Addison and Steele, by inventing the flaneur, were responding.[17]

Addison and Steele were not the first to present the city through the eyes of a detached Cynic or naive philosopher who, while walking and wandering, claims to be writing down whatever he encounters. Nor were they the first to deal with such staples of later urban spectatorial literature as the incongruity of London signs, the absurdity of London dress, the cacaphony and human variety of London streets and marketplaces, and the fascination and profusion of London types. In their attention to this subject matter, they were anticipated by Tom Brown, Ned Ward, and the English Lucian. Addison and Steele did, however, bring together features of earlier urban spectatorial modes in order to create a new one. They established, more than anyone else, the ethos and style of urban spectatorship that Benjamin was to discover in the French *feuilletons* in the 1830s.

In order to understand the historical significance of the mode of urban spectatorship they originated, it is necessary to recognize that the original readers of the *Tatler* and the *Spectator* cannot help but have been aware that what they were reading was a cleaner, more dignified, and more edifying version of the kind of urban literature that was most popular at this time. Addison and Steele were unquestionably influenced by their cruder colleagues, but they also apparently perceived that there was a market for a peripatetic spectator whose adventures were somewhat less interesting than those found in the *English Lucian* or the *London Spy*, but whose city was substantially more coherent, less shocking and surprising. In his book *The Function of Criticism*, Terry Eagleton has suggested that Addison and Steele contributed in a variety of ways to the forming and consolidation of the idea of the "gentleman," a new model of behavior for the men of England's increasingly dominant haute bourgeoisie, a model whose posture toward social life combined features of the attitudes of a mercantile class with features of the attitudes of the aristocracy. The entertaining yet edifying moralism of the *Spectator*, Eagleton suggests, helped to create what he calls, following Habermas, a "public sphere," an area of discourse, physical, social, and rhetorical, that would reflect the shared assumptions of the bourgeoisie. As Peter Stallybrass and Allon White have suggested, an important part of the creation of this bourgeois "public sphere" was the cleaning up and reconceptualization of urban public space. Stallybrass and White argue that "the *Tatler* and the *Spectator* had a central role" in this process, that they served a kind of policing function. They write: "Concomitant with the establishing of the 'refined' public sphere and its distinct notion of professional authorship was a widespread attempt to regulate body and crowd behavior so as to create conditions favorable to the sphere" (83–4). Through behavior modification brought about by satire and through the selective presentation of the urban spectacle, White and Stallybrass suggest, social hygiene as practiced by Addison and Steele made urban life tolerable for the bourgeoisie. In the end the process of which Addison and Steele were a part enabled "the creation of a sublimated public body without smells, without coarse laughter, without organs, separate from the Court and the Church on the one hand and the market square, alehouse, street and fairground on the other – this was the great labour of bourgeois culture, complementary to that institutionalizing inventiveness of the same period which Foucault has mapped in *Madness and Civilization* and *Discipline and Punish*" (93–4).

If Addison and Steele are understood to have been an important part of such a process of cleansing, then their modification of the genre of what I have called the carnivalesque spectator can be understood in these terms as well. Addison and Steele did not simply try to clean and regulate what they or any eighteenth-century observer would have seen, heard, or smelled in the city; they were also trying to change, in relation to an existing periodical tradition, the way in which London was being represented for literary consumption. It is clear, however, from their essays, that they were unwilling to go back to the sort of clean and magnificent survey of writers like Stow, whose appendix in praise of "urban" values suggests that the process of creating a bourgeois "public sphere" may have begun at least a century before Addison and Steele. Nor do their essays recall the fixed character of the Theophrastian character books. What Addison and Steele seem to have attempted, rather, is a fusion of some of the features of the survey books and Theophrastian character books on the one hand and the features of the carnivalesque urban spectator on the other. Their city takes the form suggested by periodical publication. It is discontinuous and presented by a spectator who claims to be entirely open to the randomness of urban experience. Yet the *Spectator* offers, throughout the series, a perpetual reassurance. While offering access to a fluid and apparently incoherent spectacle, the Spectator always claims to be in control. He can read and interpret whatever comes forward. In order to combine the ideal of the Panopticon with the ideal of the passive spectator, open to randomness, Addison and Steele suggest the possibility of a spectator who is able to impose order, continuity, and coherence *in the act of watching* what appears to be chaotic. Rejecting the bumbling picaresque model of the spectator that emerges in the earlier, carnivalesque periodical tradition, they introduce the innovation of a powerful gaze that provides a spectator with a panoramic equanimity available on the spot, obviating the need to present the city itself as fixed and frozen. To accomplish this fusion, Addison and Steele create the flaneur, as Benjamin found him. They create a spectatorial persona who enjoys diversity without grossness, randomness without danger, amusing bustle of mild interest rather than terrifying chaos of profound fascination. They recognize, however, that such an individual is only conceivable if, unlike the narrator of the coney-catching book or the carnivalesque sketch, he is imagined to possess extraordinary powers of interpretation that are in fact an introjection of the implicit power of the panoramic typologies of the Theophrastian character books.

So that he can plausibly exercise this degree of power, Addison and Steele give their Spectator the social privilege of a bachelor with a moderate independent income. Like virtually every other subsequent flaneur, their Spectator enjoys a maximum degree of detachment from social, economic, and familial obligations. His distance from such concerns, which gives him a panoramic perspective and which helps to make his interpretive powers more credible, is implicit in the idea of the Cynic philosopher but is never actually brought off in the earlier essay serials that made use of this device. These earlier Cynic philosophers tend to lose much of their detachment and virtually all of their ability to read, once they actually immerse themselves in London life. The Spectator, by contrast, much more successfully preserves, throughout the series, the kind of posture he describes himself as having adopted, in his original description of himself. In "The Spectator's Account of Himself," the first number of the *Spectator*, he writes:

> Thus I live in the World, rather as a Spectator of Mankind than as one of the Species; by which means I have made my self a Speculative Statesman, Soldier, Merchant, and Artizan, without ever meddling with any Practical Part in Life . . . I have acted in all parts of my Life as a Looker-on, which is the Character I intend to preserve in this Paper. (1:4–5)[18]

As he describes it, in several passages like this, the Spectator's ability to feel a sense of power over the urban spectacle partly derives from his unencumbered yet central position. He is, as he writes, in *Spectator* no. 10, a member of a "fraternity" (1:45) of those who look upon London as if it were a theater. But the Spectator's power is more than a matter of attitude and position. As he claims, and demonstrates, at various points in the essay series, he has special powers of interpretation. At one point, for example, explaining the fact that he has renounced speech, he claims that the benefits that have accrued to his intellectual vision are comparable with the superior hearing of a blind person. He writes that his silence has given him "a more than ordinary Penetration in Seeing" so that he may claim "to have looked into the Highest and Lowest of mankind, and made shrewd Guesses, without being admitted to their Conversation, at the inmost Thoughts and Reflections of all whom I behold" (1:19–20).

The power that the Spectator claims to have, as a result of his silence and detachment is, as he observes elsewhere, comparable with the power claimed by a skilled physiognomist. Although the Spectator, in no. 86, expresses some doubt about the degree to which character can be determined from physiognomy, he insists that a gifted and detached observer like himself can indeed interpret the "air" of an individual through careful scrutiny of his face. He writes: "I am so apt to frame a Notion of every Man's Humour or Circumstances by his Looks, that I have sometimes employed my self from Charing-Cross to the Royal-Exchange in drawing the Characters of those who have passed by me" (1:365). This ability to "draw characters" is represented by the Spectator as one of the main advantages of urban life, as a special kind of solitary pleasure, comparable with that of reading a book, that is not available elsewhere. As the Spectator writes in *Spectator* no. 131, affirming his intention to return to London after a visit to Sir Roger de Coverley at his country seat, the country

> is not a Place for a Person of my Temper, who does not love Jollity, and what they call Good-Neighbourhood. . . . I shall therefore retire

into the Town, if I may make use of that Phrase, and get into the Crowd again as fast as I can, in order to be alone. I can there raise what Speculations I please upon others without being observed my self, and at the same time enjoy all the Advantages of Company, with all the Privileges of Solitude. (2:20–1)

In this passage, the Spectator looks forward to Baudelaire who writes, in his prose poem "Crowds" in *Paris Spleen*: "Multitude, solitude: identical terms and interchangeable by the active and fertile poet. The man who is unable to people his solitude is equally unable to be alone in a bustling crowd" (20).

"Rais[ing] what Speculations [he] please[s] upon others," the Spectator empties others of any meaning or mental life they may have independently of his consciousness. His activity is therefore appropriately called "speculation," as it turns a crowd into a mirror.[19] In this respect, the Spectator anticipates another of Baudelaire's observations in *Paris Spleen*. In the poem "Windows," after inventing a history of an old woman he sees from a window, Baudelaire writes: "Perhaps you will say 'Are you sure that your story is the real one?' But what does it matter what reality is outside myself, so long as it has helped me to live, to feel that I am, and what I am?" (77). As Baudelaire formulates it in this passage, the main advantage of the adoption of such a "speculative" relation to urban reality is that it offers a form of vivid imaginative pleasure, an existential delight in which the flaneur, feeling what he "is," exults in his power to invent the world around him.

The peculiar process of reading that is so central to the conception of spectatorship in Addison and Steele is, apparently, a form of consumption. It is an activity that permits a spectator to transform public life into a private spectacle, in which he can always be alone, and always at home, as he uses his power of "speculation" to appropriate everything that passes. In spite of the moralism of many of the pieces of the *Spectator* and in spite of his assertions that he actually learns something from his readings, the Spectator asserts at several points that the pleasure that may be gained from consuming the urban spectacle in this way is sufficient to justify the activity. He writes: "It is an endless and frivolous Pursuit to act by any other Rule than the Care of satisfying our own Minds in what we do" (1:18–19). And so "Thus the working of my own Mind, is the general Entertainment of My Life" (1:21).

By demonstrating the possibilities of this form of detached consumption, the Spectator creates a specific niche for himself in relation to the commercial economy of London. He is suited to become the poet of capitalism. One essay in which this is particularly evident is *Spectator* no. 69, in which the Spectator demonstrates that "There is no place in the

Town which I so much love to frequent as the Royal Exchange" (1:292). In this paradise for the flaneur, the Spectator revels in the human diversity of the traders, feeling himself to be a true "Citizen of the World" (1:294). Observing their activities, he experiences feelings that would have been entirely alien to Ward, Brown, or the English Lucian. He writes:

> This grand Scene of Business gives me an infinite Variety of solid and substantial Entertainments. As I am a great Lover of Mankind, my Heart naturally overflows with Pleasure at the sight of a prosperous and happy Multitude, insomuch that at many publick Solemnities I cannot forbear expressing my Joy with Tears that have stolen down my Cheeks. For this reason I am wonderfully delighted to see such a Body of Men thriving in their own private Fortunes, and at the same time promoting the Publick Stock; or in other Words, raising Estates for their own Families, by bringing into their Country whatever is wanting, and carrying out of it whatever is superfluous. (1:294)

For his carnivalesque predecessors, the Royal Exchange is a fabulously slimy place where foreign merchants snare the unwary English, where quacks and whores market their merchandise, and where young women are kidnapped and sold into slavery. If there was legitimate commercial activity taking place there at the time, they did not think it worthy of mention. For Addison and Steele the legitimate commercial activity going on in the Royal Exchange is all that is worthy of mention. Their merchants are honest, comical, and benevolent types, not water rats, hawks, and white slavers. By cleaning up commercial spaces, Addison and Steele's Spectator, like so many flaneurs after him, represents it as a wonderfully safe and comprehensible place to take a walk.

The most self-conscious presentation, in the *Spectator*, of the structure and rewards of urban spectatorship can be found in *Spectator* no. 454. In this essay, as well, Steele represents the paradoxical nature of the flaneur's relationship to the commercial culture and spaces in which his mode of consciousness develops. At the beginning of this essay, the Spectator describes how, finding himself afflicted by a nervous restlessness that made him unable to sleep, he went into London from Richmond in the early morning hours. Through an entire day he moves from marketplace to marketplace, from Covent Garden to the Royal Exchange, observing the infinite profusion of goods available in them. By presenting his trip as a cure for a restless insomnia, Steele suggests the degree to which the spectacle of urban commercial life is all-absorbing, the way in which a true appreciation of it demands and creates a restless consciousness in search of distraction, incapable of rest. As he moves through this rich spectacle, the Spectator seems to observe all of the rich goods on display,

and yet he never buys anything for himself. At a central point in the
essay, he makes an implicit comparison between himself and a species
of female spectator called "silkworms," who "infest" silk and fabric
shops, asking to see samples of the most beautiful merchandise but never
buying anything. At the end of his day-long excursion, the Spectator
confesses to his reader that:

> When I came to my Chamber I writ down these Minutes; but was
> at a Loss what Instruction I should propose to my Reader from the
> Enumeration of so many insignificant Matters and Occurrences;
> and I thought it of great Use, if they could learn with me to keep
> their Minds open to Gratification, and ready to receive it from any
> thing it meets with. This one Circumstance will make every Face
> you see give you the Satisfaction you now take in beholding that
> of a Friend, will make all the Good which arrives to any Man, an
> Encrease of Happiness to your self. (4:103)

Trying to define what "profit" may be had from his purposeless
spectatorship, Steele is only able to describe the mental "Gratification"
that can be derived by the mind "from any thing it meets with." His
inability to interpret or attach a moral to what he has discovered illustrates
the fact that, although the flaneur represents himself as capable of reading
everything he encounters, there are moments in which his appropriative
response to what he sees takes the form not of a reading but of an ecstatic
response to the unreadable, inexpressible magnificence of some portion
of the urban spectacle.

Steele's tongue-tied "gratification" does not at first glance seem to
have any relevance to the values of the marketplace. Yet in this essay,
Steele is describing and celebrating Benjamin's conception of *Erlebnis*,
experience as consumption and collection, the "phantasmagoria of the
idler." Here and in his subsequent manifestations, the flaneur is not a
shopper but a window-shopper. By maintaining an independence from
commercial activity that corresponds to his independence from social
and familial responsibilities, the flaneur is even able to create a sense of
the benign benevolence of commercial activity. By focusing on the beautiful show that merchants put on for anyone with the eyes to see it, he
obscures, if he cannot entirely hide, the fact that they have designs on
people's money. What he proposes, however, is a new model for experience that will, by making commercial life pleasurable and by making
its spaces clean and desirable, serve in the long run to induce people to
buy. In this way, the Spectator suggests a possible way for intellectuals
to be integrated into the culture of the marketplace, as portrait painters
of commercial spectacle, as exemplars, in the manner of the flaneur, of

the equanimity, control, and independence that may be enjoyed in the sheltered spaces of commercial life.

Insofar as he can accomplish this, the flaneur becomes one of the agents of the process by which, in the formulation of Guy Debord, society becomes dominated by the principle of the "spectacle." Steele illustrates, in this essay, the quality of modernity that Debord addresses when he writes that "The spectacle presents itself as an enormous unutterable and inaccessible actuality. It says nothing more than 'that which appears is good, that which is good appears.' The attitude which it demands in principle is this passive acceptance, which in fact it has already obtained by its manner of appearing without reply, by its monopoly of appearance" (12). What Debord calls "the basically tautological character of the spectacle" (13) exercises an enormous power over a consciousness that is willing to accept, in the manner of the Spectator, the self-justifying value of the immense spectacle of commercial life in the modern city.

It is this acceptance of "the basically tautological character of the spectacle," of the value of novelty, change, and the flood of objects in and of themselves that orients human beings to the rhythms and character of a consumer society. As McKendrick, Brewer, and Plumb observe in *The Birth of Consumer Society: The Commercialization of Eighteenth-Century England*, the full-scale development of consumer society depends on specific changes in consciousness that the flaneur is particularly suited to help bring about.

> During the eighteenth century extraordinary economic and social changes swept through Britain and brought into being the first society dedicated to ever-expanding consumption based on industrial production. For this to succeed required men and women to believe in growth, in change, in modernity; to believe that the future was bright, far brighter than the past; to believe, also, that what was new was desirable. . . . Novelty, newfangledness, must be matters of excitement for an aggressive commercial and capitalist world: ever-increasing profit is not made in a world of traditional crafts and stable fashions. Appetite for the new and different, for fresh experience and novel excitements, for the getting and spending of money, for aggressive consumption lies at the heart of successful bourgeois society. (316)

By suggesting the intrinsic sufficiency of novelty and spectacle, by suggesting that everything that is encountered in a rapidly changing commercial city can be read, appreciated, or otherwise rendered clean and harmless, the flaneur may have contributed to the process by means of which "a successful bourgeois society" established itself in England.

In the eighteenth century, at the same time as the flaneur was accommodating the bourgeoisie to the friendly spectacle of the city, by offering the example of an ideal relationship to it, ideal urban spaces were simultaneously being created that expressed many of the same utopian aspirations as are evident in the genre of the flaneur. Just as the flaneur cleaned up the city of the carnivalesque urban spectator, the pleasure gardens of Vauxhall and Ranelagh offered a cleaned-up version of the carnival space itself. Vauxhall Gardens, the larger, more elaborate, and more popular of these two ancestors of the amusement park, was a series of garden walks lined by pavilions, fountains, illuminations, transparencies, and stages for spectacles.[20] The price of admission was such as to ensure that only a well-dressed, well-behaved crowd, a pleasant spectacle in itself, could enter. As carefully and entirely designed environments, offering a controlled exposure to decorous novelty and spectacle, the pleasure gardens embodied a utopian ideal of a city that could never be disorienting or threatening. The utopian ideal implicit in these spaces also made itself manifest in the new commercial spaces that were being created by the developing consumer culture of eighteenth-century London. Long before Baron Haussman plowed the great boulevards of Paris through the dense medieval streetscape, destroying the economy of the *quartiers* and creating a new urban morphology in which the city was a spectacle, accessible to the bourgeoisie in carriages or on foot on the broad sidewalks, the old commercial districts of London were superseded by the broad boulevards of Oxford Street, Regent Street, and Piccadilly[21] (see Clark). Along with the development of residential squares in this period, these London boulevards made possible the creation of specifically bourgeois spaces within the city, spaces adapted to the needs and requirements of the consciousness epitomized in the figure of the flaneur. The new wide boulevards of London and the illuminated shop windows that lined them brought the quality of spectacle developed in the enclosed space of the pleasure gardens out into the actual city (Altick, 227–8). The development of the arcades, late in the century, was also part of this process. To stroll down Oxford Street, or through the Burlington Arcade, looking into the shop windows, watching the well-dressed and prosperous crowd, was an experience not very different from that of walking down the garden walks of Vauxhall, looking at the transparencies and cosmoramas, observing the crowd that could afford the price of admission.

The essays of the *Spectator* were a part of a series of related social processes by which the bourgeois metropolis, the site of modern consumer culture, was coming into being in the eighteenth century. In these essays, the flaneur, as Benjamin describes him, was fully developed. Throughout the eighteenth century, the subjectivity of the Spectator was endlessly imitated, with remarkably little variation (Graham, 144; Law,

28; Watson, 29). Most of the essay serials in the periodical press were unified by a version of the Spectator or Isaac Bickerstaff, the "author" of the *Tatler*. Like their originals, the "connoisseur," the "lounger," the "man of the town," and numerous "reflectors," "inspectors," "philosophers," and "wanderers" attempt to unite in themselves a receptive passivity and improbable interpretive power, social invisibility, and panoramic extensiveness.[22] The subjectivity Benjamin characterizes as that of the flaneur was not only formed in England by the end of the eighteenth century. As the most invariant convention of the century's most popular literary form, it had even become something of a cliché.

The tendency to represent the city as a legible, interiorized spectacle, perpetually gratifying to a curious, consuming mind, is only one aspect, however, of the tradition created by Addison and Steele. Some of the essay serials of the eighteenth century do give particular emphasis to the flaneur's tendency within the *Spectator*, the tendency that is so clearly represented by Steele's no. 454. The *Connoisseur* (1754–6), written mostly by George Colman and Bonnel Thornton, and the *World* (1753–6), written by Edward Moore, Horace Walpole, Philip Stanhope, and others, are good examples of this strand of the Addisonian tradition in the way in which they express an unapologetic and nonmoralistic delight in the spectacle of London. Yet in addition to this privatization of public space, there is also, within the Addisonian tradition, the strand that Eagleton has identified with the "public discourse," that which "involves" the "substantial" matter of moral and philosophical instruction. In the eighteenth-century essay serials, the unifying persona who presents himself[23] as an idle, detached spectator of life was not always a significant presence after his introduction. In many, even most of these serials there is a genuine spirit of moral reform, as in and in spite of names like the *Rambler*, the *Idler*, and the *Lounger*. These serials are closer to the Juvenalian spirit of such eighteenth-century peripatetic urban poems as Johnson's "London" or Gay's "Trivia," and they are certainly anticipated by much of what can be found in the *Spectator*, especially though not exclusively in the essays written by Addison. This "policing" aspect of the Addisonian tradition would have operated in tandem with the flaneur, in the general effort to redesign the city and the crowd in such a way as to make the streets safe and pleasant places to walk for a tolerant yet philosophical and fastidious bourgeoisie. Nevertheless, these two aspects of the Addisonian tradition were fundamentally inconsistent in terms of tone and effect. This inconsistency between what might be called a moralistic and an aesthetic approach to the urban spectacle is not intrinsically untenable. Yet within the periodical essay tradition, the inconsistency would be resolved by the gradual weakening of the moralistic element, by the emergence of the pure Benjaminian flaneur of the first four decades of the nineteenth century.

Chapter 3

The Flaneur in the Nineteenth Century

By the beginning of the nineteenth century, urban spectators who presented London as a show had become entirely dominant over those who offered it as a lesson, although the quest for moral instruction was still a commonly offered pretext for a romp.[1] Several different kinds of urban consumption were available in the periodicals of early nineteenth-century London. One kind, exemplified by many of the essays of Leigh Hunt, is something of a guidebook genre, involving a great deal of attention to the historical and literary associations of "spots" in London.[2] Other essays focus on a writer's personal associations, or memories of specific places or subcultures. Although these genres differ in their premises and content from the flaneur's sketch, they can serve the similar purpose of privatizing or domesticating urban space. Unlike the flaneur, they do not intercept, reduce, or read the ephemeral. They do not claim to possess extraordinary interpretive powers, nor do they claim to be interested in everything. Rather, they look past the ephemeral to a permanent familiar spot, whose sacred value derives from its personal, historical, or cultural associations. These genres are essentially denials of modernity. In them, the crowd is notably and necessarily absent. It is only in the urban sketches structured according to the principles of the flaneur that the crowd and the ephemera of urban life are made available for consumption. A substantial proportion, possibly most of the urban essays that appeared in London periodicals during the first third of the nineteenth century, were structured according to what I have identified as the principles of the flaneur. They involve, that is, the comfortable appreciation of what is randomly encountered by a spectator who claims an unusual ability to read and gain access to faces and objects among which he claims to be entirely at home. The spirit of the flaneur, the spirit of modernity could, at this point, sell periodicals. This is evident in the titles and introductory notices of the magazines of the period. The *London Magazine*, one of the most important and influential magazines of the twenties and thirties, one of the richest fields for the flaneur, had the wonderful full title of *The London Magazines, Charivari and Courrier des Dames; a Proteus in Politics, a Chameleon in Literature, and a Butterfly in the World of Bon Ton.* In the prospectus in its first number it proclaims that "one of the *London Magazine*'s principal objects . . . will be to convey the very image, form, and pressure of that 'mighty heart' whose vast pulsations circulate life, strength, and spirits throughout this great Empire." The character of this title and prospectus suggest what any survey of the urban sketches in the periodicals of this time will bear out: that sketches of modern urban life written in a light and amusing tone were better sellers in an increasingly competitive marketplace than those that hung, however tenuously, to a didactic tradition and intention.

One of the main cultural factors involved in the dominance of the flaneur and related modes of urban consumption in the literary spectatorship of the period was the revival of the familiar essay.[3] The conventions of this highly personal style of essay writing were well suited to any effort to privatize public experience. John Fisher Murray, the flaneur in residence at *Blackwood's Magazine*, and one of the most prominent and talented flaneurs of the 1830s, suggests this when he describes the principle of the unnamed genre in which he was working. Referring to his "power of individualizing character by happy touches of the pen or pencil," an activity best accomplished in London, in "the inexhaustible mine of its living, moving, ever-changing people," he writes that "through the medium of works like these, we become intimate with other men, without the trouble of making their acquaintance, and without much expenditure of thinking, enlarge the sphere of our intelligence. We sit quietly at home, in our easy chair, while the student of human character goes into society, and returning, gives an account of his host, his company, and his entertainment" (4).

Murray's description of his activity, which recalls the Spectator's account of the reasons for his taciturnity, demonstrates the degree to which the emergence of the flaneur is related to a process that the sociologist Richard Sennett has identified as central to the urban culture of the early nineteenth century. During this period, Sennett observes, in *The Fall of Public Man*, "public behavior" for the bourgeoisie was transformed into "a matter of observation, of passive participation, of a certain kind of voyeurism" (195). No longer believing that certain "tasks of personality" could be accomplished through "active interchange with others," men of the upper and middle classes were able to enjoy, as a compensation, what Balzac called "the gastronomy of the eye," a state of transport in which "one is open to everything, one rejects nothing *a priori* from one's purview, provided one needn't become a participant, enmeshed in a scene" (27).[4] As Murray defines his function, the flaneur is a figure who mediates and provides a model for the marginalization Sennett describes. His sketches of human character are presented familiarly to an individual in an easy chair, an individual who is interested in the spectacle of the city, at least as it is transformed by "happy touches of the pen or pencil," yet who wishes to be saved the trouble of "active interchange with others." For Addison and Steele, the urban essay had at least a dual purpose, to make the city available as a spectacle, and to make it into a suitable sphere for "rational" and "moral" public interaction. In the works of nineteenth-century urban essayists, the latter purpose falls away. The flaneur, present earlier as an element in urban culture, becomes a dominant form. The aesthetic values of spectacle become predominant over other considerations, because reform, as Charles Lamb points out in "A Complaint upon the Decay of Beggars in the Metropolis," does not always improve the spectacle.

Charles Lamb's first essay, "The Londoner," written three decades before the heyday of the flaneurs in the French *feuilletons*, is a better example of Benjamin's conception of the flaneur than anything Benjamin himself cites. In the essay, an ostensible letter to the *Morning Post* dated February 1, 1802, the "Londoner" repeatedly exemplifies Benjamin's observation that for the flaneur "the street becomes a dwelling . . . he is as much at home among the facades of houses as a citizen is in his four walls" (37). He writes that he loves "the very smoke of London, because it has been the medium most familiar to my vision" (325). "Born under the shadow of St. Dunstan's steeple" (324), the Londoner was "nursed amid her [London's] noise, her crowds, her beloved smoke" (326). Nurtured by this maternal metropolis, the Londoner has grown to become its imaginative master. He refers to himself as the "speculative Lord Mayor of London" (325). The extent of his speculative dominion is evident in the extraordinarily benign image of London he presents. There is an uncanny harmony between the Londoner's complacent regard and the happy city that offers itself and its meaning to it. The opportunities offered by urban life for social, judicial, and commercial conflict are seemingly nonexistent for someone who can refer to Temple Bar as a place where "the eastern and western inhabitants of this two-fold city meet and jostle in friendly opposition" (324). Obviously such an observation is ironic but there is no sign in this essay or in any of the letters Lamb wrote on the topic of urban life that the purpose of such irony is anything other than to entertain.

Lamb's essay also exemplifies what Benjamin identified as the flaneur's function of legitimizing the economic and social order. Commercial life is represented as a wonderfully benign source of spectatorial pleasure: "The endless succession of shops where Fancy miscalled Folly is supplied with perpetual gauds and toys, excite in me no puritanical aversion. I

gladly behold every appetite supplied with its proper food. The obliging
customer, and the obliged tradesman, things which live by bowing, and
things which exist but for homage – do not affect me with disgust; from
habit I perceive nothing but urbanity, where other men, more refined,
discover meanness" (325). Even a public execution becomes, for the
Londoner, an occasion for indulging in complacent meditation: "The
salutary astonishment with which an execution is surveyed, convinces
me more forcibly than a hundred volumes of abstract polity, that the
universal instinct of man in all ages has leaned to order and good government" (325).

In Murray's sketches, there is a similar representation of the harmony
and rightness of social and commercial life:

> Thus, although society in London is individually discordant it forms
> a universal harmony; and although the interests of any one man
> may appear directly in opposition to the interests of any other man,
> as regards the whole mass they are really the same. I regard the
> crowds of human faces who
> > "Come like shadows, so depart –"
> who flit by me in the streets like the faces of a dream, never to be
> again seen, as my very good friends: they lower the price of the
> necessaries of life for me; they enable me to hear an excellent concert
> for a shilling, which, without their kind assistance, I could not
> attend for less than a hundred pounds, if at any price. Their com-
> petition with another, with the tradesman and with me, enables
> every one of us to have every thing cheaper and better, and what
> is of equal importance, more ready to our hand, than anywhere
> else; and thus we are each of us under general obligation to all,
> without being under particular obligations to any. (1:25)

Observing the same crowd that Wordsworth, in the 1805 *Prelude*, saw
as "flitting . . . like a second-sight procession," Murray does not feel, as
Wordsworth does, that "every face that passes by is a mystery." Like
Lamb and all of the other flaneurs of this period, he certainly would have
been puzzled by Benjamin's assertion that "Fear, revulsion, and horror
were the emotions which the big-city crowd aroused in those who first
observed it" (131). Murray is not bothered by the mystery of others,
and like virtually everyone else who wrote in the London magazines of
the first four decades of the nineteenth century, he is quite at home in
the big-city crowd.

The sense, in these passages by Murray and Lamb, of the plenitude
of life in London, of the universal goodness of everything within one's
purview, of the harmony of the city's motion, is one of the most standard
features of the sketches of the nineteenth-century flaneurs. It looks back

to Steele's celebration of Covent Garden and Addison's celebration of the Royal Exchange. It looks forward to what Baudelaire writes of the artist Constantin Guys in "The Painter of Modern Life":

> So out he goes and watches the river of life flow past him in all its splendor and majesty. He marvels at the eternal beauty and the amazing harmony of life in the capital cities, a harmony so providentially maintained amid the turmoil of human freedom. He gazes upon the landscapes of great cities. . . . He delights in fine carriages and proud horses, the dazzling smartness of the grooms, the expertness of the footmen, the sinuous gait of the women, the beauty of the children, happy to be alive and nicely dressed – in a word, he delights in universal life. (11)

In these moments of benevolent urban ecstasy, the flaneurs seem to see the "invisible hand" that Adam Smith saw as guiding the market system. They experience a benign, even democratic, impersonal love of the entire crowd. They also experience a sense of the self-justifying sufficiency of the spectacle, an experience of passive, unutterable approval, which, according to Guy Debord, is one of the means by which consumer society establishes its hegemony.[5] The retrospective canonization of those who did not see or experience such things in early nineteenth-century London should not blind us to the fact that for decades this was one of the most conventional ways to represent the great wen of London. For the flaneurs who wrote in the *London Magazine*, the *London Quarterly*, the *Gentleman's Magazine*, *Blackwood's Magazine*, the *New Monthly Magazine*, *High Life in London*, *Bell's Life in London*, the *Edinburgh Review*, the *Westminster Review*, and in all of the newspapers of the city, this *was* London. This was the way it was to be written about: from this perspective, in this mood, and with what Murray defended as the necessary "excursive irregularity" (40) that befitted a genre built around the structural principle of taking a walk on a busy street.

In his essay "The *Flaneur*," Benjamin wrote that anything so at odds with actual experience as the flaneur's benign image of the crowd was doomed by its self-evident absurdity. In order to have any understanding of the nineteenth-century flaneur it is necessary to recognize that when dealing with cultural assumptions of this type, there is no such thing as self-evident absurdity. As I will consider later, the flaneur would indeed become less popular in the middle of the nineteenth century. This decline in popularity had nothing to do, however, with his absurdity or even with changes in the nature of metropolitan life. It had to do with the fact that for a variety of commercial, social, and technological reasons, the conventions of representing cities were changing. In the 1830s, however, the flaneur's style of spectatorship was so pervasive and conventional that it was a central feature of the first published work of Charles Dickens, an author not usually identified with the view of urban life it implies. In the *Sketches by Boz*, the tradition of the English flaneur reaches a kind of culmination. It is a culmination, however, at a point of imminent dissolution. In response to a series of pressures, the flaneur was about to dissolve into several new genres of urban consumption that would each have a different use for his fragments. Some of the tensions that would lead to the metamorphosis of the flaneur are dramatically evident in Dickens's earliest work.

By the time Dickens, as a newspaper reporter in his early twenties, began to produce the urban sketches that would eventually be collected in the *Sketches by Boz*,[6] he knew and admired not only Addison and Steele[7] but Leigh Hunt, Charles Lamb, and various other urban spectatorial essayists who wrote for metropolitan newspapers and magazines like those in which his own sketches appeared.[8] Considering his familiarity with what had become such a dominant tradition in London journalism, it is not surprising to find the characteristically nonchalant tone of the flaneur in the following introductory paragraph to the sketch that would be published as "The Prisoner's Van":

> We have a most extraordinary partiality for lounging about the streets. Whenever we have an hour or two to spare, there is nothing we enjoy more than a little amateur vagrancy – walking up one street and down another, and staring into shop windows, and gazing about as if, instead of being on intimate terms with every shop and house in Holborn, the Strand, Fleet-Street and Cheapside, the whole were an unknown region to our wandering mind. – We revel in a crowd of any kind – a street "row" is our delight – even a woman in a fit is by no means to be despised. . . . Then a drunken man –what can be more charming than a regular drunken man?[9]

Although there is presumably some irony and self-parody in Dickens's expression of such an apparently callous attitude toward the suffering that may be observed in a city, this tone is not only conventional, it is also the most consistent feature of the *Sketches by Boz*. It recalls Elia's question in Lamb's "A Complaint Of the Decay of Beggars in the Metropolis": "And what else but an accumulation of sights – endless sights – is a great city; or for what else is it desirable?" (100), and it is part of the introduction of virtually every sketch. Every chance he has, Boz asserts that the sole object of his urban wanderings is "amusement." He observes that "It is very generally allowed that public conveyances afford an extensive field for amusement and observation" (138). Of "Brokers' and Marine-Store Shops," he suggests that "if an authentic history of their contents could be procured, it would furnish many a page of amusement" (177). "All public dinners," we are told elsewhere, "are amusing scenes," though "the annual dinner of some public charity is the most amusing" (163). Even the House of Commons, on the evening of an important debate, attracts Boz's attention as likely to "be productive of some amusement" (152).

The "amusement" that can be derived from the urban spectacle is not freely open to everyone. As Boz writes in the introduction to a sketch entitled "Shops and Their Tenants":

> What inexhaustible food for speculation do the streets of London afford! We never were able to agree with Sterne in pitying the man who could travel from Dan to Beersheba and say that all was barren; we have not the slightest commiseration for the man who can take up his hat and stick, and walk from Covent Garden to St. Paul's Churchyard and back into the bargain, without deriving some amusement – we had almost said instruction, from his perambulation. (59)

Amusement and instruction must be derived and Dickens's word for the process of that derivation is the same as Steele's. What the "speculative pedestrian" (190) consumes is the "inexhaustible food for speculation." He derives his amusement by using the faculties of interpretation that he exercises as his birthright and that are magically associated with his unusual degree of authoritative detachment. In his sketches, Boz interprets, classifies, and organizes London with remarkable grace and ease. Claiming an outrageous degree of interpretative power, he "reads" the city to his readers, assuring them by his casual tone that all of the necessary signs are available to be read, if only one looks at the city in the right way. Boz sees a man in the park and decides that "there was something in the man's manner and appearance which told us, we fancied, his whole life, or rather his whole day, for a man of this sort has no variety of day" (216). Boz then proceeds to "sketch" the man's day in extraordinary detail. Elsewhere, in a secondhand clothing shop, Boz demonstrates how "a man's whole life" was "written as legibly on [some] clothes, as if we had his autobiography engrossed on parchment before us" (75).

Like the Spectator and other figures in the history of the flaneur, Boz associates his unusual powers of interpretation with the position of authoritative detachment he assumes with respect to the urban spectacle. Like the ninety-nine-year-old narrative persona of the *Characters* of Theophrastus, who "having observed human nature a long time" has "thought it incumbent" (37) upon himself to record what he has observed, Boz consistently refers to himself as an elderly man who has seen a great deal and who now enjoys the disinterested spectatorial privileges of comfortable old age.[10] Throughout the sketches, Dickens takes advantage of the great variety of metaphors for authoritative detachment that the nineteenth century afforded, as compared with the seventeenth. He need no longer simply present himself as a Cynic philosopher. He can also assume the powers and privileges of a scientific observer, a scholarly unbiased positivist, observing the flora and fauna of London as if he were Humboldt in the South American rain forest. There are numerous examples of his pseudoscientific tone. In a sketch called "Scotland Yard," for example, Boz writes that:

> When this territory was first accidentally discovered by a country gentleman who lost his way in the Strand, some years ago, the original settlers were found to be a tailor, a publican, two eating-house keepers, and a fruit-pie maker; and it was also found to contain a race of strong and bulky men, who repaired to the wharfs in Scotland Yard regularly every morning, about five or six o'clock, to fill heavy wagons with coal, with which they proceeded to distant places up the country, and supplied the inhabitants with fuel. When they had emptied their wagons, they again returned for a fresh supply; and this trade was continued throughout the year. (64)

Maintaining this tone, Boz observes that since "the settlers derived their subsistence from ministering to the wants of these primitive traders," Scotland Yard "bore strong outward marks of being expressly adapted to [the coal traders'] tastes and wishes" (64). Elsewhere, in the "The Streets–Morning," Boz assumes the pose of a naturalist, describing the "rough, sleepy-looking animals of strange appearance, something between ostlers and hackney-coachmen" who "begin to take down the shutters of early public houses" (48). In "Gin-Shops" he adopts the interpretive posture of a physician, observing that "It is a remarkable circumstance, that different trades appear to partake of the disease to which elephants and dogs are especially liable, and to run stark, staring, raving mad, periodically" (182). As a detached yet interested diagnostician, he then enumerates the symptoms of this malady. In virtually all the sketches, Boz enters an environment like an explorer, observing and describing its particular features and customs as if it were a place no one had ever seen before, rather than a familiar part of London.

From such vantages, Dickens is able to function very effectively as, in Benjamin's words, a "botanist on asphalt." Using the techniques that he has inherited from the long tradition of "character writing," Dickens is able to impose an artificial consistency upon urban experience that makes it readily available for reading and collecting. The city of the *Sketches by Boz* is filled, first of all, with definable human types. The inhabitants of Monmouth Street, for example, "are a distinct class" de-

fined by a series of seemingly invariable characteristics, ranging from
"peaceable and retiring habits," to "countenances" that "bear a thoughtful and a dirty cast" (74). One of the pieces in the "Characters" section
of the sketches is devoted to the delineation of the defining characteristics
of "Shabby-Genteel People" who are identified as one of several classes
of people who "appertain exclusively to the metropolis" (262). Elsewhere, we encounter a "class of men, whose recreation is their garden"
(93), the "numerous race" of the contentious "red-faced men," one of
whom may be found inhabiting every "parlour, or club room, or benefit
society" (239), the "old fellows with white heads and red faces, addicted
to port wine and Hessian boots" (217), and the London apprentices who,
on Sunday, may be recognized by their swagger, their thick walking
sticks, their "light trousers of unprecedented patterns" and their "coats
for which the English language has no name" (218). Each of these classes
is defined by a few easily recognizable physiognomical and behavioral
traits. The apparent ease with which they can be defined lends credence
to Boz's assertion that he can read a man's entire life and character from
his appearance and manner.

In the *Sketches*, Boz also constructs typologies of places, institutions,
and commercial establishments. As in the case of his human typologies,
his presentation of the typology of urban space obscures the possibility
of variation within a type. In a sketch entitled "The Pawnbroker's Shop,"
for example, Boz begins by acknowledging the diversity of London
pawnshops. The diversity can be organized, however, like all forms of
diversity in the *Sketches by Boz*: "There are grades in pawning as in
everything else" (188). Different types of pawnshops reflect different
classes of impoverished people. In this sketch, Boz informs us, he will
be concerned with a relatively humble class of pawnshop, and he has
"selected one" (188) as typical. After offering a brief account of the
external aspect of his specimen, Boz lists the objects that may be found
in it. He then catalogs the characters one would expect to find in such
a place and he has them act out a series of representative tableaux. All
of this is presented as if it were the description of a particular pawnshop
at a particular point in time. Yet the framework of the description, and
of the "London Sketches" as a whole, implies that we can substitute this
particular for the general class. *This*, we are urged to believe, is what a
pawnshop is like. It will typically contain a certain set of objects and a
certain set of characters who will act out a certain set of tableaux. The
configuration of typical objects, people, and tableaux will constitute the
physiognomy of this or any other urban space. Gin-shops, brokers' and
marine-store shops, private theaters, hackney-coach stands, criminal
courts, Seven Dials, omnibuses, and the House of Commons are all
typologized in a similar way. The relatively uniform technique of these

sketches implies that all of the little worlds that constitute London, however superfically diverse, are capable of being described according to the
same principles.

In addition to those he constructs for people and places, Boz develops
a typology of urban time. In the sketches, "The Streets – Morning" and
"The Streets – Evening," he describes representative moments of the
city's life. The implication, in these sketches, that one moment can stand
for all other such moments, is given credibility by the fact that much of
what can be seen in the city is part of an occupational or household
routine. In "The Streets – Morning," the only sign of life in the hour
before dawn is the policeman walking his beat. The city itself begins to
stir with the men who "take down the shutters of early public houses"
(48) and set up breakfast tables. The streets first come to life as carts
bearing produce are driven into Covent Garden market. Sweeps and
servants soon appear and begin to perform their morning duties. They
are followed by "apprentices and shopmen" (51) preparing the shops for
the day. Soon the city is filled with people on their way to work. The
sketch concludes with shoppers descending on the city. The pleasing
regularity of the urban life represented in this sketch is produced by a
series of overlapping and intertwining individual routines. Throughout
the *Sketches*, Boz is fascinated by such regularity, wherever he can find
or impose it. Every weekday evening, he informs us, we may see the
bricklayers' laborers, dressed in fustian, leaning against posts in St. Giles
(71). Every Sunday the same men may be seen, dressed in their best
clothing, leaning against the posts in Seven Dials. Every winter evening,
the housewives in the London suburbs emerge briefly from their homes
to obtain muffins at suppertime and beer at nine. After purchasing these
goods from their respective vendors, "they all pop into their little houses
and slam their little street-doors" (54). A similar mechanical regularity
is characteristic of the life of the man Boz presumes to read in "Thoughts
about People." Like "the dial over the mantel-piece" in his office, "whose
loud ticking is as monotonous as his whole existence" (216), this man's
life is entirely regular and predictable. He works at the same desk every
day, eats dinner at the same restaurant at the same hour every evening,
returns to the same room and has a cup of tea prior to going to bed.

Even if there is a critical component to Boz's representation of the
monotonous regularity of much of urban life, there is also an unmistak-
able appreciation throughout the *Sketches* of the aesthetics of mechanical
regularity. It is particularly entertaining to see the women come out at
nine, buy from the vendors, and then "pop" back into "their little houses
and slam their little street-doors." Dickens's sense of pleasure in this
mechanical regularity is evident in the fact that he consistently imposes
the quality of a mechanical routine on urban events that are not naturally

understood in such terms. In "The Streets – Morning," for example, Boz introduces the apparently unique elements of the urban scene with such generalizing terms as "occasionally," "here and there," "now and then." "Now and then," we are told, "a rakish-looking cat runs stealthily across the road and descends his own area with as much caution and slyness – bounding first on the water-butt, then on the dust-hold, and then alighting on the flag-stones – as if he were conscious that his character depended on his gallantry of the preceding night escaping public obser-vation" (49–50). "Occasionally," one may observe "a little knot of three or four schoolboys on a stolen bathing expedition rattle merrily over the pavement, their boisterous mirth contrasting forcibly with the demeanor of the little sweep" (48). The use of such adverbs and adverbial phrases before such apparently contingent particulars gives them the reiterable quality of the occupational routines that constitute the rest of the image of a London morning. By means of such a device, Boz is able to suggest that everything he sketches in a representative moment is, in fact, typical of all London mornings.

In the *Sketches by Boz*, a carefully constructed moment is made to stand for a series of similar moments, a carefully constructed place or establishment is made to stand for an entire class of places or establish-ments, and a carefully constructed individual is made to stand for a particular class of individuals. The adequacy of the substitution of the typical elements for their respective classes is implied by the fact that Boz never feels the need, after sketching a pawnshop, to show us what another pawnshop looks like at another point in time. In this respect, the *Sketches by Boz* are the culmination of the tradition of linguistic model-building that begins with the Theophrastian character books. Boz's Lon-don offers the same utopianism as this earlier genre. It suggests that signs can deliver all that they refer to, and that an anthology of signs can stand for an entire city, world, or universe.

In these respects, the *Sketches by Boz* resembles a whole class of rep-resentations that expressed a similar utopianism and that were enjoying their greatest popularity at the same time as the flaneur. The London of the *Sketches* has the same character as the London represented in the panoramas, dioramas, cosmoramas, eidophusikons, magic lanterns, and camerae obscurae that, as Richard Altick describes in his encyclopedic *The Shows of London*, were the most popular forms of visual represen-tation in London at the same time as the flaneur was the dominant mode of representing London in the magazines.[11] In spite of their differences, all of these forms of representation produced images that resembled those produced by the flaneur. More often than any other subject matter, each was used to represent either the city of London or foreign cities. The next most common subjects of representation were battles, natural disasters, or particularly complex landscapes (like the Holy Land or the entire length of the Mississippi), scenes that, even if not urban, might be said to have an urban density. In order to represent such potentially overwhelming multiplicity, each of these forms of representation made use of the same techniques of typological and schematic reduction as the flaneur. They would offer the impression of seeing the "whole" by presenting a few recognizable structures and features interspersed with "typical" objects, establishments, and individuals. In all cases, the observer positioned at the center of a cylinder or with an eye in front of a peephole would have the same sense of enjoying a privileged vantage as the flaneur typically claims to have.[12] The panoramas and the dioramas were a figurative rendering of the flaneur's view of the world. In the heyday of the flaneur, they, along with the explicitly panoramic image of the frame story of The Devil upon Two Sticks were the most frequently invoked metaphors for the flaneur's ideal sense of visual encompassment of the city.

Some of these forms of representation were capable of movement or changes in lighting. If they were, their movements were invariably of the kind represented in Dickens's sketches. The stagecraft was only sophisticated enough to represent a scene like that in "The Streets–Night" where a group of women come out of their houses when the clock strikes nine, to buy muffins, and then pop back through their doors. As the light changed, in a diorama, to represent the progress of a morning, different "types" could appear on the scene, to be succeeded by the next group, all moving in predictable, legible, and what are represented as "typical" ways, just as they do in "The Streets – Morning." By domesticating change, both the flaneur and this panoramic culture may have legitimized and familiarized the various industrial, commercial, and even bureaucratic rhythms of modern life.

The history of the flaneur and the history of the panoramic shows of London are interestingly parallel. Each appears in rudimentary form in the seventeenth century, consolidates into recognizable form in the eighteenth century, and reaches its peak of sophistication and popularity in the 1830s. Benjamin observed that what the flaneur offered was a "panorama literature," but this is, as he appears to have recognized by collecting citations about panoramas and dioramas, more than just a metaphor. The flaneur and the culture of panoramas appear to have been complicit historical processes. It is not only their history and strategies that are parallel. They have in common the fact that they were both believed.

The Sketches by Boz were advertised by the book's subtitle as a collection of "scenes of everyday life." Presented as such, the sketches invite readers to recognize their "own" experiences within them. At the same time, however, they give a specific and highly detailed form to what the reader will recognize as familiar experience. This feature of the flaneur's representation of everyday life is also evident in Murray's observation to his *Blackwood's* readers that his sketches of "familiar scenes of metropolitan life" are so purely a transcription of that of which "few take notes, but many take notice," that "If any one should be fortunate enough to find, in the following essays, pictures of life, observation, or reflection, which may have struck him in his own solitary rambles through town, he will have the goodness to consider himself the author, and the author merely his amanuensis" (1:3). Everyday life, reality in its most mundane form, is, as Murray's formulation suggests, that which we could all potentially author. We all see it. There is no controversy about it. It is what the flaneur – the descendant of the character writer, the contemporary of the panoramist, the predecessor of the photographer – shows us through his clear and honest lens.

The degree to which the flaneur's city was convincing to his audience as a mere transcription of "everyday life" is suggested by the fact that the best flaneurs were universally praised for the fidelity and not for the creativity or cleverness of their productions. As J. Hillis Miller has observed: "From the contemporary reviews down to the best recent essays [the *Sketches*] have been praised for their fidelity to the real" (5). The same success was achieved by the panoramas and dioramas. According to Richard Altick, "At a conservative estimate, 90 percent of the criticism of panoramas throughout their history was concerned with their success or failure as realistic representation" (188). Although even the very best of panoramas and dioramas flattened, stopped, silenced, and simplified what they represented, and even moving panoramas and dioramas were capable of nothing more than the most simple and repetitive motion, these generic inadequacies received no more attention than those of the flaneur. The ability of panoramas and dioramas to determine the way in which the city was perceived is actually noted by Dickens within the *Sketches by Boz* themselves. In the sketch "Greenwich Fair" Boz notes how visitors to Greenwich, observing London through the telescopes of the pensioners, respond to the city in the distance as if they were observing Thomas Horner's "Panorama of London from the top of St. Paul's," in the Colosseum in Regent's Park.[13]

The convincing quality of these forms of representation derived from the way in which their representations combined the features of a sign and an image. In a sketch by Dickens or Murray, readers would recognize a "gin-shop" as if they were reading letters on a page. As the reader recognized the sign, the entire class of things it referred to would be invoked and would take on the character of the image in the sketch. The reader would simultaneously think: "I recognize this" and "This is what this kind of thing is like." By suggesting that everyday reality could be represented as it was, through the presentation of conventionalized, "typical" scenes and portraits that would have the detailed quality of an image and the referential inclusiveness of a sign, the sketches of the flaneur and the images of the panoramas and dioramas may have lent credence to each other. They would also have claimed an analogous authority deriving from their respective claims to be relatively unmediated images of reality. Another component of their credibility would have been their apparent completeness. By conveying a sense of the whole, they would imply that nothing had been left out. In each of these ways, these traditions of representation anticipated the photographic culture that would supersede them. Photography, television, and cinema also combine an experience of recognition with a highly detailed, allegedly unmediated image, causing the viewer to associate what they recognize with the specific image in the photograph or on the screen.

Just as different aspects of photographic culture, like television news and film, reinforce each other's claims to credibility, creating an interlocking closed system that constructs the sense of "everyday life" in a late twentieth-century society, the flaneur and the culture of the panoramas may have accomplished something similar in the early nineteenth century.[14] As is evident in Murray's claim that he is merely an amanuensis recording the urban experiences of his readers, the "everyday life" recorded by the flaneur is an apparent consensus that is in fact the creation of image makers who reinforce each other's credibility so as to maintain the illusion of consensus from which their own credibility derives. Within the culture enclosed by these systems, it is difficult to evaluate the credibility of the ideas that constitute "everyday life" because individual experience is only assumed to have authority when it makes intermittent contact with the images provided by what are believed to be more authoritative sources than one's own eyes and ears. It is for this reason that there is no such thing as self-evident absurdity when one speaks of a particular view of everyday life. It is for this reason as well that the flaneur and the panoramas only lose their credibility when new images of the city, produced by new traditions of urban representation, begin to dominate the social consensus that constructs "everyday life."

Some of the new traditions of urban representation that would weaken the hegemony of the flaneur, like photography or modern crime journalism, were the product of social or technological developments in the 1830s and 1840s. Others, however, were the product of instability, inadequacy, or paradox within the tradition of the flaneur itself. One such crack within the flaneur's construction of reality is particularly evident within the *Sketches by Boz*. By presenting the city as orderly and coherent, spatially and temporally encompassed, the flaneur and the panoramist unintentionally create an effect of incongruity deriving from the fact that something that is known to be ephemeral and dynamic is being represented as if it were eternal and immutable. By eliminating all contingency, panoramas, dioramas, and the sketches of the flaneur produce an uncanny sense of death in the thing. A realistic painting does not produce this sense of incongruity because it is more explicitly represented and perceived as a work of art, as the artist's imaginative apprehension of reality. Panoramas, dioramas, flaneur's sketches, and, later on, photographs contain the incongruity because they are represented and perceived as direct and comparatively unmediated "slices" (to use a common metaphor in the literature of the flaneur) of reality. The viewer is struck by the fact that what he or she observes is "real" and yet it does not change, or if it does, it changes in an endlessly repeated cyclical way. The existence of this effect explains why, in the midst of what appears to be the flaneur's preternatural complacency and happiness with his prospect, there are often moments of melancholy like the following passage from James Grant's panorama of London entitled *The Great Metropolis*:

> Xerxes wept when he surveyed his fine army of a million of men from an eminence, at the thought that in a hundred years afterwards not one of the soldiers who stood vigorous and healthy before him would be alive. The theme was a fitting one on which to moralize, and the tears of that great general were natural and comprehendable on the occasion. I have often thought what must be the emotions of a man ... were he to station himself on the top of St. Paul's, which is 480 feet above the general level of the metropolis, and look down on the houses and streets within a circle of five miles. The painful and humiliating thought would intrude itself on his mind, that in those houses and streets there were no fewer than two millions of his fellow-beings, and yet that of this vast number, though now as busy and bustling as if this world were to be their eternal home, there will not, in all probability, ere the lapse of a century, be one solitary individual whose body is not mouldering in the dust. London will no doubt be as populous then as now; but its inhabitants will be a race who have not as yet any local habitation or a name; who have not, indeed, even an existence. (1:18–19)[15]

As the poet of capitalism, the connoisseur of its dynamism, the flaneur must deny the destructiveness of that dynamism. He must control and sanitize change, just as he must control and sanitize the crowd. Dickens tries to achieve this traditional effect of the flaneur when he suggests that the motion of the city falls into predictable and observable patterns that give it something of the character of a frozen, graspable process. Yet this is where the contradictions within the *Sketches* become manifest. In Dickens's dioramic representation of the real and the random, all of which seems to be and is presented as if it were amusing, playful, and trivial, there is a constant awareness of mortality, a constant sense of the discrepancy between the fixity and regularity of the image and the ephemerality of what is represented. A substantial proportion of the *Sketches by Boz* are concerned with the theme of individual social and economic decline. "Shops and Their Tenants" describes the doomed enterprises that successively occupy a single shop. "Scotland Yard" deals with the obliteration of an urban subculture because of the construction of a new bridge across the Thames. Stories of decline figure prominently in "The Pawnbroker's Shop," "Meditations in Monmouth Street," "The Drunkard's Death," "Shabby-Genteel People," and "Broker's and Marine-Store Shops." Throughout the sketches, Boz even seems to conceive of decline as the inevitable direction of urban life over time. In "Hackney-Coach Stands," he considers the prospect of hackney coaches having memories. If they did, he exclaims, "How many stories might be related of the different people it had conveyed on matters of business or profit, pleasure or pain! And how many melancholy tales of the same people at different periods! The country-girl – the showy, over-dressed woman – the drunken prostitute! The raw apprentice – the dissipated spendthrift – the thief!" (84). Each of these stories of decline takes place within a vast and indifferent flux. As Boz observes, at the opening of "Thoughts about People," "It is strange with how little notice, good, bad, or indifferent, a man may live and die in London. He awakens no sympathy in the breast of any single person; his existence is a matter of interest to no one save himself; he cannot be said to be forgotten when he dies, for no one remembered him when he was alive" (215).

The unresolved coexistence of the flaneur's posture on the one hand and an obsessive awareness of the ravages of time and social processes on the other produces some bizarre moments of contradiction in the *Sketches by Boz*. In "Hackney-Coach Stands," for example, Boz's speculations about the "melancholy tales" a hackney coach might relate if it had a memory are introduced by the following sentences: "What an interesting book a hackney-coach might produce, if it could carry as much in its head as it does in its body! The autobiography of a broken-down hackney-coach would surely be as amusing as the autobiography of a broken-down hackneyed dramatist" (84). These melancholy tales, Boz conjectures, would be "interesting" and "amusing." A reader might wonder at this point if Boz's distance from the city has made him an aesthete of human suffering. We are again tempted to think this when, in the sketch "Shops and Their Tenants," Boz describes the failure of a stationer's shop and the gradual decline of the stationer's consumptive daughter. He describes the eviction of the family and expresses some degree of sympathy: "What became of the last tenant we never could learn; we believe the girl is past all suffering; and beyond all sorrow. God help her! We hope she is" (62). Having said this, Boz begins his next paragraph: "We were somewhat curious to ascertain what would be the next stage – for that the place had no chance of succeeding now was perfectly clear. The bill was soon taken down, and some alterations were being made in the interior of the shop. We were in a fever of expectation; we exhausted conjecture" (62). "Somewhat curious," "in a fever of expectation" – Boz has returned to the position of watcher, and his attention has returned to the "interesting" progression of diverse establishments that successively occupy a single shop.

Dickens's consciousness bore the scars of the rapid and unpredictable changes of London economic life. Yet for him, as he once wrote to John Forster, London and its crowds were a "magic lantern," essential to his creativity.[16] Boz therefore insists upon the flaneur's prerogative of observing change from a position of detachment. But by refusing to sanitize the change, and by allowing himself to express emotions about urban change that would have been alien to the flaneur, he suggests several ways in which the figure of the flaneur might be transformed. Boz displays, first of all, an emotional response to the pathos of reductive realistic representation that anticipates an emotional dynamic that would gain particular prominence in the culture of photography. Boz looks at his fixed and frozen sketches and panoramas and experiences, as Murray did, with a sense of the poignance of the urban moment, a revelation of transience in the freezing of the urban flux. He also becomes vividly aware, from his position of detachment, of the plenitude of life in a city. The *Sketches* are filled with moments in which Boz stops his walk simply to marvel at the immense amount of human life and emotion in a library of wills, behind the windows of a hospital, behind the walls of a prison, within the walls of a hackney coach, in the objects of a pawnshop, or in the clothes in a secondhand shop. In these moments he is like the flaneur angels in Wim Wender's film *Wings of Desire* who, sitting in an automobile showroom, exchange descriptions of the human events they have collected, stunned by the multiplicity of life in Berlin, incapable of interpreting it, capable only of a distanced yet powerful sentiment of compassion. In a fascinating and significant response to this powerful, indefinite feeling, Boz often sets himself up as a salvager of human identity. He anticipates the detective in the way in which he transforms the flaneur's unusual ability to interpret urban signs into a fantasy of a consciousness that can find anything and anyone who is lost, who can reveal the hidden skeleton of a narrative behind the mute urban trace.

By reading the story "contained" within the object, Boz offers his readers some degree of reassurance against their awareness that vanished people and ways of life do not always leave traces of themselves in urban objects. He also suggests the possibility of an aesthetic exploitation of the city through narrative and ultimately, through a panoramic interlocking of narratives that would address the experience of time in a way that the flaneur's sketch or the panorama could not. In the *Sketches by Boz*, Dickens strains against the limitations of the flaneur's sketch in ways that may have been very productive for his development into a novelist.

Dickens's discovery opens up new avenues of consumption of the city, focusing not on the power of an image arrested from time, but on time itself, on the narratives contained in the images. Narrative creates the possibility of representing time, of transcending the flaneur's imprisonment in the momentary and the ephemeral. It appears, within the *Sketches* themselves, to promise what they would in fact come to offer, a more popular and more versatile medium for the representation of everyday life than anything that the flaneur could provide. But the development of the urban panoramic novel, visible in the *Sketches*, reflects only one of the ways in which the paradoxes and inadequacies of the flaneur are leading to the development of rival forms of urban representation.

Another inadequacy of the tradition of the flaneur is evident in the most popular English book of the 1820s. Like the *Sketches by Boz*, Pierce Egan's *Life in London* self-consciously invokes the conventions of the flaneur. In his introduction, Egan refers to *The Devil upon Two Sticks* and he promises the reader "a Camera Obscura View of London, not only because of its safety, but because it is so snug, and also possessing the invaluable advantages of seeing and not being seen" (46). Viewed in this way,

> the Metropolis is a complete Cyclopedia, where every man . . . may find something to please his palate, regulate his taste, suit his pocket, enlarge his mind, and make him happy and comfortable. . . . In fact every Square in the Metropolis is a sort of map well worthy of exploring. . . . There is not a street also in London but what may be compared to a large or small volume of intelligence, abounding with anecdote, incident, and peculiarities. A court or alley must be obscure indeed, if it does not afford some remarks; and even the poorest cellar contains some trait or other, in unison with the manners and feelings of this great city, that may be put down in the notebook, and reviewed, at an after period, with much pleasure and satisfaction. (51–2)

In *Life in London*, as in the contemporary urban familiar essays, the sheer pleasure afforded by urban spectatorship is exalted above any of its other conceivable uses and products. Egan's use of these conventions suggests once again how pervasive the stock attitude of the flaneur had become in the first few decades of the nineteenth century. Yet Egan breaks away from the flaneur's tradition by extending his spectatorship into those areas of London life that had been purged from the literature of urban spectatorship by the flaneur. Egan, in essence, revives the carnival city of Ward, Brown, and the English Lucian. His book is an extravagantly slangy account of the bawdy and discontinuous adventures of Corinthian Tom, an elegant "man about town," his country cousin Jerry Hawthorn, and Bob Logic, a purported wit. While it was not unusual for a flaneur to carry his lucid equanimity into a few carefully designed back alleys and gin-shops, Egan sends his perpetually drunken characters into whorehouses, gambling dens, and the sort of places where a trained monkey might fight a dog. The energy of all of their frenzied motion is spectatorial consumption. One of Egan's heroes is referred to as "an out-and-outer for continually scouring the back slums . . . in search of something new" (322). This consumption is not in any respect intellectual or "speculative." When Egan makes the stock comparison of London to a book, he emphasizes that it is a "volume . . . abounding with anecdote, incident, and peculiarities" (51), one that offers, without any apologies, nothing more substantial than "pleasure and satisfaction" (52).

Reviving the subject matter of the carnivalesque urban spectators, Egan also revived their language and rhetorical style. *Life in London*, like its predecessors, is written in a democratic and subversive slang. Its prose style is a form of linguistic slumming. The gentlemen protagonists are not protected by the distancing effect of educated prose. Instead, they and the reader seem to be brought by the language into the world of the streets. In this world, as in Ward's *London Spy*, anything can happen at any time. Everything is exaggerated, and nothing is continuous. In a world described in this way, novelty and spectacle are present everywhere and it is hardly necessary for the heroes of *Life in London* to "scour the back slums" in search of it. In the tradition of the carnivalesque urban spectator, Egan suggests that there is a continuity between the most fashionable places in London and the underworld of illicit amusements, as both serve to accommodate extravagant appetites for pleasure. Yet writing after and in the context of the flaneur, Egan finds enough appeal in the luxury and absurdity of the bourgeois city. He is not as concerned as his carnivalesque predecessors to emphasize its corruption. Joining the flaneur's love of luxurious spectacle with the carnivalesque spectator's penchant for repetitive and cumulative ecstasies of exaggeration, Egan may have invented the gushing tabloid style of description of haute bourgeois luxury that survives in the rhetoric of Robin Leach's "Lifestyles of the Rich and Famous." Egan writes, in one typical passage, that:

> The Italian Opera (this luxurious wardrobe of the great, this jeweller's shop of the nation, this *scent* and *perfume* repository of the

world, and Arabian Nights' spectacle of Fortunatus's cap) is one of the most brilliant collections of portraits of Life in London. It possesses such fascinations, and the *spell* is so powerful, that to be "*seen there*" is quite enough, the performances being mere dumb show to most of the visitors. (24)

In this passage, Egan presents the flaneur's landscape in something other than the flaneur's style. His extravagance and his uninhibited revival of the forbidden features of the city suggest that whether or not contemporary audiences found the flaneur's city to be credible, they may not have found it sufficiently satisfying. Egan's bawdy and raucous image of London life may have been a self-conscious rejection of the flaneur's fantasy of social control, of a coherent "indoor" urban landscape. In this way it may have exposed a contradiction that had been present in the genre of the flaneur from the beginning. It is not easy to reconcile a professed love of randomness, novelty, and spectacle with a conviction that the city one loves to watch is predictable, compartmentalized, and benign. The emergence and immense popularity of Egan may suggest that this balance is impossible to maintain particularly if, within the tradition of the flaneur, the values of spectacle have eclipsed the moral concerns that may have helped to maintain the principles of social order.

In spite of the unprecedented popularity of *Life in London*, its mode of representing the city did not survive beyond the death of the monarch, George IV, to whom it is dedicated. In the decades that followed it was referred to, if at all, as a characteristic text of "Regency London," thereby connoting a libertine picturesqueness no longer acceptable. The rejection of Egan on prudish grounds continued well into the twentieth century.[17] A radically different popular view of London succeeded Egan's in the Victorian period, a view that is best exemplified by a work that enjoyed a popularity in the 1840s analogous to the popularity of *Life in London* in the 1820s.

G. W. M. Reynolds's *Mysteries of London* (1846) was the chief English representative of a "mysteries" genre that originated with Eugene Sue's *Mysteries of Paris*, and which was eventually to be found throughout the Western world, including the United States, in the 1840s and 1850s. Less political and more fastidious than Sue's *Mysteries*, the *Mysteries of London* was a serial presentation of scandals and atrocities set in a London whose character was quite different from that of the flaneur or of Egan. The following atmospheric description of the setting of an atrocity is typical of the book's style and subject matter. Reynolds writes:

However filthy, unhealthy and repulsive the entire neighbourhood of West Street (Smithfield), Field Lane, and Saffron Hill may appear at the present day, it was far worse some years ago. . . . The knackers' yards of Cow Cross, and the establishments in Castle Street where horses' flesh is boiled down to supply food for the dogs and cats of the metropolis, send forth now, as they did then, a foetid and sickening odour which could not possibly be borne by a sensitive stomach. At the windows of those establishments, the bones of the animals are hung to bleach, and to offend the eye as much as the horrible stench of the flesh acts repugnantly to the nerves. ... As if nothing should be wanting to render that district as filthy and unhealthy as possible, water is scarce. There is in this absence of a plentiful supply of that wholesome article an actual apology for dirt. Some of the houses have small backyards, in which the inhabitants keep pigs. A short time ago, an infant belonging to a poor widow ... died, and was laid upon the sacking of the bed while the mother went out to make arrangements for its interment. During her absence a pig entered the room from the yard, and feasted upon the dead child's face!

In that densely populated neighborhood that we are describing hundreds of families each live and sleep in one room. When a member of one of these families happens to die, the corpse is kept in the close room where the rest continue to live and sleep. ... The habit of whole families sleeping together in one room, destroys all sense of shame in the daughters: and what then remains of their virtue? But, alas! a horrible – an odious crime often results from that poverty which thus huddles brothers and sisters, aunts and nephews, all together in one room – the crime of incest! (1:43)

In the introduction to the *Mysteries of London*, Reynolds offers the flaneur's traditional promise to project the city through a magic lantern for an audience that wishes to preserve its detachment. Like Egan, Reynolds modifies this classic promise by promising to show his audience things they would not normally be able to see without sacrificing some of their precious comfort and safety. Yet while Egan's city is a carnival, a grab bag of novelties, incoherent and discontinuous, but always avowedly amusing, in Reynolds, human misery has become the main focus of the spectator's consuming interest. Reynolds's back alleys do not have any subversive, carnivalesque quality to them. They are repeatedly condemned as a disgrace and in this respect they are, along with the novels of Dickens, an example of a literature that may owe some of its tone and subject matter to reformers' texts like those of Mayhew and Chadwick, works whose exposure of the living conditions of the lower classes may have further eroded the credibility of the flaneur. Yet although there certainly may have been a sincere reform impulse behind some of the literature that focused on these conditions, I think it would be impossible for anyone to read through much of the *Mysteries of London* and conclude that it reflected a view of urban life that was any more compassionate than Egan's. For all of the pious rhetoric that accompanies it, Reynolds's Gothic rendering of hidden London is a kind of pornography of human misery. Like the images of the flaneur, or of Egan, Reynolds's work is designed to be consumed as a spectacle by a socially distanced audience. Yet because Reynolds's spectacle derives its appeal from its ability to produce a sense of disgust and horror, it implies an even greater degree of social distance between the reader and the spectacle than can be found in the flaneur or in Egan.

In the *Mysteries of London*, Reynolds achieves a sense of social distance in several different ways. The language of the text is radically different from that of earlier representations of the London slums. Ward and Egan wrote in an extravagantly lively, amoral, and democratic slang that suggested a linguistic and therefore psychological immersion into the world they were exploring. Reynolds, however, writes in a language that belongs exclusively to the educated classes, a language that reminds a reader at every point of the disapproving distance between the narrative voice and what it describes. In addition to this linguistic difference, there is an effect of distance produced by Reynolds's focus on the physically repulsive quality of the London streets. The flaneur and the carnivalesque spectator are either indifferent to or amused by the loathsomeness of London, which is so prominent a feature in Reynolds's work and in much of the urban literature written after 1840. For Reynolds, this physical filth is used to figure the city's moral filth, something that, again, was ignored by the flaneur and was a subject of amusement to the carnivalesque spectator. Although the cosmopolitan generosity of the flaneur and the manic playfulness of the carnivalesque spectator may have sanitized London, they did not produce the socially destructive recoil that Reynolds would have produced in his audience. By removing all humor and generosity from his mudbath, Reynolds exemplifies the development of the bourgeois disgust for the city in the Victorian period. He offers a conception of the city as a place where the bourgeoisie is continually assailed by the moral, physical, and linguistic filthiness of the urban poor, the crowd that is represented in passages like the following, passages that can never be found in Egan, Ward, or the writings of the flaneur:

> Towards eight o'clock the crowd had congregated to such an extent that it moved and undulated like the stormy ocean. And oh! what characters were collected around that jibbet. Every hideous den, every revolting hole – every abode of vice, squalor, and low debauchery, had vomited forth their horrible population. (1:101)

It is descriptions like these that have caused twentieth-century writers like Benjamin to write that "Fear, revulsion, and horror were the emotions which the big-city crowd aroused in those who first observed it" (131). There is a kind of moralism in here, but it is the kind of moralism that encourages the abandonment of the ideal of socially diverse public space. It is a moralism that does not result in a more just, humane urban social order, but in Haussmanization or, in England and America, in suburbs, places for the bourgoisie to flee the contagion of the lower classes.

Although London, in the middle of the nineteenth century, was probably becoming less menacing,[18] it was perceived otherwise by the bourgeoisie who began to consume, in the middle decades of the century, a steady diet of lurid crime journalism,[19] reformers' texts like Mayhew and Chadwick, and panoramic novels of city life like those of Dickens. It was the accumulated weight of this new culture of urban consumption and the conception of everyday life that it produced that more than anything else deprived the flaneur of his dominant position as the creator of "everyday life" in the metropolis. The idea of what constituted a "realistic" image of London life was changing. Yet in the journalism of this period, the flaneur did not entirely disappear. Rather, he had to share the field with new, contradictory images. There was still a need and a market for him, because the commercial culture in which he had his origins continued to expand. As a representative of certain cosmopolitan ideals, of a certain way of responding to the city, the flaneur continued to have meaning within the culture of Great Britain. It was at this point of culmination and dissolution that the flaneur began to be a significant figure in the culture of the United States, where he had many of the same meanings, and some different ones as well.

Chapter 4

The Flaneur in America

Studies of the perception of cities in eighteenth- and nineteenth-century American culture have usually proceeded from the assumption that America was, and is, a fundamentally antiurban culture. This view has often seemed particularly convincing because it has produced a canon of images and texts that, when invoked, support the very assumptions that are responsible for the fact that they are so familiar. Discussions of American antiurbanism invariably make use of the letters and writings of Jefferson, the nature philosophy and social experiments of the Transcendentalists, paintings like Thomas Cole's *The Progress of Empire*, and various texts, from Charles Brockden Brown's *Arthur Mervyn* to Herman Melville's *Pierre*, that are shaped by negative conceptions of urbanity as ancient as the Bible or Juvenal or as recent as Rousseau or Wordsworth.

No one can deny that America has produced a distinguished, diverse, and influential antiurban tradition. In the writings of Jefferson and de Crèvecoeur, the opportunity to build a civilization free of the corrupting effects of urban culture is represented as an important part of the historical meaning of the United States. As Jefferson wrote in a letter to James Madison, a system of government as morally challenging as constitutional democracy would only be able to function as long as the nation's pursuits remained primarily agricultural, "and this will be as long as there remains vacant lands in any part of America. When they get piled upon one another in large cities, as in Europe, they will become corrupt as in Europe" (918). In his *Notes on Virginia*, Jefferson describes what should, etymologically at least, be a contradiction: a civilization that has no cities, and no apparent need of them. Jefferson's antiurban ideal has remained influential throughout American history. It is a major component of what Frederick Jackson Turner identified as one of the central ideals of American culture, the imperative to move out to the frontier, to settle a continental wilderness with a network of small and thriving farms and towns.[1] The strength of this antiurban tradition may also be evident in the degree to which antiurban archetypes like Babylon, Pandemonium, Elijah's Jerusalem, Juvenal's Rome, and Bunyan's Vanity Fair dominate the representation of city life in both canonical and noncanonical literature written in the United States before the Civil War.[2]

Although I have no quarrel with Leo Marx's assertion that "the pastoral ideal has been used to define the meaning of America ever since the age of discovery" (3), and though I certainly hear the "antiurban roar" that Morton and Lucia White amplify in their account of attitudes toward the city in American intellectual culture, I nevertheless believe, along with several other recent historians and cultural critics, that the dominance of antiurbanism in nineteenth-century American culture has been greatly overstated.[3] Despite the distinction of some of its products, and its enormous impact on American political rhetoric, American antiurbanism, particularly in the period 1830 to 1860, was essentially a minority tradition, a tradition of intellectuals formulating their objections to a society built on commerce and industry. It was never representative of the complexity or diversity of American popular attitudes toward the city in the first half of the nineteenth century. As Charles Glaab and Theodore Brown have written, in their *History of Urban America*: "Although the anti-urban philosophers and novelists of the nineteenth century intrigue the contemporary mind, the defenders and prophets of the material city perhaps reflect more exactly the early popular view of the city" (72). As their book and others make clear, however, interest in cities was not confined to the unintellectual populace. According to Carl Bridenbaugh, American culture had been urban in its location and outlook as early as the colonial period. It was inevitably in the cities that presses and readership were to be found, and the urbanity of early American culture – that is to say, its cosmopolitanism, secularism, and interest in European style and culture – was amply evident in the journalism of the coastal cities. This interest continued and grew into the nineteenth century, alongside native and imported traditions of antiurbanism. Jefferson notwithstanding, most Americans in the first half of the nineteenth century appear to have understood that the United States could not thrive without ports or centers of commerce and manufacture.[4] Jefferson's dream was a practical impossibility. It was, as Thomas Bender has described it, a literary convention transformed into a political philosophy, doomed to become as it did become, irrelevant to the way in which the new nation would develop (*Toward an Urban Vision*, 4).

If Jefferson's ideal of an agrarian civilization represented one utopian vision of America's future, the periodical press of antebellum America also contained another. In the newspapers and magazines of New York and other large cities, the destiny of America was not represented to be the taming of a continental wilderness with a new form of agrarian civilization. It was represented to be the establishment of large, cosmopolitan cities that were connected to, rivaled, and would eventually surpass those of Europe. In New York in particular,[5] there was, as Perry Miller describes, a number of writers who, even during the heyday of American Romantic antiurbanism, insisted that America's growing cities should be viewed as an intrinsic part of, not a threat to, an indigenous American culture.[6] As one of these New York intellectuals, Cornelius Mathews, had written in a preface to one of his plays, it was only fitting, considering the way in which America was developing, that American literature should include among its subjects

> the crowded life of cities, the customs, habitudes, and actions of men dwelling in contact, or falling off into peculiar and individual modes of conduct, amalgamated together into a close but motley society, with religions, trades, politics, professions, and pursuits, shooting athwart the whole live mass, and forming a web infinitely diversified. (Cited in Miller, 93)

Even if America did not precisely rise to Mathews's challenge, it did have some familiarity with how the "crowded life of cities" was being represented on the other side of the Atlantic. Americans, who enjoyed the virtually unlimited access to British books and periodicals that the lack of an international copyright agreement made possible, encountered the flaneur in the American reprints of the most popular English magazines and books.[7] The *Sketches by Boz*, like all of Dickens's works, was extremely popular in America. Addison and Steele's work was widely read (Mott, 41) as were the essays of Lamb, Egan's *Life in London*, and the London sketches of Leigh Hunt and John Fisher Murray. It was through the writings of these authors and their lesser contemporaries that most literate Americans had some familiarity with the metropolises of Europe, and with the flaneur's characteristic way of looking at them.

Although American writers and journalists, from the colonial period onward, had produced essays that incorporated certain of the features of the Addisonian tradition, none of these essays have the characteristic features of a flaneur's sketch.[8] Until the 1840s, all American cities were quite small compared with the metropolises of Europe, and although it might seem as if a city would not have to be very large in order to provide enough for a flaneur to watch, it does appear that this was considered a deterrent. In the American press, it was understood to be necessary for a flaneur, in order to function as a flaneur, to be able to assert that he was at the center of the action, in a place that could plausibly be said to offer the most varied spectacle of objects and human types in the world. The first American sketches in the style of the flaneur were travel pieces, descriptions of London and Paris. One of the most conventional features of these sketches was the contemptuous dismissal of American cities as places where one might enjoy the access to an immensely diverse spectacle that was possible in London or Paris.

Accounts of foreign travel, and particularly accounts of travel in foreign cities, were an important staple of American magazines in their first great period of expansion, which began around 1820 (Mott, 340ff.). Washington Irving's *Sketchbook of Geoffrey Crayon* (1820) included several sketches, which, like other American travel sketches of the time, were written in the traditional style of the flaneur. This is partly due to the way in which they were inevitably influenced by representations of London that appeared in English periodicals. But, as is evident in Irving's *Sketchbook*, there is a natural analogy between the conventional situation of the flaneur and that of the American traveler in Europe. Crayon sees London as he does because, as he notes, he is "a stranger in the land" (22). The American in Europe, like the flaneur, is a detached and interested observer, interpreting and appreciating a world in which he does not play a part. An American journalist in London, an acquaintance of Poe, described the advantages of this social invisibility when he wrote to his readers that the period between one's arrival in a foreign metropolis and the delivery of one's letters of introduction is the best time for observation. "While perfectly unknown," Nathaniel Parker Willis wrote,[9] "the stranger feels . . . a complete willingness to be amused in any shape which chance pleases to offer, and his desponding loneliness serving him like the dark depths of a well, he sees lights invisible from the higher level of amusement" (306).

Nathaniel Parker Willis was the most prominent and influential American literary traveler in London in the period after Irving's *Sketchbook*. He was the first journalist to be employed by a single American periodical specifically to travel and send back travel sketches for publication (Auser, 33). His first series of sketches for the *New York Mirror*, entitled *Pencillings by the Way*, were a great success on both sides of the Atlantic. Willis followed up the success of *Pencillings by the Way* by writing other series of travel sketches interspersed with short stories that were themselves travel sketches. These pieces appeared in a variety of magazines, and when collected and published in book form were given such titles as *Inklings of Adventure*, *Loiterings of Travel*, and *Dashes at Life with a Free Pencil*.

In his sketches of London, Willis is a quintessential flaneur, transforming a large and complex city into a collection of pleasant impressions that are easily mastered and consumed. Unlike Boz, whose sketches he very much admired, Willis, as a flaneur, is in no way paradoxical. He is, rather, a true, if modestly talented, descendant of Lamb's "Londoner." His London is a varied and harmless spectacle, a distanced source of speculative amusement. The arcades, the glass-covered nineteenth-century antecedents of shopping malls that Benjamin identifies as the classic milieu of the flaneur, were a favorite haunt of Willis. He writes in one of his sketches:

> It was the close of a London rainy day. Weary of pacing my solitary room, I sallied out as usual to the Burlington Arcade. . . . The little shops were brightly lit, the rain pattered on the glass roof overhead, and to one who had not a single acquaintance in so vast a city, even the passing of the crowd and the glittering of lights seemed a kind of society. I began to speculate on the characteristics of those who passed and repassed me in the turns of the short gallery; and the dinner-hours coming round, and the men gradually thinning off from the crowd, I adjourned to the Blue Posts [a chophouse] with very much the feeling of a reader interrupted in the course of a novel. (30)

In another sketch, Willis writes:

> I would rather walk Regent street of an evening than see ninety-nine plays in a hundred; and so think, apparently, multitudes of people, who stroll up and down the clean and broad London side-walks, gazing in at the gorgeous succession of shop-windows, and by the day-bright glare of the illumination exchanging nods and smiles – the street, indeed, becoming gradually a fashionable evening promenade, as cheap as it is amusing and delightful. (538)

The London Willis presents to his American readers is frequently compared to a book or a play. The pleasures it offers derive from a combined effort of interpretation and appreciation. "Observation," as Willis chose to call it, his "silent studies of character," were his principal "amusement" in the city of London (306). Every great thoroughfare of London offered special delights for a secure and authoritative observer. In one London sketch, he writes of "the various shifting, motley group that belong to Oxford street, and Oxford street alone! What thoroughfares equal thee in the variety of human specimens! in the choice of objects for remark, satire, admiration!" (555). Bond Street, we are told in the same sketch, "is a study for such observers, as, having gone through an apprenticeship of criticism upon all the other races and grades of men . . . are now prepared to study their species in its highest fashionable phase" (555).

In his sketches of London, Willis adds nothing to the tradition of the English flaneur. He simply reproduces its most conventional features. The only element that can be found in his sketches that cannot be found in those of his British contemporaries is the implied American audience.

Willis glamorizes London for educated and would-be cosmopolitan English-speaking readers who are unlikely to have ever seen it. In the writings of Willis and other American travelers, there is a perpetual envy of the density, cosmopolitanism, and romance of the European metropolises, a sense that no American city could possibly measure up to it. Sometimes there is a surreal quality to such representations, as travel writers exaggerate to an often comical degree the qualities of European cities that Americans would not have known firsthand. By the time Poe wrote "The Man of the Crowd," American journalistic effusions on the subject of London's immensity had become a cliché. As an anonymous correspondent for the *New York Mirror* humorously observed in a "Letter from London," dated July 20, 1839:

> Everyone who enters London, even if it be for the twentieth time, thinks it necessary to say something of the innumerable streets, the endless, interminable, and bewildering rows of gas-lamps, and the unceasing fermentation which is continually going on amid the immense and restless population of the modern Babylon and to express his wonder thereat. I will spare you all this, taking it for granted that you have had a sufficiency of foreign correspondents to enlighten you amply about these matters.

Poe himself may have satirized the hyperbole of American correspondents in London, as well as the available American standards of comparison, in a piece entitled *English Notes*, a humorous sketch attributed to him that was published in a Boston newspaper (under the pseudonym Quarles Quickens) as a rebuttal to Dickens's *American Notes*. In this piece, Poe pretends to be an American traveler in London who, in order to convey a sense of the magnitude of the English metropolis, asks his readers to multiply familiar people and places in Boston by absurd magnitudes.[10]

This American tradition of exaggeration may explain why Hawthorne, who had never seen London by this point, describes Wakefield as living in a city whose crowds are so vast that a person walking undisguised past his own home would not need to fear detection. Poe, in "The Man of the Crowd," asks his readers to imagine that his story is set in a city so crowded that on a minor London street, late on a rainy night, "the passengers had gradually diminished to about that number which is ordinarily seen at noon in Broadway near the Park – so vast a difference is there between a London populace and that of the most frequented American city" (512). London, of course, was not this crowded – no city has ever been. But for Americans before 1840, the density and romance of the European metropolis was something that could only be imagined. The disorientation possible in such unimaginably crowded cities was thought to be capable of driving a normal American insane. In the midst of a Paris *flânerie* published in the *Knickerbocker* in January, 1836, in which the ability of the Paris streets to induce a state of drunkenness in a wandering spectator is described, the editors of the *Knickerbocker* include a note in which they cite someone named Campbell, who, in a piece on London in the *New Monthly Magazine* noted that not only a common state of drunkenness, but also "several cases of insanity, of considerable continuance" (7:31), had been traced to the experience of sightseeing in London by "strangers in the British capital."

Just as Poe and Hawthorne explain that "The Man of the Crowd" and "Wakefield" cannot be imagined to be taking place even in New York, Willis and the other travel writers revel in the cosmopolitan splendor of London in such a way as to suggest that what they are describing cannot be experienced on any American street. Yet although most writers in the journals of the 1830s seem to share this sense of America's cosmopolitan insufficiency, there were some who refused to wait until New York looked or felt like a metropolis in order to begin writing about it as such. Prominent among such Americans were what Perry Miller has called the "would-be boulevardiers" (29) who edited and wrote for the *Knickerbocker*, the New York magazine that was the most influential American journal of the 1830s and 1840s (Miller, 12), a journal that was regularly read by Poe, Hawthorne, and Whitman.

As Miller has described them, the writers associated with the *Knickerbocker* "were not worshippers of rural landscape, they did not want to range the wilderness with Natty Bumppo, they were not savages. What they wanted was that Nassau Street and Gramercy Park be rated equivalents of Fleet Street and Grosvenor Square" (29). Their urbanism was a reaction against the antiurban romanticism of New England intellectuals and was in this respect an assertion of New York's growing cultural dominance as America's intellectual and publishing center. Even though it was nationalist, their "cryptic revolt was" necessarily cryptic for fear of not seeming nationalist, especially since Americans had demonstrated, in their strong negative reaction to James Fenimore Cooper's critical *Home as Found*, that they were especially sensitive on this issue. Having such nationalist intentions, colored as they were with a profound appreciation for and envy of London, writers for the *Knickerbocker* filled their magazine with numerous sketches of London and New York written in the characteristic style of the flaneur.

In the continuing serials entitled "Odds and Ends – From the Port-Folio of a Penny-a-Liner," "The Leisure Hunter," "Mephistopheles in New York," "Ollapod," "Town and Country," "Loaferiana," and "The Editor's Table," the contemporary clichés of cosmopolitan spectatorship were reproduced with little variation. In each of these series, socially

invisible spectators, gifted with unusual powers of observation, wrote
celebrations of the immensity, diversity, and spectacle value of London
and New York, which is referred to on several occasions as the "London
of America." The most durable of these, the author of "Odds and Ends
– From the Port-Folio of a Penny-a-Liner," offers a succinct definition
of his activity, and that of the entire tradition in the following paragraph:

> One of my chief pleasures is, at the close of the day, to go forth
> into the street, and meet and mingle in the crowds that throng it,
> on their thousand various pursuits of business and pleasure; "to be
> with them, and yet not of them" – to see, and yet not be seen –
> to observe, and yet not be observed – to know and comprehend,
> and yet not be known or comprehended. (8:92, July 1836)

In all of these columns there is the familiar affected laziness, as well
as the vaguely ironic and self-mocking moral detachment, as when one
of these spectators, after describing his failure to find a beggar boy who
had affected him more than most, remarks that he "(tender creature that
I am!) felt miserable until after tea" (7:372, April 1836). All of the traditional techniques and references of the genre are present, from invocations of Asmodeus to the comparison of the city to a panorama.
Although there is nothing new in the flaneur's sketches in the *Knickerbocker*, what is new is the fact that after 1835, most of them are set in
New York. Before 1835, almost all are set in London or Paris. After
1835, there is a mixture, to the point where New York is unquestionably
dominant by the end of the decade. In the *Knickerbocker*, it is possible to
trace the developing self-consciousness of New York as a setting suitable
for the flaneur.

Even if there is little that is original (except for locale) in the writings
of the *Knickerbocker* flaneurs of the thirties, it is possible to find evidence,
in this substantial body of material, of the fact that the situations of urban
spectatorship represented in the works of Poe, Hawthorne, and Whitman
would not have been unfamiliar to their readers. In the *Knickerbocker* of
June 1835, for example, a serial featuring a flaneur who calls himself
"The Leisure Hunter," contains an anticipation of the plot of "The Man
of the Crowd." Referring to himself as one "of the school of Walking
Philosophers," the Leisure Hunter describes his faith in the ability of
those like himself to, in their "occasional communings with men...
unloose the mask of virtue, and disclose the hollow eye of crime: we
may survey the rewards of pleasure in the furrowed brow and sallow
cheek, or in the wretch stooping beneath the burden of complicated
misfortunes." "Filled with such reflections as these," the Leisure Hunter
describes how he "strolled the other evening into a secluded coffee-

house, – determined in my mind to elicit a history from the first vagrant whom chance or dissipation might direct thither" (5:497, June 1835).

The December 1836 column of the "Odds and Ends" series is so extraordinarily similar to "The Hotel" chapter in *The Blithedale Romance* that it is almost impossible to believe that Hawthorne had not read it and used it in his novel fifteen years later. In it, the committedly cosmopolitan author of the column describes returning to the city after "a month or two" of "experimenting in rural felicity." Pleased "once more to return to the city, to join the busy crowd – to resume [his] accustomed occupations – to feel again the excitement of business, the throes of ambition, and the lures of pleasure!" he describes how "inexpressibly comfortable" it felt to return to his bachelor quarters, where he observes: "There were my books, my favorite chair, my table, my papers, just as I had left them." Resuming his seat at his table he listens to the sounds he has not heard in the country: the ironing and brushing of some nearby hatters, the pressing, cutting, and stitching of tailors, the laying of a foundation for a nearby building. Interspersed with his descriptions of the sounds of the city is his account of the sounds that can be heard from a neighboring dioramic exposition. The "Penny-a-Liner" hears the thunder and rain of the Deluge, the "martial music of Napoleon's army as it is entering Moscow; then . . . the reports of the artillery, the booming of the cannon, and finally, the usual explosion, and the falling of the Kremlin. Next in order is the Great Fire of New York. The ringing of the bells – the rattling of the engines – the sudden flashes of light, etc." After describing the thoroughly familiar and predictable sounds of the diorama, the author of the column observes that: "My rear windows overlook a complete little world. Poverty, affluence, industry, profligacy, and vice, are all assembled beneath them." The remainder of the sketch consists of his detailed descriptions of the scenes he "typically" observes from his window, proving his assertion that "I have a species of eye-acquaintance with all my neighbors in the rear" (8:710–11, December 1836).

The structural similarity between the empathic personalities of the American flaneurs of the *Knickerbocker* and Walt Whitman's poetic persona is evident in one of the "Odds and Ends" pieces, in which the "penny-a-liner" describes the amusements and activities available in New York to someone who is "poor and unknown" and "without a character," in a way that is significantly similar to sections of *Song of Myself.*

I, with my poverty-stricken brethren, make the journey of life on foot. We hasten not on our way; we take it easy; we cull the flowers which grow along our path. . . .

Oftentimes . . . I have taken my station in front of Colman's window . . . for the purpose of examining at my leisure the various specimens of the arts which he daily displays for the gratification of the public. . . .

If at the next corner I discover a fight, I join the ring, and take upon myself the duties of master of ceremonies. I hold the hats and coats of the combatants. . . .

I am always on hand when a man is run over, or falls from a building, help carry him to the nearest apothecary's shop and am always inside when the door is closed. . . .

I attend the parades of the "Light Guards," and the "Tompkins Blues," . . . I am not too proud to march along with the boys on the side-walk, and keep step with the music. It does me good. It excites my martial spirit; it arouses my "American feelings" . . . in short, it makes me a more patriotic citizen and a greater lover of my country.

I attend all the fires. . . . I help females and small children to escape from the flames, take care of valuable packages that are thrown into the street, pick up pieces of china and looking-glasses that are cast down for preservation from the upper stories, and see how a stop is finally put to the flames.

I go very frequently to funerals. . . . I mourn for each and every one who dies, for I am sorry that they are obliged to leave this pleasant world of ours, the pursuits which engrossed them, the pleasures which occupied them, and all the thousand endearing ties which draw upon the hearts even of the most lonely and desolate.

I take great interest in the improvement and increase of the city. No citizen, public or private, has been more solicitous than I about the green posts and chains in the Park. . . .

These are a few of my occupations and amusements; and they are such as the man of character or the proud man knows not. (June 1836, 8:597–9)

These selections from what Perry Miller has called America's most influential journal in the 1830s and 1840s indicate that however anomolous their attitudes may appear to us in the twentieth century, the urbanism of the passages they resemble in Poe, Hawthorne, and Whitman would not have been as anomolous to contemporary readers. By reading sketches like the ones cited, Poe, Hawthorne, and Whitman were familiar with a way of looking at cities that was virtually as prevalent in their culture as it was in Baudelaire's. New York was not yet Paris, but the flaneurs in the *Knickerbocker* were confident that it was moving in that direction.

After 1840, no one writing in the New York press seems to have had any doubt about the suitability of New York as a venue for the flaneur.

In journals like *Arcturus*, the *Broadway Journal*, *Putnam's Monthly Magazine*, the *Dollar Magazine*, the *Home Journal*, the *Aurora*, and in newspapers like the *Mirror* and the *Tribune*, the New York flaneur was prominent and plentiful in the 1840s and 1850s.[11] Instead of the sheepish sense of inferiority that still can be found in the New York flaneurs of the 1830s, one finds an amusing sense of rivalry with London and Paris. As George G. Foster, arguably the best and most characteristic of the New York flaneurs of the 1840s, the author of *New York in Slices: By an Experienced Carver* (1849), *New York Naked* (n.d.), *New York by Gaslight with Here and There a Streak of Sunshine* (1850), had written in a wonderfully characteristic passage: "Most of our readers have doubtless had 'slices' from the Markets before now. But they furnish abundant mental food as well as physical, to one who has learned the grand secret of eating with his eyes. We scarcely know where so much and such varieties of human nature can be encountered as in a walk through the Markets. Every face you meet is a character, every scene affords a piquant contrast. Talk of your Eastern bazaars and Parisian arcades!" (*New York in Slices*, 40).

The exotic types that can be found in these locales, Foster assures his readers, are nothing compared to those that may be encountered in a New York market. As a flaneur, offering "slices" to his readers, Foster makes use of the latest metaphor for the flattening, collectable image of the flaneur's sketch. In his *New York in Slices: By an Experienced Carver* he promises his readers a "pen-and-ink daguerrotype" (54)[12] of what he "eats" with his eyes, what he consumes of the urban spectacle. As an apparently self-conscious participant in the flaneur's tradition, Foster insists on the importance of speculation, the act of interpretation involved in his "slicing": "There is plenty of philosophy in omnibus-riding, if you have but the wit to find it out" (65). Like other flaneurs, he presents his slices as a collection which, in its entirety, resembles a panorama: "A New York eating-house at high-tide is a scene which would repay the labors of an antiquarian or a panoramist, if its spirit and details could be but half-preserved" (67). With his panoramic view, Foster lays claim to what he calls his "Asmodean privilege."[13]

The natural suitability of the flaneur to the culture of New York was evident in the degree to which he was associated with and easily assimilated into the culture of spectacle that was as prominent in New York as it was in any city of Europe. The New York flaneurs were always comparing their productions to panoramas, dioramas, and daguerrotypes. One of the earliest and best of the New York sketchbooks was even written to accompany the exhibition of a scale model of New York built by its author. E. Porter Belden's *New York: Past, Present, and Future* (1849), which attempted to provide a survey of New York as comprehensive as Stow's survey of London, was written as a guide not to the city itself but to what was advertised on the title page as a:

CARVED MODEL
OF
NEW-YORK & BROOKLYN
EXECUTED BY
E. PORTER BELDEN
WITH ONE HUNDRED AND FIFTY
ASSISTANTS
Is intended to be exhibited in the
various Cities of the Union
THIS MODEL IS A PERFECT
PIECE OF MECHANISM
Representing every building and other object in the city. It was
constructed at a cost exceeding
$20,000
OVER THE WHOLE MODEL IS AN
IMMENSE CANOPY
Of Carved and Ornamental Work in Gothic
Architecture,
Representing in the finest Oil
Painting
The Leading Business Establishments of
the City

Writing shortly after Belden, Cornelius Mathews, in *A Pen-and-Ink Panorama of New York City* (1853), maintained the conceit of unrolling a spool panorama of New York for his audience.

The connection of the culture of the flaneur with the culture of the exhibition is also evident in the fact that the most frequently mentioned and extensively described place in New York in most of the books written about it in the 1840s and 1850s was P. T. Barnum's American Museum on Park Row. This institution has the same peculiar prominence in New York literature of the period that the Royal Exchange had in the literature of London 150 years earlier. The reasons, I suspect, are similar. These panoramic spaces, containing the entire multiplicity of the world and presenting it as a spectacle to be consumed, appeared to spectatorial narrrators to be the most representative spaces in their respective cities, the one true metaphor for the whole. Cornelius Mathews's *A Pen-and-Ink Panorama of New-York* and George G. Foster's *New York by Gas-Light* both begin in exactly the same way, with views of the variety and spectacle of Broadway, leading seamlessly into the similarly various and odd spectacle of Barnum's museum. Barnum's museum has a similar centrality in E. Porter Belden's *New York: Past, Present, and Future* and Joel H. Ross's *What I Saw in New-York; or a Bird's Eye View of City Life.* In the last of these, the significance of Barnum's museum to the public image of New York is evident when, in an effort to describe the importance of a place he is sketching (a match factory), he says of it that it "is as much a part of New-York, as is Trinity Church, or Barnum's Museum, or Tom Thumb." The idea of New York as a collection of novelties and specimens reached a culmination in this period in the outpouring of New York books that accompanied the opening of the Crystal Palace exposition in 1853. As an all-containing spectacle of great novelty and diversity, the Crystal Palace was able to temporarily replaced Barnum's museum as the most popular synechdoche for the city. The sense of the Crystal Palace as the central metaphor for the city, continuous with and representative of all of its spectacles, is most evident in this passage from Foster's *Fifteen Minutes around New-York*: "For some blocks we have been aware, by the accumulation of coffee houses, grog shops, 'saloons', peep-shows of living alligators, model-artists and three-headed calves, that we were approaching the newly discovered, Sedgwickean centre of the metropolis. 'Fortieth street, – Crystal Palace' – says the conductor, stopping the cars handily on the crossing" (11). Elsewhere, after surveying the immense luxury and ostentation of New York, Foster refers to the city as a "universal human crystal palace" (*Fifteen Minutes around New-York*, 23).

As these examples demonstrate, New York was understood to resemble a vast exhibition hall, a spectacle, a panorama. Presenting this panorama, the New York flaneurs use the same techniques and structuring metaphors as their European counterparts and as the first American flaneurs in the *Knickerbocker*. The only thing that distinguishes them is their proud, perpetual, if still occasionally defensive insistence that New York is now a metropolis on a par with London or Paris. Nathaniel Parker Willis who, after 1840 turned his flaneur's perspective toward his native city, provides an example of this when he boasts, in a piece he wrote in 1850 for his own *Home Journal*: "But New-York hereafter may as well be spelt New-Yolk, for Paris, or what makes Paris the world's golden centre, is positively coming here!" because New York has become "the point where money is spent most freely for pleasure." After a proud catalog of the world-class singers, musicians, and dancers expected to appear in New York in the upcoming season, Willis observes:

But generally, as to the imminent Parisification of New-York: – There is a floating population of seekers of the world's pleasantest place, who, as it will appear to every connoisseur of European capitals, are very sure to follow the sweetest voices, most bewildering legs, best players, boldest riders, etc. These independent idlers, in turn, are sure to be followed by the best cooks, the prettiest glove-fitters, etc. . . . and the many ministers to taste and luxury who follow the garden of refinement on its "Westward course." – for whom Paris has been what Bagdad was, and for whom New-York is to be what Paris is." (*The Rag Bag*, 47)

The "Westward course" of the garden of refinement was accompanied, to judge from the periodicals of the period, by a flowering, in the West, of the types of individuals traditionally found in that garden. The literature of the New York flaneur is filled with astonished and even quite proud essays on the extraordinary profusion of dandies in New York. Foster writes, in an entire chapter devoted to New York dandies, in *New York in Slices*:

Since the lamentable failure of the whisker-crop on the Boulevard des Italiens, New York is the only City and Broadway is the only street in which any thing like a respectable assortment of live Dandies can be found. – As to the bucks of Bond-Street and the swells of St. James, we regard them not. In short, as Paraguay is said by travellers to be the paradise of monkeys, we regard New York as destined to become the metropolis of Dandies. (76)

A culture that can furnish dandies can necessarily furnish the flaneur. Although they are profoundly different, even opposite types, they can always be found together. It is only when a city can produce a fashionable spectacle in which dandies can participate that it is capable of producing a spectacle of sufficient richness for a flaneur to observe.[14]

The sense of the inevitability of New York's emergence as the preeminent metropolis of the world, as a habitat for spectators of human typology and extravagance without compare, suggests the nature of the importance that the figure of the flaneur may have had in America. The flaneur, to many Americans, may have suggested that America promised to become what it would in fact become, not a network of independent homesteads and small towns, but the world's foremost industrial consumer society, producing and consuming the greatest number and concentration of spectacles, products, and images, and containing the greatest diversity of human types. New York was to be, in the view of influential journalists like Willis and Foster, the new Paris, something even greater than a new London, and certainly nothing at all like a new Arcadia. In Europe, the flaneur had been the most representative spokesman for the pride of the bourgeoisie in the kind of world that they and the economic system associated with them were able to create. It is only fitting that this figure would thrive in America, where his glorification of commerce, his benign sense of the crowd, and his sense of society as involving, in the words of the English flaneur Murray, the "universal harmony" (25) of competitive trade, would have placed him more definitely in the ideological mainstream than he would have been in Europe.

Even if he was undeniably and even slavishly derivative of his London and Paris models, the particular meaning of the American flaneur was that he represented the destiny of America to be not the recapturing of an imaginary premodern innocence, but the culmination of the forces of modernity that were transforming life throughout the larger industrial civilization of which America was a part. It was in this context, as the representative of America's still tenuous urbanism and cosmopolitanism, that he was encountered by Poe, Hawthorne, and Whitman, who were as interested as any of their European contemporaries in the effect of "modern" urban life upon the imagination.

Chapter 5

From the Flaneur to the Detective: Interpreting the City of Poe

In his essay "The *Flaneur*," Walter Benjamin refers to Poe's story, "The Man of the Crowd" as "an x-ray picture of a detective story." In it, Benjamin writes, "The drapery represented by the crime has disappeared" and we are left with "the mere armature, . . . the pursuer, the crowd, and an unknown man" (48). Here, as elsewhere, Benjamin makes a brilliant association whose full meaning is inaccessible because of a historical misunderstanding. It is true that "The Man of the Crowd" contains the "armature" of a detective story, but in this context it is extremely important to recognize that Poe wrote "The Man of the Crowd" *just before* he wrote the first detective story, "The Murders in the Rue Morgue." "The Man of the Crowd" is therefore more of an embryo than an x-ray. In this chapter, I will try to show how writing "The Man of the Crowd" may have led Poe to develop the genre of the detective story. In this story, Poe offers a critique of the flaneur's method of representing modern cities. This will enable him, in the detective stories, to develop a new method that will serve some of the same functions, while transcending some of what are understood to be the flaneur's limitations. Inventing a new genre, and a new urban spectator, in response to changes that may have been taking place in the public understanding of cities, Poe offered new models for reading and consuming the modern city.

Edgar Allan Poe would have been familiar with the tradition of the flaneur from a variety of sources. He had written an extremely favorable review of the *Sketches by Boz* for the *Southern Literary Messenger* in 1836.[1] In a review of Hawthorne's *Twice-Told Tales*, Poe compared Hawthorne's essay style to that of Addison, Steele, Lamb, Hunt, and Irving.[2] Killis Campbell has documented Poe's extensive familiarity with each of these authors, a familiarity that would hardly have been surprising for an English-speaking man of letters in the early nineteenth century. As a journalist, Poe was undoubtedly familiar with the most prominent English and American magazines,[3] and at several points in his career, he had even written urban sketches of his own. He wrote pieces for various periodicals on such subjects as cabs, omnibuses, and paving stones[4] and in the spring of 1844, he wrote a series of "letters" to a Pennsylvania newspaper entitled *Doings of Gotham*. These letters in the *Columbia Spy*, with their elegiac attention to urban ephemera, are particularly reminiscent of the tone of several of the pieces in the *Sketches by Boz*.

In addition to Boz, the most important antecedent of the flaneur narrator of "The Man of the Crowd" is likely to have been Nathaniel Parker Willis, the most prominent American flaneur of the 1830s and indeed the most prominent magazine writer at the time "The Man of the Crowd" was written. Poe knew Willis as a colleague and rival, and he had written about his work on several occasions.[5] Though Poe had some personal regard for Willis, and although he had a limited admiration for some of Willis's work, in general he disliked what he considered to be Willis's "dazzling" affectations. As Poe wrote in one of his letters to the *Columbia Spy*: "Mr. Willis . . . is well-constituted for dazzling the masses— with brilliant agreeable talents – no profundity – no genius" (*Doings of Gotham*, 34). On at least two occasions, Poe had even parodied the precious, cosmopolitan style of Willis's magazine pieces, in "The Duke de l'Omelette" (Thompson, 44–5; Daughrity, 55–62) and in "Lionizing" (Benton, "Lionizing," 239–44). Willis's London sketches, which I briefly considered in the previous chapter, are among the best examples of his precious, presumptuous, and quintessentially flaneuresque style. In them, Willis represents himself as an idle walker in the gaslit streets of London, pursuing what he calls his "silent studies of character" (306), appreciating the "various shifting, motley" components of the crowd, "the variety of human specimens" (555), confidently reading the rapidly changing and moving world that he represents in the following description of the Strand:

> You would think it the main artery of the world. I suppose there is no thoroughfare on the face of the earth where the stream of human life runs with a tide so overwhelming. In any other street in the world you catch the eye of the passer-by. In the Strand, no man sees another except as a solid body, whose contact is to be avoided. You are safe nowhere on the pavement without all the vigilance of your senses. Omnibuses and cabs, drays, carriages, wheelbarrows, and porters, beset the street. Newspaper-hawkers, pickpockets, shop-boys, coal-heavers, and a perpetual and selfish crowd dispute the sidewalk. If you venture to look at a print in a shop-window; you arrest the tide of passengers, who immediately walk over you; and if you stop to speak with a friend, who by

chance has run his nose against yours rather than another man's, you impede the way, and are made to understand it by the force of jostling. (553)

Willis's London sketches, written in 1834 and 1835, were published together in book form for the first time in 1840 in a collection entitled *Romance of Travel*, a book that received a great deal of attention in the New York press because of the prominence and popularity of its author. Nine months after the appearance of this volume, "The Man of the Crowd," was published in *Graham's Magazine*. Poe's story is narrated by a figure that many of his readers would have associated with Willis, and perhaps with Boz, or any of the other figures mentioned in the previous chapters who approached the prospect of modern urban life in a similar way. Poe's narrator is an idle observer of London life who, from the vantage of a coffeehouse window, observes a crowd very much like the one described in the passage just quoted. Like Willis, this narrator is a silent student of character, a connoisseur of the "variety of human specimens." In the midst of a potentially overwhelming yet reassuringly legible crowd, his epistemological composure is so strong that he claims an ability to look at a face and to read in the "brief interval of a glance, the history of long years" (2:511). In the opening pages of "The Man of the Crowd," Poe offers one of the fullest portraits in literature of the figure of the flaneur. He creates his narrator out of material from sources with which he was familiar. In order to understand why Poe may have been interested in such an urban spectator at this particular moment in his career, it may be useful to consider the resemblances between "The Man of the Crowd" and the other stories he wrote at about the same time. When Poe wrote "The Man of the Crowd," he had recently completed "The Fall of the House of Usher" and would soon begin to write "A Descent into the Maelstrom." The classic flaneur is perfectly suited to serve the function of a specific type of Poe character, who is also represented by the narrator of "The Fall of the House of Usher" and by the fisherman in "A Descent into the Maelstrom." He is someone who tries to orient himself in a world he cannot understand, by thinking that he can read its most superficial aspects.

Each of the narrators in these stories encounters a chaotic and opaque environment. These environments are so similar that they can be considered versions of each other. Often the same words and phrases are used to describe them. In Poe's London, "the rays of the gas lamps... threw over everything a fitful and garish lustre. All was dark and splendid – as that ebony to which has been likened the style of Tertullian" (2:510–11). The Norwegian fisherman observes how the "rays of the full moon ...streamed in a flood of golden glory along the black walls...

the wide waste of liquid ebony" (2:590). In Roderick Usher's painting, "A flood of intense rays" fills a dark, subterranean tunnel and "bathe(s) the whole in a ghastly and inappropriate splendor" (2:406).

Observing his splendidly yet garishly illuminated darkness, the narrator of "The Man of the Crowd" notes "the rapidity with which the world of light flitted before the window" (2:511) and he describes the "jostling" and uneven motion of the "tumultuous sea of human heads" (2:507). The fisherman in "A Descent into the Maelstrom" notices that the diverse array of spinning objects moves "not with any uniform movement – but in dizzying swings and jerks" (2:591). The narrator of "The Fall of the House of Usher" watches as storm clouds, "glowing in the unnatural light" emanating from the mansion, "flew careering from all points against each other" because of the "frequent and violent alterations in the direction of the wind" (2:412). In all three of these stories, a mist often obscures the bizarrely illuminated objects that move rapidly and unevenly through the ebony medium.

Like the narrator of "The Man of the Crowd," the fisherman, as he is drawn into the maelstrom, abandons himself to an unusual mood of calm "interest" in which he finds "amusement in speculating" (2:591) upon the objects spinning past him. He speculates about their relative velocities in much the same way as the flaneur narrator speculates about characters and professions. The narrator of "The Fall of the House of Usher" achieves a similar composure by reducing his impressions of the house to "superstitions" (2:399), the storm to "mere electrical phenomena not uncommon" (2:412), and Usher's behavior to "the inexplicable vagaries of madness" and "the tottering of . . . lofty reason upon her throne" (2:406).

Each of these narrators imposes a familiar set of categories upon what would otherwise be unfamiliar and terrifying. The narrator of "The Man of the Crowd" treats the crowd as a collection of identifiable physiognomical and professional types. The narrator of "The Fall of the House of Usher" encompasses his experience with a crude set of scientific and psychological formulas. The fisherman extricates himself from the maelstrom by making use of the principles of physics and geometry. In "The Fall of the House of Usher" and in "The Man of the Crowd," however, the effort of the narrator to impose coherence upon what he sees is undermined by the obsessive fascination each develops with a consciousness that reflects and is reflected by the chaotic environment. Encountering the old man, the narrator of "The Man of the Crowd" finds "a countenance which at once arrested and absorbed [his] whole attention" (2:511). Usher too has "a countenance not easily to be forgotten" (2:402) and after Lady Madeleine has been put in her tomb, he is described as "roam[ing] from chamber to chamber with hurried, unequal, and objectless step" (2:410). This obsessive motion, so similar to that of the old man, suggests to the narrator that Usher's "unceasingly agitated mind was laboring with some obsessive secret" (2:411). The narrator of "The Man of the Crowd" has the same suspicions of the man he observes.

Though distanced from and unable to read Usher's consciousness, the narrator begins to identify with it. Observing Usher constantly, he says that "It was no wonder that his condition terrified – that it infected me. I felt creeping upon me, by slow yet certain degrees, the wild influences of his own fantastic yet impressive superstitions" (2:411). In "The Man of the Crowd," the identification of the narrator with the old man is equally intense. The old man, absorbed by his desire to be surrounded by human activity, moves through the streets of London without stopping for over twenty-four hours. The narrator "follow[s] him in the wildest amazement, resolute not to abandon a scrutiny in which I now felt an interest all-absorbing" (2:515). Like the narrator of "The Fall of the House of Usher," the narrator of "The Man of the Crowd" has been "infected" by his subject, and his behavior has taken on some of the same obsessive qualities.[6]

In "The Man of the Crowd," Poe represents a modification of the same narrative and psychological situation as he had explored in "The Fall of the House of Usher." In each story, an individual with an excessive faith in his ability to systematically reduce chaos to coherence develops an obsessive identification with an individual whose behavior calls into question the very possibility of such coherence. Neither of these narrators emerges from his encounter with any understanding either of the individual he has been "following," or of the obsession that makes him follow. By representing the specific character of the obtuse obsession of the narrator of "The Man of the Crowd," Poe offers a complex and multifaceted analysis of the entire tradition of urban spectatorship with which the narrator is associated.

One aspect of the meaning of the old man to the narrator is that he is the one illegible face in a crowd of legible ones. When he sees the old man, the narrator is forced to interrupt his reading. The narrator relates that the old man had "a countenance which at once arrested and absorbed my whole attention, on account of the absolute idiosyncrasy of its expression." As he tries "to form some analysis of the meaning conveyed" by the old man's face, the narrator says that "there arose confusedly and paradoxically within my mind, the ideas of vast mental power, of caution, of penuriousness, of avarice, of coolness, of malice, of blood-thirstiness, of triumph, of merriment, of excessive terror, of intense, of supreme despair. I felt singularly aroused, startled, fascinated." The fact that he cannot form a coherent analysis of the old man's face may suggest to the narrator that his entire system of interpretation is inadequate. The desire to close this gap in his reading of the urban crowd, to place the old man in a panoptic niche along with everyone else, may be part of what might motivate a convalescent to risk his life by pursuing an old man through cold and rainy streets for twenty-four hours. But another part of his motivation may be the fact that the narrator wishes to close the gap in his reading of himself. The narrator cannot form an analysis of his own fascination with the old man. This inability may be due to the fact that, to the narrator, the old man represents a variety of things he wishes to repress about himself and his activity.[7]

The old man is, first of all, an example of the type of metropolitan individual described by Wordsworth in his preface to the second edition of *Lyrical Ballads*. "The encreasing accumulation of men in cities," Wordsworth wrote, produces people who are incapable of mental excitement "without the application of gross and violent stimulants." Such individuals become slaves to a "craving for extraordinary incident" and they are in this way reduced "to a state of almost savage torpor" (*Prose Works*, 130). Even "the highest minds" among city dwellers, Wordsworth writes in the seventh book of *The Prelude*, cannot escape this reduction of consciousness to a "perpetual flow of trivial objects" (701–2). For such a consciousness, the greatest fear is of an arrest of the flow because there is no interior resource from which new objects can come. This is the dilemma of "the man of the crowd." "He refuses to be alone" (2:515) because his mind has lost the ability to produce experience synthetically. Without this ability, either he can be conscious of external stimuli or he must experience a pure emptiness, a terrifying and intolerable ennui. It is the terror of the prospect of this emptiness that drives the old man through the London streets. It is the source of his anxiety when he perceives that a group of people he has been following through an increasingly empty city has begun to disperse. It is the reason he emits "a half shriek of joy" (2:515) when he finds an open gin-shop in the early morning hours. The old man, like the narrator, is trying to close a gap in the field of his experience.

The gap in the old man's experience is, however, an absence of stimuli, not the absence of a reading. The pursued man is not, therefore, a flaneur.[8] He is more analogous to a figure Benjamin defines in a footnote, the *badaud*, or gaper, the individual who compulsively watches, but cannot assimilate or represent the urban spectacle. The *badaud* can only experience his need for the urban spectacle, and when the need is satisfied, he becomes the spectacle. He does not preserve his individuality, because he is not in any way separate from what he experiences. As such, he represents the possibility of disintegration that is raised, but never directly confronted, by the flaneur. The flaneur, insofar as he is a flaneur, denies that there is anything dangerous about his openness to random experience. He presents himself as someone who, by reading and appreciating what he sees, preserves the sense of individuality and distance implicit in his acts of interpretive observation and connoisseurship. Yet for the flaneur narrator, the spectacle of the old man's obsessive, uncomprehending spectatorship raises the possibility that he may not be as different from the old man as he believes himself to be. He too may be in search of nothing more than temporary satisfaction of a restless desire for the pleasure of a spectacle. If his understanding of the crowd is not "true," if all of his readings are part of a game, in which he merely pretends to see the history or character of a person in the brief moment their face passes his window, then the readings of the flaneur narrator are essentially indistinguishable from the "gross and violent stimulants" sought by the old man. They may represent a more sophisticated form of amusement than the pleasures sought by the old man, but they are nothing more than amusement. Poe suggests that the flaneur, as much as the *badaud*, seeks, in a crowd of fellow human beings, nothing more than a stimulating spectacle to relieve his boredom.

In order to enjoy his own spectacle of changing lights and moving forms, the narrator, like the old man, assumes a posture of receptive passivity. He says that he feels a calm interest in "everything." The old man is also interested in everything. Although the narrator, at the opening of the story, remains calm and preserves his individuality by reading the crowd, his indiscriminate openness to what passes by the window endangers both his composure and his selfhood. It is possible that his desire to receive stimuli may develop to the point that it exceeds his desire or capacity to organize them. If this were to happen, he would be reduced to the mental condition of the old man. Like the narrator of "Usher," contemplating Usher's morbid acuity of the senses, the narrator of "The Man of the Crowd" is likely to find the prospect of such reduction both terrifying and appealing. His obsession with the old man may reflect his ambivalent fascination with the latter's passive, thrill-seeking consciousness, which is essentially a more advanced version of his own mood of passive, indiscriminate interest in the urban spectacle.

Although the narrator's pursuit of the old man may illuminate some similarities between them, the narrator never becomes aware of these similarities. On the contrary, in order to repress any awareness of a resemblance, and in order to extricate himself from his obsession, the narrator imposes a reading upon the old man that stresses his absolute otherness. At the end of the story, he solemnly pronounces that "This old man is the type and genius of deep crime" (2:515). On the face of it, it does not seem as though the reader has been adequately prepared for this interpretation. Although it is true that the narrator thinks he sees a diamond and a dagger under the old man's coat, these are not certain signs that any crime has been committed and the narrator does not see the old man commit any crimes. Among the profuse and conflicting readings the narrator attaches to the old man are some qualities, such as "avarice," "coolness," "malice," and "blood-thirstiness," that are conventionally associated with crime, but none of these readings are borne out by the events of the story. The events of the story do, however, suggest several possible explanations for the narrator's labeling of the old man as "the type and genius of deep crime."

One possible interpretation of this labeling suggests yet another similarity between the narrator and the old man. The identity of the old man is disintegrated into the crowd. The urban criminal also wishes to be lost in the crowd. Although the two forms of identity loss referred to here are quite different, their effects can be similar. By immersing themselves in the crowd, both the criminal and the old man become outsiders in terms of the crowd. For the criminal, the crowd becomes nothing more than a concealing environment. For the old man, it becomes nothing more than a spectacle, a source of stimuli. For the narrator, who can see the social outcast in the old man but not in himself, the crowd ceases to be a community of individuals to whom he is in any way connected.

The similarity between the urban spectator and the criminal in hiding may also have been suggested to Poe by a novel he admired greatly and often referred to in his critical writings (Pollin, 237–53). In William Godwin's *Caleb Williams*, the main character is a young man who, having been wrongly accused of a crime, flees to London and attempts to lose himself in its "inexhaustible reservoir of concealment" (254). Disguising himself as a Jew, Caleb Williams says that he "shrunk from the vigilance of every human eye. I dared not open my heart to the best affections of our nature. I was shut up a deserted, solitary wretch in the midst of my species" (255). Distanced from and concealed among his fellow human beings, Godwin's protagonist finds that the profession that suits him best is that of writing essays for newspapers "in the style of Addison's Spectators" (259).

In this extraordinary image, in which he associates the fleeing criminal, the Wandering Jew, and the Addisonian spectator, Godwin illustrates the paradoxical quality of the social abstraction enjoyed by the flaneur. The invisibility of the urban spectator is the premise of his power, but it is also a condition of isolation analogous to that of what was probably, in the early nineteenth century, the most popular mythic example of compulsive spectatorial isolation. As a compulsive wanderer unable to rest, Poe's "man of the crowd" has also been associated with the Wandering Jew (Bonaparte, 421), and he may be associated with Cain, another figure, often associated with the Wandering Jew (Anderson, 3) who

wanders, excluded from the society of others by a crime he has committed.[9] Identifying the old man as the type and genius of deep crime,
the narrator may once again be seeing in him something that he would
be afraid of acknowledging in his own activity. To abandon all connections with the human community in order to enjoy the pleasure of watching it is to commit a transgression whose punishment is nothing more
than the natural consequence of the act: an isolation as deep as that of
Cain or the Wandering Jew.

Whether or not the old man is literally a criminal, his behavior resembles that of an urban criminal because it involves isolation in the
midst of an urban crowd. There is also an analogy between the consciousness of the old man and that of the urban criminal, as Poe appears
to have understood it. In a later story, "The Imp of the Perverse," a
narrator who has committed a murder with a poisoned candle is seized,
several years after his crime, by a desire to confess it. He conceives this
"perverse" intention while walking along a city street. In an unsuccessful
effort to suppress what he is thinking, he begins to walk faster until, he
relates: "I bounded like a madman through the crowded thoroughfares,
knowing that to think, in my situation, was to be lost" (3:1226). Bounding like a madman through crowded thoroughfares, the "man of the
crowd" may also be trying to avoid thought. Like that of the criminal
in "The Imp of the Perverse," his absorption in urban stimuli may
represent an effort to be free not only from the human community, but
from any internalization of its laws and customs. Embedded in this
connection is a notion that someone who abandons himself entirely to
the reception of urban stimuli loses his capacity for both intellectual
activity and moral response. Such an individual, as Baudelaire might
suggest, would be capable of committing an act of criminal violence
simply in order to relieve his boredom. The narrator does not seem to
be on the point of committing any such crime but his casually aesthetic
attitude toward urban vice and criminality, which anticipates Dupin's
approach to the murders he solves, may be an intellectual version of the
thrill-seeking amorality that could lead to criminality in a less intellectual
being like the old man. Once again, the activity of the old man represents
a potential consequence of the flaneur narrator's apparently innocuous
activity.

Even if one understands the narrator's association of the old man with
crime as an acknowledgment and repression of some of the most extreme
consequences of his spectatorial isolation, it is still difficult to interpret
the strength of the narrator's association of the old man not just with
crime but with "deep" crime and with the "worst heart of the world"
(2:515). Even if one can perceive analogies between the behavior of the
old man and that of a criminal, this still seems to be an uncommonly

severe moral judgment to pronounce upon an old man who may be, on the basis of the evidence presented, guilty of no more serious crime than an inability to be alone.[10]

A possible explanation for the hyperbole of this association is that it expresses the intensity of the emotion that has sent the narrator on his pursuit of the old man. The hyperbole may be a vague and yet powerful response to the fact that the old man cannot be read. "The Man of the Crowd" begins and ends with the narrator associating "deep crime" with illegibility. This reiterated association implies that illegibility is itself a form of crime. It is a transgression against the laws imposed by the flaneur upon the city. In the opening paragraphs of this story, the narrator finds that superficial crimes do not disrupt the order established by such laws. The narrator easily identifies pickpockets, gamblers, con men, and prostitutes. Finding them transparent, he views them with detached amusement. They cause him no anxiety. Given the flaneur's nearly exclusive concern with interpretative mastery, only that which he cannot read can cause him anxiety. When the narrator encounters a face that "does not permit itself to be read," he associates it with that which is unintelligible in moral behavior. In this way, he demonizes the gap in the urban text. By linking unintelligibility with "deep crime," the narrator fuses the chief source of epistemological anxiety in the city with a chief source of physical anxiety. The opacity of the urban crowd ceases to be merely confusing; it becomes actively threatening. The narrator's association of "the type and genius of deep crime" with the abstract "man of the crowd" indicates that his conception of the source of this malevolence is neither localized nor defined. Rather, the old man's unintelligibility has opened up the possibility that no man or woman of the crowd can be read as the narrator has presumed to read either one. If this is so, then the entire crowd threatens the physical and epistemological well-being of the narrator.

Ultimately, "The Man of the Crowd" suggests that the urban crowd cannot be reduced to comfortable transparency. The crowd is physically threatening and possibly unreadable. It is also psychologically threatening, offering an urban spectator the terrifying yet appealing prospect of dissolution into its stream. By representing this encounter between the narrator and the old man, Poe shows what the flaneur cannot read, in the crowd and in himself. As in several other Poe stories, a limited narrator stands in the ruins of his system, unsure of what has happened. In this particular story, the narrator is able to recognize that there is a gap in his interpretative control of reality. He does not interpret this gap. Instead, he leaves the old man with the observation that "perhaps it is but one of the great mercies of God" that "the worst heart of the world"

(2:515) cannot be read. The flaneur, the domesticator of the urban crowd, remains unable to read the unlocalized malevolence he has discovered.

As a critique of the interpretative strategies of the flaneur, "The Man of the Crowd" lays the groundwork for their transcendence. The story implies that an urban observer is needed who can read and in some sense master what the flaneur cannot. It may, in this respect, be a demonstration by Poe that the flaneur had not and could not adapt to the dramatic changes that were taking place at this time in the perception of the metropolis. Whether or not cities in the nineteenth century were in fact becoming more dangerous, it was perceived that they were becoming more dangerous.[11] They were certainly getting larger. Whether or not this meant that they were becoming more illegible or that the conditions of social alienation in them were intensifying, they were perceived as more illegible and alienating.

In America as in England, perhaps the single most significant reason for this change in the perception of the city was a more widespread exploitation, by an increasingly diverse array of media, of the fascination of urban violence and illegibility.[12] The technological changes that led to the explosive growth of a cheap urban press created a cultural phenomenon that Poe himself identified as enormously influential on the literature of the period. In his essay on "The Literati of New York City" Poe had written that the rise of penny newspapers in the 1830s had an influence on American literature that was "probably beyond all calculation" (Poe, *Essays and Reviews*, 1214). Beginning with the appearance of the New York *Morning Post* and the New York *Sun* in 1833, these penny papers specialized in sensational accounts of urban crimes and scandals. Around the same time, trial pamphlets and criminal biographies, genres that depended on the same sudden reduction in the cost of mass printing as had made the penny papers possible, focused on the same subject matter. The popularity of these new forms of consumption was overwhelming. As David Reynolds has written, "puritanical protests could not stop the trickle of popular crime narratives from swelling into a broad river by the 1830s and to a virtual flood by the 1840s. By then, almost every sensational trial, besides being played up in the penny papers, produced its own cheap pamphlet that was hawked in street bookstalls and railway depots" (175). This popular literature created a climate in which the "mysteries" genre could become popular in America. In the 1840s, Sue and G. W. M. Reynolds were widely read, as were such American imitations as Edward Zane Carroll Judson's *The Mysteries and Miseries of New York* and George Lippard's *Quaker City*.[13] This extremely accessible genre would become the main form of literary exploitation of the new sense of the city fostered by the penny press. Yet even before these works appeared in America, Poe, with his interest in the aesthetics of sensation, and his active involvement in the world of New York journalism, seems to have perceived some of the potential that a more threatening view of urban life held for literary exploitation. One aspect of what Poe considered to be the incalculable influence of cheap crime literature on American literature and culture was that it created the opportunity for the kind of character, and the kind of literature, that Poe was to create in the story he wrote immediately after "The Man of the Crowd."

In "The Murders in the Rue Morgue," Poe tried to adapt what he could salvage of the flaneur to what he found most aesthetically promising in the increasingly popular view of the city as a threatening and impenetrable mystery. If "The Man of the Crowd" is Poe's demonstration that urban life is too terrifying and opaque to be read by the flaneur, "The Murders in the Rue Morgue" contains his proposition that a literary approach was needed that could exploit the fascination of such cities, and that an urban interpreter was needed who could provide a more credible and complex assurance of urban legibility than could be found in the literature of the flaneur. It is in this sense that "The Man of the Crowd" can be considered an embryo of the detective story.

In "The Murders in the Rue Morgue" and "The Mystery of Marie Roget," that which the flaneur leaves out of his city is given special prominence. "Deep crime" and illegibility, two concepts the flaneur uncomprehendingly joins at the end of "The Man of the Crowd," are powerfully combined in images of brutalized corpses whose murders cannot be understood. From shortly after the beginning of either of these stories, the reader knows that he or she is not in the safe, legible, and predictable city of the flaneur. Poe, in fact, does everything he can to increase the reader's anxiety. The corpses are graphically described. Each victim appears to have had no expectation of her murder and each appears to have been particularly helpless at the hands of her murderer. The nature of these murders is such as to make the reader acutely aware of his or her vulnerability to brutal and unpredictable urban violence. This awareness is heightened by Dupin's reference, in "The Mystery of Marie Roget," to "the great frequency, in large cities, of such atrocities as the one described" (2:736).

In addition to representing the unpredictable and violent nature of urban life, the murdered corpses figuratively represent what Benjamin refers to as "the obliteration of the individual's traces in the big-city crowd." The fascination with such obliteration, which is a significant aspect of *Caleb Williams*, the *Sketches by Boz*, and all of Dickens's later works, is identified by Benjamin as the "original social content of the detective story" (43). Living in almost complete seclusion, Mme. and

Mlle. L'Espanaye were, in life, virtually unknown to the crowd that takes such an interest in them as corpses. Marie Roget has a much wider circle of acquaintances, but her anonymity in a city as large as Paris is hardly less extreme. Refuting the comforting suggestion of a newspaper reporter that "It is impossible that a person so well known to thousands as this young woman was, should have passed three blocks without someone having seen her" (2:749), Dupin observes:

> For my part, I should hold it not only as possible, but as very more than probable, that Marie might have proceeded, at any given pe-riod, by any one of the many routes between her residence and that of her aunt, without meeting a single individual whom she knew, or by whom she was known. In viewing this question in its full and proper light, we must hold steadily in mind the great disproportion between the personal acquaintance of even the most noted individual in Paris and the entire population of Paris itself. (2:749–50)

Although social invisibility is an important precondition of the fla-neur's assertion of power, the type of invisibility described here is a condition of vulnerability. While the flaneur chooses his invisibility, which sets him apart from everyone he watches, the urban anonymity referred to here is not chosen and it is universal. Its fundamental meaning, in stories of this type, is that anyone can disappear without a trace in cities so huge and so entirely composed of strangers.

The population of Poe's Paris is not only anonymous and vulnerable, it is also opaque. The mystery surrounding the corpses is emblematic of the opacity of urban individuals to each other. Like Dupin and the nar-rator, Mme. L'Espanaye and her daughter shut themselves off from social interaction and from the scrutiny of others. No one knows enough about them to have any idea of why they would be murdered. The motivations and activities of Marie Roget are also mysterious. No one is sure where she was going, who she was meeting, or what she was doing. As illegible corpses, the murder victims may suggest the general illegibility of faces in an urban crowd. Without the possibility of access to their conscious-ness, each appears to be an empty representation of a human being. The clues they offer can be read in a variety of ways, according to a variety of interpretative systems. They can never be read as easily as the flaneur would have one believe.

The sense of the opacity of urban individuals to each other is further heightened by the fact that Paris, in each of these stories, is represented as a sort of Babel. Most of those who hear the voices of the alleged murderers of Mme. L'Espanaye and her daughter are foreigners. Each speaks a different language and each interprets the shrill voice of the ape differently. In "The Mystery of Marie Roget," there is a similar though figurative profusion of languages. Each newspaper has a different interpretation of the case and each vies with the others to establish the superior credibility of its theory. There is no discussion and no consensus, only the discordant competition of incompatible theories.

By beginning the development of his detective stories with graphic journalistic descriptions of the murdered corpses, Poe confronts the reader with an image that condenses a range of urban anxieties. In this way, Poe's detective story differs markedly from the flaneur's sketch. In the literature of the flaneur, the reader is shielded from all potential sources of anxiety at the moment he or she first encounters them. The resolution of the mystery of another person is instantaneous; we can know everything we need to know as soon as the person's face comes into view. In the detective story, on the other hand, the resolution of the murders is achieved only after some effort and some time. By representing the original traumatic experience prior to (rather than simultaneously with) its resolution, Poe postpones the action of the defenses, which, in the form of a "reading" of the corpses, will protect consciousness from the shock they produce. In this way, he exploits the aesthetic appeal of the shock. The structure of the detective story permits the reader to experience both the thrill of epistemological and physical anxiety in the city and the pleasure of its resolution.

By inventing a literary genre that could exploit the aesthetic appeal of urban anxiety, Poe was not, however, inventing the aesthetic itself. In fact, an important aspect of the content of these detective stories is Poe's representation of the exploitation of urban anxiety, in response to public demand, by big-city newspapers. The unprecedented amount of attention given by the New York press to the unsolved murder of Mary Rogers in 1841 was one of the most prominent early instances of the kind of journalistic exploitation that was spreading at this time from the penny press to virtually all American newspapers. As John Walsh writes, in his book about the case and its influence on Poe, Mary Rogers "was, it is clear, among the first to gain celebrity as a by-product of journalism's dawning self-consciousness. Within a week of her death, the *New York Daily Express* gave the story a front-page headline, explaining that the murder was of such an atrocious character as to demand that it be taken forth from the ordinary police reports, to be made a matter of special attention, to arouse inquiry as to the murderers" (8).[14]

Despite the laudable aims expressed, the intention of the *Daily Express* and of the various "French" newspapers cited in Poe's stories was apparently to take an "interesting" unsolved murder and turn it into the focus of a new form of commercially profitable mass entertainment. The attempt to solve the murder of Mary Rogers appears to have occupied newspaper readers in New York in 1841 in much the same way as the effort to apprehend the Son of Sam preoccupied newspaper readers in the same city in 1977. That Poe recognized the nature of the public interest in such murders is evident in the terms he uses to describe it. The narrator observes that "The atrocity of this murder . . . the youth and beauty of the victim and, above all, her previous notoriety, conspired to produce intense excitement in the minds of sensitive Parisians. I can call to mind no similar occurrence producing so general and intense effect" (2:726). In "The Poetic Principle," Poe argues that the value of a poem should be determined by the amount of "elevating excitement" (*Complete Works*, 14:266) it produces in the minds of its readers. In "The Philosophy of Composition," Poe emphasizes the importance and priority of the "effect" a literary work is intended to produce. Describing the impression made by the murder of Marie Roget upon the public mind in terms of two of the most important concepts of his aesthetic theory, Poe identifies what were to become the conventions of tabloid journalism as a legitimate urban aesthetic form. He also implicitly acknowledges the nature of the aesthetic appeal of the genre he was in the process of inventing.

If the purpose of a work of literature is understood to be the production of a high level of excitement in a reader through the communication of a powerful effect, then a brutal and illegible murder is certainly a legitimate aesthetic subject. As it was coming to be understood in the first half of the nineteenth century, the metropolis, like other enigmatic and terrifying environments in Poe (the maelstrom, an Antarctic ocean, the house of Usher, etc.), offered constant exposure to "exciting effects." Baudelaire correctly perceives, in Poe's works and aesthetic theory, an anticipation of the aesthetics of "decadence," an aesthetics that depends upon the exploitation of surprise, of the most extreme form of novelty (Baudelaire, "New Notes on Edgar Poe," 121). In his valorization of these qualities, both in his work and in his aesthetic theory, Poe develops an aesthetic capable of embracing the phenomenological qualities of urban experience, at least as they were coming to be understood. In this way, he confirms Wordsworthian fears about the tendencies of a modern urban imagination. Poe has no apologies about producing "excitement" by means of "gross and violent stimulants." His aesthetic is related to the aesthetic of those who attend St. Bartholemew's Fair in the seventh book of *The Prelude*. It is drawn to "All out-o'-the-way, far-fetched, perverted things" (687).

But the aesthetic appeal of Poe's detective stories only begins with the presentation of a shock in the midst of a romantically threatening environment. It also derives from the progressive control of the shock and the deliverance from its attendant anxiety. In order to allow a controlled exposure to urban anxiety, Poe invented the ratiocinative detective, a figure capable of mastering the urban environment without inhibiting its capacity to produce anxiety or terror.

Numerous sources have been proposed for C. Auguste Dupin. Several scholars have suggested that his method derives from that of Voltaire's Zadig, a hermit who, in the romance that bears his name, demonstrates an unusual ability to read animal tracks (Messac, 17; Allan, 67–8). W. T. Bandy suggests that, in Dupin, Poe "drew a self-portrait, romanticized perhaps, but completely recognizable" (2:509). Another frequently acknowledged source of the Dupin stories is a series of four articles entitled "Unpublished Passages in the Life of Vidocq, the French Minister of Police", which appeared in the *Gentlemen's Magazine* from September to December 1838 (Arthur Hobson Quinn, 310). These appear to have been based on a version of the spurious memoirs of François Eugène Vidocq, an ex-criminal who, in 1811, did in fact become Paris's first Chief of Security.[15] Poe certainly read this series, but it is difficult to determine the precise nature of his debt to it. Nothing in the character of Vidocq himself, as he appears in these installments, could have served as a model for Dupin. Poe makes this clear when he has Dupin, in "The Murders in the Rue Morgue," dismiss Vidocq as nothing more than a "good guesser" (2:545). Vidocq, in these "Unpublished Passages," is a policeman whose only special gift is an extraordinary ability to always be in the right place at the right time. He demonstrates no acute powers of detection.

Although the character of Vidocq may not have made much of an impression on Poe, his profession and activity may have. The idea of an individual whose task it was to "solve" a crime was a very new one. The world's first professional police force came into existence in London only twelve years before "The Murders in the Rue Morgue" was published.[16] The world's first detective department came into being in 1842, the year after the publication of this story. In fact, when this first detective story was published, the word "detective" did not even exist in the English language (*Oxford English Dictionary*, 1:704). Given Poe's interests in problem solving and in crime, his exposure, in this series, to the novel figure of the crime solver may very well have played a role in his creation of C. Auguste Dupin.

Although all of these sources may have contributed to Poe's invention of the detective, it seems to me that critics of Poe, in their discussion of the detective's origins, have neglected Benjamin's suggestive linking of the detective and the flaneur, which he himself only sketchily pursues. That Poe may have made use of the tradition of the flaneur, in his creation of Dupin, is suggested by the fact that Dupin shares a number of personal qualities and habits conventionally associated with this figure. Secluding himself by day in a mansion with closed shutters, Dupin explores the

Paris streets by night, associating with no one except a narrator with no distinctive character traits of his own. Like the flaneur, he is therefore distanced from and invisible to the inhabitants of the city through which he moves. Like the flaneur also, Dupin has an appetite for urban observation. Every evening, the narrator relates, he and Dupin "sallied forth into the streets . . . roaming far and wide until a late hour, seeking amid the wild lights and shadows of the populous city that infinity of mental excitement which quiet observation can afford" (2:533). Like that of the flaneur in "The Man of the Crowd," Dupin's appetite for urban observation has become an absorbing obsession. As Dupin says at one point in "The Murders in the Rue Morgue," "observation has become with me, of late, a species of necessity" (2:535). Such an obsession, like that of the narrator of "The Man of the Crowd," is preferably pursued by gaslight.

The narrator observes that the "energy of Dupin's character" has succumbed to the decline in his family's fortunes. Accordingly, "he ceased to bestir himself in the world or to care for the retrieval of his fortunes" (2:531). His decayed social and economic situation breeds in Dupin a detached passivity ideal for a flaneur. The world no longer concerns him but it continues to interest and amuse him. He is perpetually open to the refined yet morally indifferent pleasures traditionally sought by the flaneur. After reading of the murders in the Rue Morgue, Dupin says to the narrator: "As for these murders, let us enter into some examinations for ourselves, before we make up an opinion respecting them. An inquiry will afford us some amusement." The narrator, writing what the reader is presumably thinking after this statement, adds, "(I thought this an odd term, so applied, but said nothing)" (2:546).

At certain points, even Dupin's techniques of reading resemble those of the flaneur. Like the flaneur, he will occasionally assert that reality may be read by looking at its commonly accessible surface in the proper way. Dupin says to the narrator, in "The Murders in the Rue Morgue," that "as regards the more important knowledge, I do believe she is invariably superficial" (2:545). In order to be able to read reality "the necessary knowledge is of what to observe" (2:530). In his lengthy discussion of the game of whist, at the opening of "The Murders in the Rue Morgue," the narrator describes how a particularly proficient player of the game makes use of physiognomical reading, one of the traditional tools of the flaneur. The crucial things a whist player must observe are very close to what the narrator of "The Man of the Crowd" observes. The cardplayer notices the "countenance," the "air," and the changes in facial expressions of his opponents. By reading these external signs, he will be "in full possession of the contents of each hand," after "the first two or three rounds have been played" (2:530).

Soon after the narrator's introductory remarks, Dupin demonstrates his own proficiency at this sort of reading when, during one of his nocturnal rambles, he astonishes the narrator by correctly deriving an entire chain of thought from the latter's facial expressions and gestures. Dupin's improbable proficiency at superficial interpretation resembles that of the narrator of "The Man of the Crowd," who claims to be able to read the professions, motivations, and histories of individuals by observing their external traits. In the introductory pages of "The Murders in the Rue Morgue," the narrator offers a theory of how it is possible for Dupin to make such readings. He asserts that someone who possesses particularly acute "analytic" faculties of mind is able to "throw himself into" a person and by "identify[ing] himself" with him, may understand and even predict his behavior (2:529). This, apparently, is how Dupin traces the narrator's chain of thought. He "throws himself" into the narrator and follows an "inevitable" progression from street stone to stereotomy to Epicurus, to recent theories of cosmogony to Orion, to an actor named Chantilly. A similar technique is described in "The Purloined Letter," when Dupin describes a schoolboy who is successful at the game of "even and odd" because he is able to "throw" himself into the minds of his playmates by imitating their facial expressions.

The narrator is so impressed by Dupin's ability to perform this trick that he incorrectly assumes that it exemplifies Dupin's method in general. After describing the technique of the proficient whist player, the narrator suggests that his account of how Dupin solved the mystery of the murders in the Rue Morgue "will appear to the reader somewhat in the light of a commentary upon the propositions just advanced" (2:531). Although the story he is about to tell may in fact be a commentary upon the narrator's opening "propositions" about the analytical mind, it is hardly the illustration the narrator assumes it is. It is true that Dupin is capable of accomplishing sleights of hand worthy of the flaneur. Yet only in "The Purloined Letter" does he solve a mystery by "throwing" himself into someone else's consciousness and in that story, the consciousness he throws himself into is that of a virtual double. Dupin's derivation of the narrator's chain of thought is also a unique instance of interpretation that cannot be generalized into a method for solving mysteries like that of the murders in the Rue Morgue. The narrator's conventional mind is entirely familiar to Dupin, who has largely absorbed the narrator's identity into his own. When Dupin traces the progression of the narrator's thoughts, several of the crucial connections in the chain consist of observations Dupin had made to the narrator in the conversations that have become the narrator's only form of human contact. To read the narrator is, for Dupin, to read a text that he himself has been writing.[17]

Many critics of these stories have accepted the narrator's description of Dupin's method as authoritative,[18] possibly because it does accurately describe his method in "The Purloined Letter." It is important to recognize, however, that Dupin's description and implementation of his method in "The Murders in the Rue Morgue" and "The Mystery of Marie Roget" not only do not correspond to the narrator's account, they are at odds with it.[19]

The method of the whist player and the method of Dupin when he reads the mind of the narrator depend upon being able to recognize a definable and predictable correspondence between a facial expression or bodily gesture and the thought it signifies. In "The Man of the Crowd," Poe discredits the assumption that it is possible to gain access to the consciousness of others by reading external features and mannerisms. In "The Purloined Letter," after he uses the example of the schoolboy to illustrate how he has outwitted D., Dupin expresses contempt for this as a general method when he says that the schoolboy's technique "lies at the bottom of the spurious profundity which has been attributed to Rochefoucault, to La Bruyère, to Machiavelli, and to Campanella" (3:985). As a system that reduces the complexity of gesture and expression to the simplicity of signs, the technique of the whist player or the schoolboy is only suited to the reading of what is already known or what follows certain conventions. Yet Dupin repeatedly stresses, in his own descriptions of his method, that he solves mysteries like those of Marie Roget and the murders in the Rue Morgue by reading the anomalous and the undefined. This principle is so important to Dupin's method that Poe has Dupin make the following observation in *both* "The Murders in the Rue Morgue" and "The Mystery of Marie Roget": "I have observed that it is by deviations from the plane of the ordinary, that reason feels her way, if at all, in her search for the true. In investigations such as we are now pursuing, it should not be so much asked 'what has occurred?' as 'what has occurred that has never occurred before?'" (2:540, 736–7).

Although the narrator transcribes what Dupin says about his method, and although, in his own description of Dupin's method, he repeats Dupin's fundamental principle that the "necessary knowledge is of what to observe," the narrator has no more understanding of Dupin's method than the narrator of "The Fall of the House of Usher" has of Usher's mental disorder or than the narrator of "The Man of the Crowd" has of the old man's motivations. The narrator's example of the whist player completely distorts the point Dupin had been making when he said that the "necessary knowledge is of what to observe." The whist player does not observe what has never occurred before. He observes what is conventional and readable in his opponent's expressions and gestures. The narrator's assumption that Dupin is simply an unusually proficient flaneur, throwing himself into the minds of others, is analogous to the comparably obtuse pronouncements made by the other, equally limited narrators. The narrator of the detective stories may even serve a function analogous to that of the other Poe narrators. He is a conventional mind with a conventional conception of how a mystery can be reduced to coherence, and he is fascinated by an unconventional mind he cannot fully comprehend. In "The Man of the Crowd," the narrator's system is unraveled and shown to be inadequate. In the detective stories, on the other hand, the system elucidated by the narrator is not even applied. Its inadequacy is demonstrated by the apparent success and superiority of the detective's very different system for solving the mysteries of urban life.

In order to solve the mysteries, Dupin chooses as his text those elements of urban experience that appear as gaps in the reading of the flaneur. The flaneur, seeking to reduce the crowd to a set of types, always looks for what has already been seen and defined. As "The Man of the Crowd" demonstrates, an encounter with the unprecedented and undefined only makes him anxious. Believing that truth can only be discovered by reading what the flaneur cannot assimilate, Dupin begins to solve the murders in the Rue Morgue by trying to interpret the ways in which it differs from an ordinary robbery or murder. The normal examination of acquaintances, possible motives, and so on would not have led to a solution. The solution can only be found by reading such "deviations from the plane of the ordinary" as the fact that a drawer of linens was rifled while several valuable objects were in plain view. Such "deviations" as the unnecessary brutality of the murders and the preternatural agility required of the escaping murderer also contribute to the solution of the case. Dupin's method, we are led to believe, is effective because it assumes what the nature of these murders illustrates about urban experience. Life in a giant city, Poe's audience believes, is filled with encounters with the unprecedented and undefined. It is a perpetual exposure to the breaking of social and epistemological laws. The murder of the two women is a deviation from human law. The character of these murders is itself a deviation from what is conventionally expected of murders. The method of the flaneur, which organizes urban experience by codifying expectations into law, is entirely inadequate to interpret an environment in which deviation from all forms of law is believed to be the norm. If Poe is willing to go much further than previous authors in developing an aesthetic of urban shock, he also develops a "technique" for reading the shocks. The gaps and ruptures in the flaneur's framework are no longer a source of anxiety. They are, for the detective, the means by which "reason feels her way . . . in her search for the true" (2:736).

In his effort to solve the murders in these stories, Dupin accepts yet another nineteenth-century perception of urban life that the flaneur denies. For the flaneur, his own is the only language in the city. Every object or person has no life or meaning other than that which the flaneur attributes to him, her, or it. No other interpretations are apparent within the flaneur's text. The city of Dupin, on the other hand, is filled not only with different interpretations, but also with different languages for interpretation. In these two stories, the detective accepts the multiplicity of languages and develops a way of reading reality by reading the interaction between the languages. Once again the detective takes what the flaneur represses and uses it as the basis of a reading that is more complex than any that the flaneur could have offered.

The simplest example of this technique is Dupin's determination that the shrill voice heard by those who climbed the stairs to the apartment of Mme. L'Espanaye and her daughter was not that of a human being. Dupin comes to this conclusion by integrating the different interpretations of the voice by speakers of different languages. Among those who testify is a Frenchman who thinks that it was the voice of an Italian. A German believes the shrill voice to be French and an Englishman and an Italian hear it as a Russian. None of these individual readers can correctly interpret the voice. Each is imprisoned within his own language. Dupin, on the other hand, is able to function as a metareader. His perspective, which enables him to interpret the differing interpretations, permits him to construct an interpretation beyond the scope of any of the respective languages.

Dupin's role as a metareader of urban languages is more complex in "The Mystery of Marie Roget." In this later story, Dupin derives the crucial facts about the case by analyzing the different interpretations of it in the different newspapers. The bulk of this long story is devoted to Dupin's demonstration of the way in which each newspaper uses a different and, in each case, limited language to interpret the murder of Marie Roget. A paper entitled *L'Etoile*, for example, attempts to prove that the discovered corpse is not that of Marie Roget and that she herself has run off with a lover. Dupin observes that "it is the mingled epigram and melodrame of the idea . . . rather than any true plausibility" (2:738) that prompts the newspaper to promote it. Once it has decided on this hypothesis, Dupin goes on to show, the newspaper interprets every detail of the case in such a way as to support it. First, it tries to support its assertions by alleging apathy on the part of Marie's relatives. When this allegation is shown to be false, it asserts that Beauvais is a party to the scheme, possibly the lover himself, and it throws suspicion on his supposed attempts to prevent other acquaintances and relatives from examining the corpse.

Later, in reference to another article in *L'Etoile*, Dupin observes that "The first aim of the writer is to show, from the brevity of the interval between Marie's disappearance and the finding of the floating corpse, that this corpse cannot possibly be that of Marie. The reduction of this interval to its smallest possible dimension, becomes thus, at once, an object with the reasoner. In the rash pursuit of this object, he rushes into mere assumption at the outset" (2:738). The writer of the article assumes that if Marie left her mother's house at nine on Sunday morning, her corpse could not possibly have been thrown into the river before midnight that evening. As Dupin rather easily demonstrates, this is an unfounded assumption and constitutes a blind spot in *L'Etoile*'s theory. He goes on to show that this assumption of *L'Etoile* implies yet another assumption: that the murder was committed at some distance from the river and the corpse had to be carried to it. The assumptions Dupin refutes are preliminary to a central point in *L'Etoile*'s argument. The newspaper seeks to establish that if the corpse, which was discovered at noon on Wednesday, is that of Marie, "it could have been in the water but a very brief time" (2:740). Having established this, or as Dupin says, "having prescribed thus a limit to suit its own preconceived notions" (2:740), the journal goes on to assert that "All experience has shown that bodies . . . require from six to ten days for sufficient decomposition to take place to bring them to the top of the water" (2:740). If this is the case, then the corpse found floating on the water cannot be that of Marie Roget. This final assumption, however, as Dupin demonstrates in a lengthy discourse on the physics of decomposition, is entirely false. "All experience," he says, "does not show that drowned bodies require from six to eight days for sufficient decomposition to take place to bring them to the surface. Both science and experience show that the period of their rising is, and necessarily must be indiscriminate" (2:743). Refuting the various arguments of *L'Etoile*, Dupin concludes that there is no reason to doubt that the body discovered in the Seine is that of Marie Roget.

Dupin then proceeds to identify the unjustified assumptions and blind spots in the interpretation of the case put forward by a newspaper called *Le Commerciel*. *Le Commerciel* "wishes to intimate that Marie was seized by a gang of low ruffians not far from her mother's door" (2:749). In order to support this thesis, *Le Commerciel* offers two arguments: that Marie could not have gone far without being recognized; and that the fact that she was gagged with a strip torn from her petticoat is an indication that her murderers had no pocket handkerchiefs and were therefore of the lowest class. As he had with the arguments of *L'Etoile*, Dupin refutes these by demonstrating the weaknesses of the assumptions on which they are based. It is not true, he argues, that someone walking through a vast city at nine on a Sunday morning is certain to be recognized. It is also not true that "low ruffians" can be counted upon not to have pocket handkerchiefs. Later on, Dupin disposes entirely of the

gang theory by demonstrating the blind spots of other journalistic interpretations that attempt to support it. He shows, for example, that the
signs of a violent struggle discovered at the scene of the crime are,
contrary to what the newspapers assert, indications that Marie Roget
was not murdered by a gang. Disposing of the arguments of the gang
theory, Dupin concludes that a single intimate acquaintance of Marie's
must be responsible for her murder.

Throughout the story, Dupin's technique remains the same. He solves
a murder solely on the basis of newspaper accounts, not by combining
their insights and interpretations, but by analyzing their omissions.
Though it is far more complex, and though it is so drawn out as to have
bored many readers of this story, his method is essentially the same as
the one used to determine that the shrill voice in "The Murders in the
Rue Morgue" was not human. In each case, a correct interpretation is
put together by exploring the gaps and blind spots in the interpretations
offered by several limited languages. If this story is a failure, as has
commonly been charged, I think it is because Poe was so anxious to
demonstrate the feasibility of such a method that he neglected other
literary considerations. His own obsession with the way in which Dupin
solves this mystery is perhaps the strongest indication of his desire to
transcend the limitations of the flaneur by creating an urban interpreter
capable of reading the unexpected and unacknowledged.

As a method of solving crimes by analyzing the gaps and omissions
in the interpretations of others, Dupin's technique represents an important modification of the Panoptic model of surveillance implicit in the
flaneur's techniques of reading. The flaneur imagines himself to be central
and invisible, capable of gaining access to the consciousness of others
simply by observing what he believes to be immanent in their faces and
gestures. His attitude, toward faces and gestures as signs, is naive, at
least as compared with that of the detective. He assumes that it is possible
to gain access to the consciousness of a person by recognizing the type
to which he or she belongs or by simply, and without explanation,
"reading the history of long years in a single glance." His "technique"
is little more than a combination of sorcery and the application of de-
ceptively coherent keys for interpretation. In all cases, it is fundamentally
visual and immediate, assuming a direct correspondence between a face
or gesture and the personality it signifies.

Dupin, on the other hand, although he acknowledges that truth can
be derived from visual observation of the superficial, differs from the
flaneur in that he understands that this activity is problematic. It is precisely such conventions of interpretation as those employed by the flaneur, conventions that assume a definable correspondence between an
event and what it signifies, that often obscure what there is to be seen.

Dupin adopts an invisible centrality like that of the flaneur, but instead of conceiving of himself as a panoramic observer of the immanent, he is a panoramic interpreter of interpretations. He does not claim to find the truth by languidly surveying the cubicles of the Panopticon. He intellectually reconstructs it by analyzing what each inhabitant of a cubicle, believing his cubicle to be a privileged vantage, is unable to see. What Dupin discovers by this method remains mysterious and inaccessible, even if it is known. The murderer of Mme. and Mlle. L'Espanaye is an extremely unusual animal. Even when safely contained in a stable, he remains a powerful embodiment of the threatening mystery and unpredictability of urban life. The murderer of Marie Roget is never discovered, captured, or even named. He is simply posited, derived through an analysis of the way in which others have misread his identity and his act. Both of these reconstructed consciousnesses are deferred. They are inaccessible and distant from the traces they have left. They cannot by any means be "perceived," immediately in a sign. As much as "the man of the crowd" they remain unfathomable, representations of the dimly understood "worst heart of the world," the unlocalized malevolence at the heart of an illegible city.

The implications of this difference in method between the flaneur and the detective are extremely important. The flaneur's method of interpretation became inadequate to the needs of a nineteenth-century audience because it denied what that audience had come to believe, that faces in the urban crowd were illegible and, because of this, threatening. Rather than denying it, the detective assumes that cities are terrifying and unpredictable and he acknowledges their apparent illegibility. Having done this, he demonstrates a technique of reading that appears to be more credible because it accepts what the flaneur denies. It also has an apparent intellectual rigor that would have given it authority in a period in which science is enjoying an unprecedented prestige. Dupin is not a mere idler with no credentials other than his social invisibility. He is a gifted and qualified specialist in an arcane yet eminently useful branch of knowledge.

For all of the modifications that a figure like Dupin makes in the strategies of the flaneur, he shares, however, many of the objectives and functions of his predecessor. He makes it possible, first of all, to consume the city as a spectacle. By offering his audience a controlled exposure to what is terrifying or incoherent in urban life, he even expands the sphere of this consumption. Like *Life in London* or the *London Spy*, the detective story assumes that part of the appeal of the city lies in the fact that one never knows what will happen next. Although the flaneur always pretends to be open to randomness, his city is so predictable that he can never convincingly offer this sense. By picking up traces after a crime, and by not claiming to be in possession of a mental lexicon in which every potential experience is anticipated, the detective restores the temporal structure of carnival. Experience is neither anticipated nor continuous. Instead it is shocking, surprising, subversive of order, and in this respect profoundly fascinating. Yet at the same time, order is always retrospectively restored by a policing structure that is more nimble and resourceful, and therefore more apparently powerful than that of the flaneur.

Although the detective observes a city that is more threatening and mysterious than that of the flaneur, and although his process of reading is fundamentally different, he is therefore, like the flaneur, a reassuring figure. The detective suggests that what appears to be an increasingly opaque urban world can be grasped, even if only by a panoramic observer with superhuman powers. By resolving mysteries that are emblematic of the urban anxieties of his audience, the detective, like the flaneur, suggests that social order is a possibility. In fact, he offers a stronger assurance of this possibility than the flaneur because it seems as if the detective's methods of interpretation could actually be used in a practical way to maintain that order. The detective story suggests that if the authorities were to discover the proper scientific methods and were to pursue their investigations with appropriate rigor, they would be able to control what is threatening or unexplainable in urban social life. Dupin's fantasy is therefore an extension into the social sphere of the positivistic faith that science can ultimately solve all physical mysteries and provide the tools to eradicate what is threatening in nature. The assumptions that underlie the fantasy of a perfect policing of society are fundamentally the same as those that underlie the fantasy of a perfect policing of nature. Each assumes that there is nothing theoretically incapable of being understood, if the proper method is applied from a vantage point outside and independent of what is observed. By finding and interpreting everyone else's blind spots, Poe's detective appears to occupy such a position.

Poe was conscious of the marketability of a genre that offered the reassurance that social order could be preserved through the development of a science of crime solving. When he tried to sell "The Mystery of Marie Roget" to magazines, he therefore presented it as a demonstration of how the mystery of Mary Rogers might be solved. As he wrote, referring to his story, in a June 4, 1841, letter to George Roberts, the editor of the *Boston Notion*, "I believe not only that I have demonstrated not only [*sic*] the fallacy of the general idea – that the girl was the victim of a gang of ruffians – but have indicated the assassin in a manner which will give renewed impetus to investigation. My main object, nevertheless, as you will readily understand, is an analysis of the true principles which should direct inquiry in similar cases" (Walsh, 47; *Letters* 1:199–200).

The fact that Poe made these claims in order to sell his story should not, of course, be taken as evidence that he believed them. It seems extremely unlikely that an author who was so consistently suspicious of all systematic penetrations of the impenetrable would have been likely to have seriously believed in the "method" of Auguste Dupin. In 1846, Poe himself had remarked, in an August 9 letter to Philip Pendleton Cooke, "These tales of ratiocination owe most of their popularity to being something in a new key. I do not mean to say that they are not ingenious—but people think them more ingenious than they are – on account of their method and air of method. In 'The Murders in the Rue Morgue,' for instance, where is the ingenuity of unravelling a web which you yourself (the author) have woven for the express purpose of unravelling" (Kennedy, 195–6; *Letters* 2:328). Rather than believing, like Kennedy, that this remark represents Poe's disillusionment with the detective story, I feel that this merely states what Poe is likely to have known all along about the detective story. Certainly Poe seems to be aware of the precise nature of the detective's deception when he discusses the principles of plot construction in his two reviews (1841 and 1842) of Dickens's *Barnaby Rudge*, in which he takes Dickens to task for not having made certain that all of the details of his text are set up so as to achieve the maximum effect at the denouement – for not, in other words, having written his story "backwards," as Poe presumably wrote "The Murders in the Rue Morgue."

Poe understood the method of the detective story to be a hoax, an "air of method," just as the flaneurs who wrote for magazines presumably did not believe that they could actually read a person's entire history at a glance. The fact that the detective stories were so often considered credible or that Poe could have tried to convince editors to accept his story on the grounds that it indicated the solution of an actual, unsolved murder case, suggests the parallel role that both genres may have played, in different though overlapping periods, in the construction of the idea of "everyday life." In the "method" of the detective, the basic structure of the flaneur's credibility has even been preserved intact. As much as the flaneur, the detective presents a "reverse" deduction from a postulated conclusion as if it were an inductive discovery of the conclusion. Although the detective's fantasy is more complex than that of the flaneur, there is no absolute sense in which it can be considered more credible. It only appears more credible to an audience conditioned to share its assumptions. Just as the flaneur seemed credible to an audience that read flaneur's sketches and that was used to seeing cities represented in dioramas, the detective seemed credible to an audience that read the crime narratives in the daily newspapers, and that read the various genres of urban menace that developed around this time. Each is "realistic" only within a broad cultural construction that determines what will be understood as "realistic."

In spite of their differences, the detective is not a contradiction of the flaneur so much as a dialectical adaptation of him. Poe's problem with the flaneur stems less from the fact that he is a con than from the fact that he cons without sufficient intellectual rigor or suspense. By replacing the flaneur with the detective, Poe does not offer a critique of the premises of panoptic egotism so much as he replaces an outmoded version of it with one that is better adapted to the changing intellectual and aesthetic expectations of his audience. In his detective stories, the city is still a spectacle, and the model for the consciousness that can consume the spectacle is still a detached reader and connoisseur of a social world with which he has no desire to interact.

Nathaniel Hawthorne had a much more serious quarrel with the flaneur. Though, like Poe, he had problems with the flaneur's epistemology, his engagement with the flaneur does not lead to the creation of a new form of fiction. Whereas Poe was concerned with developing ways to exploit the possibilities of modernity, Hawthorne, in the various stories and romances in which he represents the flaneur, offers one of the fullest and earliest American critiques of the civilization that was coming into being in response to the conditions of modernity.

Chapter 6

The Urban Spectator in Hawthorne's Sketches

In his book *Nathaniel Hawthorne*, Henry James observed that Hawthorne's life "was passed, for the most part, in a small and homogeneous society, in a provincial rural community, it had few perceptible points of contact with what is called the world, with public events, with the manners of his time, even with the life of his neighbors" (1). Writing as if he felt the need to explain why he chose, as an American writer, to live in the metropolises of Europe, James invites his reader to feel compassion for Hawthorne. "When we think," he writes, "of what conditions of intellectual life, of taste must have been in a small New England town fifty years ago; and when we think of a young man of beautiful genius, of style and form and colour, trying to make a career for himself in the midst of them, compassion for the young man becomes our dominant sentiment" (28). The portrait James painted, somewhat too clearly, of the "exquisitely and consistently provincial" (143) Hawthorne, has set the tone for all subsequent discussions of Hawthorne's relation to what James calls "the world" of the mid-nineteenth century. Nathaniel Hawthorne is still widely spoken of as someone too accustomed to solitude and rural retreat to have had much of an interest in cities, as someone too vividly aware of the power and influence of the past to have had much of an interest in the effervescent features of modernity.

It is impossible to deny the fact that Hawthorne viewed the life of his time from what was, physically and mentally, a provincial perspective. Yet the Jamesian paradigm of Hawthorne's relation to modernity does not do justice to the ambivalent yet profound fascination Hawthorne seems to have had, throughout his life, with the great cities of the world, and with the form that modern life was taking in and around them. Hawthorne wrote, in his journal, that "I take an interest in all the nooks and crannies of cities" (8:496), and numerous passages in the American, English, and French and Italian notebooks offer evidence of his fascination with London, Paris, and to a lesser extent, the cities of Italy. Hawthorne's son Julian, in his biography of his parents, writes of Hawthorne's enormous "appetite" for London, which he explored in the characteristic manner of the flaneur, when he finally visited it in 1853. Julian Hawthorne writes:

> He rejoiced in the human ocean that flooded the thoroughfares and eddied through its squares and courts; he greeted as old friends its cathedrals, its river, its bridges, its Tower, its inns, its Temple, its alleys and chop-houses, – so strange were they and so familiar. . . . He cast himself adrift upon the great city, and cruised whithersoever the current took him; and when he could keep his feet no longer, he would hail a hansom and trundle homeward in happy weakness, to begin his explorations afresh the next morning. His appetite for London, which had grown during his lifetime, was almost as big as London itself; he could not gratify it enough. He enjoyed the vague and irresponsible wandering even more than the deliberate and pre-meditated sight-seeing. (2:70)

Although Hawthorne was only able to indulge his fascination with metropolitan life after he had written virtually all of his major works, he obviously did not need to have direct experience of the largest cities in the world in order to have had a fascination with them and with the form that modern life was taking in them. During the main portion of his literary career, his actual experience of urban life was limited to an occasional trip to Boston, yet like most literate Americans, Hawthorne had an extensive imaginative acquaintance with the metropolises of Europe, and particularly with London. The *Spectator* and *Caleb Williams* were among his earliest literary enthusiasms.[1] As Poe observed (*Complete Works*, 9:105), in his review of "Twice Told Tales," and as Kesselring has documented, Hawthorne was clearly familiar with the writings of Lamb, Hunt, and Irving. As Kesselring has also established, Hawthorne was a regular reader of such British periodicals as the *Gentlemen's Magazine, Edinburgh Review, Monthly Magazine, Monthly Review, Quarterly Review, Westminster Review, London Monthly Magazine,* and *Blackwood's Edinburgh Magazine,* all of which often published urban sketches written in the characteristic manner of the flaneur. Like many Americans, Nathaniel Hawthorne had an imaginative acquaintance with the flaneur's London and yet it could not be said to represent his "everyday life" in any respect. It may have been encountered as an image of how interesting, in a romantic realist way, everyday life could be if one was in the right place, viewing it from the right vantage. In a few of his early sketches, Hawthorne explores the dilemma of an American who tries to be a flaneur in an environment that is almost comically inhospitable to his efforts.

One of these sketches, "Sights from a Steeple" (1831), has received far more credit than it deserves for its charm and far less credit than it deserves for its irony. In the 150 years since this frustrating and surprisingly substantial piece was published, critics have generally agreed with, and only rarely elaborated on, Edgar Allan Poe's judgment that it is "beautiful... quiet, thoughtful, (and) subdued" (Review of "Twice Told Tales," 105). Most modern critics have also agreed with F. O. Matthiessen's assertion that once we have granted the sketch the aesthetic qualities Poe finds in it, "it seems so slight as to be almost imperceptible" (208). Yet if Hawthorne merely wanted to write a charming demonstration of what Nina Baym refers to as "the narrator's ability to embellish the reality he transcribes with pleasing and cogent fanciful touches" (*Hawthorne's Career*, 51), I do not think that he would have persistently suggested, throughout the sketch, that the narrator who climbs to the top of a steeple fails to satisfy both his own expectations and those he has created in the reader.

In the first sentence of "Sights from a Steeple," the narrator expresses disappointment with his view. He complains that though he has "climbed high," his "reward is small" (9:191). He is dissatisfied because he had hoped to use the steeple as a kind of Tower of Babel. He would have liked to have gone up as far as heaven. Or, failing that, he would at least have liked to have seen "beautiful spirits... disporting themselves" (9:191) on the clouds. Although his charming tone may nullify what his audience would recognize as the immoral and even diabolical nature of his enterprise, the narrator openly declares that he is in search of forbidden knowledge. In the next paragraph, he takes this somewhat further. Referring to himself as "a watchman, all-heeding and unheeded" (9:192), the narrator expresses a wish:

> that the multitude of chimneys could speak, like those of Madrid, and betray, in smoky whispers, the secrets of all who, since their first foundation, have assembled at the hearths within! O that the Limping Devil of Le Sage would perch beside me here, extend his wand over this contiguity of roofs, uncover every chamber, and make me familiar with their inhabitants! The most desirable mode of existence might be that of a spiritualized Paul Pry, hovering invisible round man and woman, witnessing their deeds, searching into their hearts, borrowing brightness from their felicity, and shade from their sorrow, and retaining no emotion peculiar to himself (9:192).

Wishing to be "all-heeding and unheeded," to see through the roofs of a city, spying on its inhabitants, penetrating and imaginatively participating in their inner lives, without a fixed identity of his own, the narrator of "Sights from a Steeple" expresses sentiments that are classic in the literature of the flaneur. In the quoted passage, he specifically refers to the premise of a work that had an important place in this tradition. By mentioning Le Sage's "Limping Devil," Hawthorne's narrator establishes kinship with such authors as Egan, Hunt, and Dickens, as well as a whole series of English and American flaneurs who cite the frame story of "The Limping Devil" as an illustration of the advantages an urban spectator might ideally wish to enjoy. By mentioning, in the second paragraph of his sketch, an earlier account of the adventures of a man on top of a steeple, the narrator suggests that Le Sage's book is the inspiration for his own project. The casual and nonbibliographical nature of his reference to the Limping Devil further implies that he assumes that his reader is familiar with the story of Don Cleofas. If this is so, then the reader would surely be expected to recognize that what the narrator of the sketch is trying to do is duplicate the experience of Don Cleofas on an American steeple.

Before the narrator even looks down, however, he informs his readers that he cannot see what Don Cleofas saw. It is impossible, he says, to see through "brick walls" or into "the mystery of human bosoms." This being so, he "can but guess" (9:192) what is hidden inside them. In practice, he does not even do that. At no point does the narrator describe anything that could not in fact be seen by someone on top of a steeple, and at no point does he engage in a speculation that is not clearly and unambiguously supported by what he sees. Most of what he describes (the two parades, the funeral, and the crowd of merchants at the seaport) are undifferentiated crowds organized for specific and clearly identifiable reasons. The few differentiated individuals he observes are extremely easy to interpret.

In addition to being legible, the town described by the steeple-top narrator is remarkably benign. This steeple sitter is unaccompanied by any devil and the town beneath him is certainly not Le Sage's Madrid. Instead of a chaotic world of vice and corruption, the narrator of "Sights from a Steeple" observes a world of social order, of extreme propriety. A marching band of soldiers respectfully yields to a funeral procession. The suitor and the young ladies yield to the authority of the father. The streets are broad, straight, and well maintained. In addition to being orderly, what the narrator sees is generally trivial. The narrator says that he has climbed to his height in order to penetrate the depths of human nature. Yet from his height, human nature does not appear to have the depth it seems to have on the ground. To the narrator, the militia band in their bright uniforms resemble "from the height whence I look down, the painted veterans that garrison the window of a toy-shop" (9:195). The closest thing to a "secret" the narrator uncovers is that a relatively nondescript young man is possibly in love with a young woman about

whom we know nothing more than that she is, in the narrator's judgment, more attractive than her sister. In his ruminations on parades,
funerals, commerce, and young love, the narrator is manifestly unable
to observe anything that he could not have observed from a less exalted
vantage.

After expressing his original disappointment and acknowledging his
own limitations, the narrator seems to become content with what he
describes. After the account of the funeral, however, he once again gives
vent to his frustration:

> How various are the situations of the people covered by the roofs
> beneath me, and how diversified are the events at this moment
> befalling them! The new-born, the aged, the dying, the strong in
> life, and the recent dead, are in the chambers of these many man-
> sions. The full of hope, the happy, the miserable, and the desperate,
> dwell together within the circle of my glance. In some of the houses
> over which my eyes roam so coldly, guilt is entering into hearts
> that are still tenanted by a debased and trodden virtue, – guilt is
> on the very edge of commission, and the impending deed might
> be averted; guilt is done and the criminal wonders if it might be
> irrevocable. There are broad thoughts struggling in my mind, and,
> were I able to give them distinctness, they would make their way
> in eloquence. (9:196)

If the town beneath him is as interesting as he says it is in this passage,
the narrator has given the reader remarkably little sense of it. He implies
by this digression that he is aware of this, that he is as bored by what
he is describing as the reader is. The narrator acknowledges here a failure
of his own imagination that excludes him from the subject matter he
craves. He tries to imagine the richness of the life under the roofs, broad
thoughts struggle in his mind. If only he were able to give them distinctness, he could be eloquent. He could write about birth, death, hope,
misery, desperation, sin, guilt, and crime. If this is what he really wants
to be writing about, he cannot possibly be content with what he is in
fact writing about. But the broad thoughts never acquire the necessary
distinctness and he never becomes eloquent. By his own admission, the
narrator does not fulfill the expectations he may have created in his
audience by climbing to his special vantage point.

Having implicitly acknowledged what he cannot do, the narrator proceeds to demonstrate what he can do. Raindrops begin to fall and the
reader is treated to the spectacle of a thunderstorm so carefully controlled
and charmingly artificial that it seems like a thunderstorm in a diorama.
It is proper and orderly, waiting until the young ladies are safely inside
before letting loose its full fury. It appears at just the right time, giving

the narrator the opportunity to enliven a tableau the dramatic potential of which he has otherwise exhausted. It ends at just the right time, providing a pretty rainbow to conclude the sketch. It is so contrived that the reader may take as a pleasing irony the narrator's reference to the storm as a "tumult which I am powerless to direct or quell" (9:198).[2] But the narrator's easy manipulation of the stage machinery available to him only serves to highlight what is not available to him. It is easy to summon storms. It is hard to "know the interior of brick walls or the mystery of human bosoms." The narrator's final and specious success only underlines the fact that his experiment has failed. Considering that Hawthorne was writing during the heyday of a literary tradition in which the opacity of roofs and bosoms was not considered a serious obstacle to the observation of what was within them, the steeple-top narrator's failure to offer an illusion of spectatorial omniscience is significant. There is a similarly significant failure in another of Hawthorne's sketches, "The Old Apple Dealer" (1842).

"The Old Apple Dealer" is similar to Poe's "The Man of the Crowd" in that it concerns a narrator's effort to determine the character and history of a randomly encountered old man, who is never addressed or questioned. Most critics of this sketch have assumed that the narrator's effort is successful.[3] Like certain readers of "Sights from a Steeple," they have taken the narrator's extravagant opening statements of intention as accurate descriptions of his accomplishment. Other critics, perceiving that the narrator does not accomplish what he sets out to do, have read it as a demonstration that some people are so uninteresting that they do not reward a careful reading.[4] Yet such apparently opaque individuals were particularly favored subjects for the readings of the flaneurs. In one of Dickens's *Sketches by Boz*, written seven years earlier and possibly familiar to Hawthorne, a narrator sees a similarly nondescript man and has no difficulty imagining his life in great detail.[5]

In the time-honored tradition of the flaneur, the fact that the old apple dealer is "almost hueless," that he is "faded and featureless" (10:439), is represented by the narrator of the sketch as a welcome challenge. The narrator declares that he is determined to prove that "the lover of the moral picturesque may sometimes find what he seeks in a character which is, nevertheless, of too negative a description to be seized upon, and represented to the imaginative vision by word-painting" (10:439). Without speaking to the old man, knowing nothing of his history, and unable to seize upon any distinctive or revealing physiognomical traits, the narrator proceeds to "guess" what is beneath the surface he observes. As he does this, however, he persistently calls attention to the purely speculative nature of his activity. When Hawthorne's narrator speculates that the man's "past life . . . offers no bright spots to his memory," he must add the qualification of a "probably" (10:440). At another point, the narrator observes an "indescribable shadow" upon the man's features and speculates that, "just at that instant, the suspicion occurred to him, that, in his chill decline of life, earning scanty bread by selling cakes, apples, and candy, he is a very miserable fellow" (10:441). Seeming at this point to have perceived a thought of the old man, the narrator suddenly reverses himself. He writes: "But if he think so, it is a mistake. He can never suffer the extreme of misery, because the tone of his whole being is too much subdued for him to feel anything" (10:441). Apparently the narrator had thought that he perceived an idea or emotion on the man's face. Then he realized that such a perception was inconsistent with the character of the old man as he has sketched it up to this point. So he reverses himself. In the process, the narrator exposes his own difficulty in distinguishing between what he is seeing and what he is creating. What caused him to "perceive" the old man's subjective revelation was his own subjective impression that, at a certain moment, "the expression of frost-bitten, patient despondency" on the man's face "becomes very touching" (10:441).

Throughout the sketch, the language of the narrator implies that virtually all of his "perceptions" are acts of creation and appropriation. This is clear from the very first sentence of the sketch in which he refers to what he is doing as the activity of "find[ing] what he seeks in a character" (10:439). By observing the old man, the narrator claims to have made him "a naturalized citizen of my inner world" (10:439). At the end of the sketch, however, after failing to discern the man's earlier profession and fortune with any degree of specificity, the narrator remarks, in frustration:

> To confess, the truth, it is not the easiest matter in the world, to define and individualize a character like this which we are now handling. The portrait must be so generally negative, that the most delicate pencil is likely to spoil it by introducing some too positive tint. Every touch must be kept down or else you destroy the subdued tone, which is absolutely essential to the whole effect. (10:444)

Like any flaneur, Hawthorne's narrator is painting, he is not seeing. Unlike the flaneur, this narrator refuses to hide his oils and easel and he complains of the difficulty of what the flaneur claims is easy. His self-consciousness is sufficient to restrain his speculations. To an audience accustomed to the speculative freedom of the English flaneurs, Hawthorne's portrait of an old apple dealer would have seemed disappointingly tentative and meager. In the end, like the steeple-top narrator, the narrator of "The Old Apple Dealer" is in the embarrassing situation of having discovered almost nothing of what he said he was going to discover at the opening of the sketch.

In both "Sights from a Steeple" and "The Old Apple Dealer," Hawthorne reaffirms the opacity of the world by showing how little an honest flaneur or panoramic spectator would actually accomplish. Such a reaffirmation would be of a piece with Hawthorne's well-known suspicions and doubts about the moral and epistemological character of the activity of the artist. It would also fit in with Hawthorne's evident respect for privacy and the rights of individuals to be opaque, complex, and mysterious. Yet at the same time, Hawthorne's focus on the frustration of his narrators as they "write" sketches that they themselves find unsatisfactory suggests that Hawthorne may be representing a frustration of his own: the frustration involved in trying to make art out of the ephemera of everyday life when one is far from the urban, European centers in which this is being done, and in which conventions have taken root that appear to make it possible.

The narrator of "Sights from a Steeple" is someone in the wrong place at the wrong time. He presents himself as someone who, through his reading, possesses the tools of metropolitan spectatorship. He has, however, no metropolis to look at. Briefly, he contemplates turning the small town beneath him into a metropolis. In language that would be conventional if he were looking at London, the narrator marvels at the variety, diversity, and proximity of what he feels must be going on under the roofs of a town that seems rather spread out and not terribly diverse, a town to which he never gains the access he originally hopes to have. When the frustrated narrator describes the darkening sky as being as "gloomy as an author's prospects," forcing him "to resume [his] station on lower earth" (9:198), he may be expressing Hawthorne's understanding of himself as an American artist at a time when America cannot yet produce or consume modern realist art, although it can produce artists capable of conceiving this ambition. In the one sketch in which he deals extensively with what was still understood to be the foreign, yet prospectively American issue of urban modernity, it was necessary for Hawthorne to choose a foreign metropolitan locale.

Although no one has ever judged "Wakefield" (1836) to be one of Hawthorne's most aesthetically successful pieces, its setting and professed subject are such that it would be difficult to dismiss it as trivial. Yet because it has been taken more seriously, "Wakefield" has too often been read as if it had no connection to sketches like "Sights from a Steeple" and "The Old Apple Dealer," which have, for too long, been filed away as if they were trivial. In order to read the representation of the subjective conditions of urban life in "Wakefield," it is necessary to consider the sketch in the context of these other sketches, to see how it contributes

to the analysis of the dynamics of urban spectatorship that is also contained within them. In addition to resembling these other sketches,
"Wakefield" is significantly similar to Poe's "The Man of the Crowd,"
which it is likely to have influenced.[6]

Both "Wakefield" and "The Man of the Crowd" involve narrators
who, in the classic manner of the flaneur, claim to be able to read and
remain personally distant from the object of their meditations. Each
narrative is generated by the narrator's effort to interpret an identifiably
urban mystery. In each case, the narrator's original assertion of epistemological control is undermined by his own narration. As each narrator
fails to illuminate the object of his scrutiny, he becomes more frustrated
and more involved in the mystery, both out of a desire to solve it, and
out of a growing identification with the mysterious individual, upon
whom he projects some of his most powerful anxieties. In the end, each
narrator attempts to restore his control, to offer a "moral," and though
he claims to have been successful, the manifest inappropriateness of the
moral leaves the reader not with a sense of the urban interpreter's powers,
but with a sense of the menacing opacity of human beings, particularly
as perceived against the backdrop of a European metropolis whose ability
to overwhelm the composure of the would-be flaneur has been magnified
to an extraordinary degree by American authors writing for an American
audience.

The narrator of "The Man of the Crowd" never becomes fully conscious of the degree to which his opening assertions of interpretive power
are undercut by the events of his narrative. The narrator of "Wakefield,"
on the other hand, like the other Hawthorne narrators I have considered
thus far, begins to undermine his own interpretive authority as soon as
he has laid claim to it. Though he promises a "moral," he immediately
undercuts it by guaranteeing that he will provide one even if he fails to
find any in the incident (9:131). The narrator's ironic sense of his activity
is further evident in the condescending way in which he refers to the
promised "moral." It will, he writes, be "done up neatly," like a wrapped
present, and a reader can count on the fact that, whatever it is, it will
be capable of being "condensed into the final sentence" (9:131). After
emphasizing the artificial nature of his activity in this way, it seems
unlikely that the narrator's next sentence, the smug and dubious assurance
that "Thought has always its efficacy, and every striking incident its
moral" (9:131), is meant to be taken straight.

In addition to emphasizing the reductive and artificial character of his
enterprise, the narrator of "Wakefield" undercuts his authority by refusing to claim that his perspective is in any way privileged or that his
interpretive skills are especially powerful. Although the reader is invited
to accompany him on a "ramble . . . through the twenty years of Wake-

field's vagary," the narrator freely acknowledges that it might be just as valuable for the reader to "do his own meditation" (9:131). When he actually begins to sketch Wakefield's character, the narrator emphasizes the fictive quality of his characterization by writing: "What sort of man was Wakefield? We are free to shape out our own idea, and call it by his name" (9:131). Like the narrator of "The Old Apple Dealer," the narrator of "Wakefield" refuses to assume the interpretive authority that is conventionally assumed by other urban spectatorial essayists in similar situations.

After having undercut his authority, the narrator of "Wakefield" proceeds to offer a detailed description of Wakefield's subjectivity. The degree of detail with which he describes the inner life of someone about whom he claims to know nothing suggests that the narrator is identifying with Wakefield's situation, that he is exploring what his own motivations might have been if he had done what Wakefield has done. That such an identification is an important element of the sketch is indicated by the way in which the narrator repeatedly emphasizes how strong a fascination Wakefield's story has for him. He writes that it "forcibly affects [his] mind," "it has often recurred [to him], always exciting wonder" (9:131). Legitimizing his identification, the narrator observes that Wakefield's story "appeals to the general sympathies of mankind. We know, each for himself, that none of us would perpetuate such a folly, yet feel as if some other might" (9:131).

If the narrator is identifying with "Wakefield," it is particularly significant that the personality he chooses to give him is roughly identical to the personality the narrator of "Sights from a Steeple" described himself as having. Like the narrator of "Sights from a Steeple," who glorifies his own detached and purposeless idleness, Wakefield is someone whose "mind occupie[s] itself in long and lazy musings, that tended to no purpose" (9:131). His laziness, like the steeple-top narrator's, manifests itself as an imaginative, intellectual, and ultimately verbal incapacity. The narrator of "Sights from a Steeple" has "broad thoughts struggling in [his] mind," thoughts that are unable to become "distinct," that are unable to "make their way in eloquence" (9:196). Wakefield's thoughts lack the "vigor" necessary to "attain . . . purpose," "his thoughts were seldom so energetic as to seize hold of words" (9:131). In fact, "such are [Wakefield's] loose and rambling modes of thought, that he has taken this very singular step, with the consciousness of a purpose, indeed, but without being able to define it sufficiently for his own contemplation" (9:134). The activity of the narrator of "Sights from a Steeple" is comparably undefined. He has some vague and grandiose conceptions of what he would like to imagine from the steeple top, but he is never able to bring his thoughts to sufficient distinctness to be able to report them.

In addition to having similar subjectivities, Wakefield and the steeple-top narrator are engaged in similar activities. Both remove themselves from the world that is familiar to them, in order to observe it, without a clear purpose, from an unusual vantage. Neither of them has a clear idea of what they expect to learn from viewing the world in this way. The lazy and indeterminate nature of their activities suggests that their intention is more existential than epistemological. Each wishes to experience the indolent pleasure of spectatorial detachment. Each is, in this respect, a flaneur. Yet Wakefield's characterization adds a feature to the flaneur's personality that would assume a great deal of prominence in the analysis of the modern urban subjectivity found in the works of Poe and Baudelaire. Wakefield's curiosity, although it is lazy and unfocused, is also compulsive. He cannot stop once he has started, and he continues in his self-imposed exile for twenty years. His curiosity is, as the narrator writes, an example of "an influence, [which] beyond our control, lays its strong hand on every deed we do, and weaves its consequences into an iron tissue of necessity" (9:136–7). This anticipates what Baudelaire wrote of Poe's "man of the crowd": for him, "curiosity has become a fatal, irresistable passion" ("The Painter of Modern Life," 294). Just as Poe's "man of the crowd" represents the compulsive potential of the mild curiosity of the flaneur narrator, Wakefield illuminates the compulsive potential of the steeple-top narrator's effort to peer through the roofs of his neighbors. Although their differing degrees of compulsiveness give a different character to their activities, Wakefield's project is in many ways a natural development of the steeple-top narrator's desire to be central yet invisible, to encompass the sphere of his life without taking a part in it, for the purpose of satisfying an indolent curiosity.

Lazy, unfocused, and yet compulsively curious, perpetually in search of novelty, the subjectivities of Wakefield and the steeple-top narrator have much in common with what Steele and Wordsworth had identified as the characteristically modern personality. They approach their experience as spectacle and they appear to lack the means to unify their experience or produce it synthetically. The narrator of "Wakefield" is also a quintessentially modern consumer of spectacle, no less than the narrator of "The Man of the Crowd," and this is undoubtedly an important aspect of his identification with Wakefield. In the sketch, the narrator represents himself as engaged in a lazy and ill-defined act of consuming a piece of spectacular information taken from a newspaper. As encyclopedias of novelty, newspapers are, as both Steele and Wordsworth observed, vital to the modern consciousness, and they are a central component of all of Poe's parables of urban reading. Poe constructs his London out of accounts he has read in newspapers and magazines. The narrator of "The Man of the Crowd," significantly, places a newspaper aside in order to begin to read the crowd. Ultimately, Auguste Dupin, the Poe character who grows out of the narrator of "The Man of the Crowd," experiences the city and solves his mysteries primarily through newspapers. "Wakefield" anticipates all of these Poe stories in the way in which it describes an effort to interpret a newspaper article. As each of these works written at the dawn of modern journalism makes clear, it is through newspapers that all of the novelties that can be found in a giant city become available for consumption. In the age of newspapers, it is not necessary for one to have direct experience of such events as the grisly unexplained murder of the L'Espanayes or a bizarre story like Wakefield's for them to become part of the experience of everyday life.

Just as the narrator of "The Man of the Crowd" observed a frenzied, compulsive version of his own urban spectatorship in the activity of the man he followed, the narrator of "Wakefield" may observe a version of his own urban consumption in Wakefield's activity. What Wakefield does is an interesting reflection of what is involved in the act of reading a metropolitan newspaper. To read such a paper, particularly a paper of the 1830s, is to observe the life that is lived in close proximity to oneself, without being noticed by those one watches, safe from any interaction with them. Newspapers make it possible to watch what is of interest to oneself, while escaping the surveillance of others. Like the narrator of "Sights from a Steeple," a newspaper reader is in effect a "spiritualized Paul Pry." He routinely achieves a version of what the narrator of "Wakefield" refers to as "Wakefield's unprecedented fate, to retain his original share of human sympathies, and to be still involved in human interests, while he had lost his reciprocal influence on them" (9:138). A reader of newspapers, a viewer of panoramas, or any individual engaged in the modern activity of viewing images or viewing reality as if it were composed of images, is in a situation eerily analogous to that of Wakefield who, the narrator writes, "had given up his place and privileges with living men, without being admitted among the dead" (9:138).

By retaining the consciousness and mobility of a living person, while assuming the social privileges of a dead one, Wakefield carries an appetite for urban spectacle to an extraordinary, yet logical extreme. "Wakefield" is written at a time when the proliferation of images and the transformation of experience into the consumption of images are bringing about changes in the relationship of consciousness to experience that the invention of photography four years later will intensify, if not actually cause. Roland Barthes suggests, in his book *Camera Lucida*, that the invention of photography represents a major turning point in the history of civilization. "For the Photograph," he writes, "is the advent of myself as Other: a cunning dissociation of consciousness from identity" (12). Wakefield's action expresses this historically significant dissociation, and, appearing in a sketch written in 1835, it illustrates the degree to which the dissociation Barthes describes is a product of a broad and varied urban and technological revolution in the nature of experience, and not simply a product of the invention of photography by itself. What Wakefield tries to do in the middle of modern London is to see himself as Other. He wishes to observe himself as represented in the reaction of his wife to his absence. In this way he will be able to view his identity from the perspective of his consciousness, and experience his identity in the way in which he experiences the identity of others, as something that can be read off of the physiognomy of another person. Figuratively speaking, Wakefield's act expresses his desire to see a photograph of himself at a moment in which the only film available to record his impression is the visage of his wife.

As Hawthorne represents it, what causes Wakefield to attempt this transformation of life into image is the experience of urban anonymity. It is only necessary for Wakefield to step out his front door in order to "lose his individuality, and melt into the great mass of London life" (9:133). The degree of anonymity in Hawthorne's London, which like the London of "The Man of the Crowd" is exaggerated for effect by American authors writing for American audiences, is represented as a possible cause, and a possible opportunity for Wakefield's exile. His desire to see himself may reflect the anxiety about identity that an environment as crowded as this imaginary London might be imagined to produce. But it also offers thrilling possibilities for anyone who wishes to exchange their identity for the vantage point of an invisible spectator. In a city so crowded that the narrator mocks Wakefield for thinking that anyone could have detected him while he was on his way to his new lodgings, or passing by his old home, invisibility is a matter of course. Only in such a city, and not in a town like Salem, would it be possible to imagine achieving the goal of the narrator of "Sights from a Steeple": to "hover invisible around man and woman, witnessing their deeds, searching into their hearts, etc." (9:192). Wakefield, then, tries to take advantage of the opportunity provided by a modern European metropolis to view the world from an invisible vantage, as a collection of images. Yet like a voracious beast that, having consumed everything in sight, begins to consume itself, he tries to observe himself, and particularly the spectacle of his own death.

Wakefield's tale becomes a parable of spectatorial hubris, of an effort to observe what no one can observe, the effects of one's own death. And by creating a situation in which one is alive to see this spectacle, he reverses the power relationship that is normally imagined to exist when one imagines one's own death, the sense of others being aware of and observing something central to your own identity that you yourself cannot be aware of or observe. This fear, which is an intensification of a living fear of being watched and interpreted without knowing it, is obliterated, short-changed, short-circuited by Wakefield's trick. He becomes the only spectator of the spectacle of his absence. Anyone else is deceived in what they believe they are seeing.

Such an understanding of Wakefield's character and project may explain why the strongest emotions Wakefield experiences in the course of his twenty years are exaggerated fears of visibility, fears that he is in fact a spectacle when he is trying to be a spectator. The narrator's two most emphatic assertions of Wakefield's invisibility are responses to overestimations, on Wakefield's part, of the possibility that he has been seen. After reaching his lodgings in the next street from his home, Wakefield indulges himself in a whole train of paranoid imaginings. He remembers that at one point "he was delayed by the throng, in the very focus of a lighted lantern" (9:133); he seems to remember hearing footsteps following him and a voice calling his name. He becomes certain that "a dozen busybodies had been watching him and told his wife the whole affair" (133). The narrator ridicules this anxiety: "Poor Wakefield! Little knowest thou thine own insignificance in this great world! No mortal eye but mine has traced thee" (9:133). The next day, after walking by and almost entering his house, Wakefield has similarly agitated thoughts and the narrator mocks the way in which "the crafty nincompoop takes to his heels, scared with the idea, that, among a thousand such atoms of mortality, her eye must have detected him" (9:135). Finally, in order to protect himself from any possibility of detection, Wakefield adopts a series of disguises that the narrator implies, in the assertions quoted above, are unnecessary.

Trying to become an invisible watcher in an environment in which he fears he is always visible, Wakefield expresses a fear that Richard Sennett has suggested is characteristic of the period in which "Wakefield" was written, a fear that is the inverse of the fantasies of spectatorial dominion that are also characteristic of this period. Sennett argues, in *The Fall of Public Man*, that much of the urban culture of the 1830s and 1840s can be understood as an attempt to escape or elude surveillance. He asserts that the relatively new tendency of individuals to believe that personality was immanent, and therefore involuntarily revealed in a person's features and gestures, even if it owes much of its origins to an effort to alleviate epistemological anxiety, may have produced an even stronger anxiety, a fear of detection, a fear of being read. Sennett's analysis is clearly related to Foucault's paradigm of the Panopticon. In the terms provided by Foucault's image, it is possible to understand Wakefield's project as an effort to escape the clearly defined and completely visible Panoptic cubicle in which he is ordinarily situated, in order to experience the power of the invisible spectator in the tower of the Panopticon. Fearing surveillance, fearing that his personality is immanent in his face, life, and gestures, Wakefield may be seeking to escape the intrusive gaze of the other by becoming that gaze.

However one understands the constellation of Wakefield's spectatorial ambitions and motivations, it is clear that "Wakefield" demonstrates something quite similar to what "The Man of the Crowd" demonstrates: that the access to the consciousness of others, which urban anonymity seems to offer, is in fact impossible. Crowds cannot so easily be reduced to a text. The interpretive freedom of an urban spectator is simply freedom, it is not power. "Wakefield" establishes this by means of a double plot structure very much like that of "The Man of the Crowd." As Wakefield tries to read his wife's reaction to his absence, the narrator simultaneously tries to read Wakefield's motivations. The sketch consists of parallel moments of interpretive frustration. Wakefield peers into different configurations of his wife's features over time. In each instance, his questions and uncertainties are the same. Does she miss him or doesn't she? How much? How will she express it? How will his absence affect her? His compulsiveness is fueled by his inability to answer any of these questions by reading her face. Parallel to these failed moments of physiognomical reading are the narrator's unsuccessful efforts to gain access to Wakefield's consciousness. Every time Wakefield is shown trying to read his wife's features, the narrator presents himself as trying to read Wakefield's features. And just as Wakefield becomes more obsessed as he remains perpetually uncertain of the meaning of his wife's features, the narrator grows more obsessed as he remains perpetually uncertain of Wakefield's motivations. In frustration, each indulges in speculations. These, however, never bring the narrative to a rest because neither Wakefield nor the narrator are ever shown to be satisfied with the accuracy of their interpretations. And so the sketch continues, in fits and starts, as nervously and aimlessly as "The Man of the Crowd," as each spectator continues to be compulsively drawn to what he watches, remaining at all times unsatisfied by his interpretive interaction with it.

At the climax of "Wakefield," the narrator represents Wakefield's final effort to read his wife's physiognomy. Looking in through the parlor window, he observes on the ceiling "a grotesque shadow of good Mrs. Wakefield. The cap, the nose and chin, and the broad waist, form an admirable caricature, which dances, moreover, with the up-flickering and down-sinking blaze, almost too merrily for the shade of an elderly widow" (9:139). The climax of this sketch, appropriately, is a revelation of the fluidity and impenetrability of human features. It is this revelation, which is never consciously formulated by Wakefield, that causes him to finally cross his own threshold. Though Wakefield returns home, the narrator is unable to show him coming to any understanding of his twenty-year absence. The narrator himself has not penetrated Wakefield's mystery to the point of being able to offer an explanation for his behavior. In the end, having promised a moral, the narrator comes up with one, but it is every bit as inadequate a summation to the story as the moral of "The Man of the Crowd." The narrator observes that: "Amid the seeming confusion of our mysterious world, individuals are so nicely adjusted to a system, and systems to one another, and to a whole, that, by stepping aside for a moment, a man exposes himself to a fearful risk of losing his place forever. Like Wakefield, he may become, as it were, the Outcast of the Universe" (9:140). Just as the narrator of "The Man of the Crowd" has not proved that he has discovered the dark heart of the world, the narrator of "Wakefield" has hardly proved this peculiar assertion. Like the moral of the Poe story, the moral only serves to dissociate the narrator from the mysterious image with which he has become involved.

In "Sights from a Steeple" and "The Old Apple Dealer," Hawthorne undermines several of the spectatorial assumptions that form the basis of the tradition of the flaneur. In "Wakefield," he examines some of the potential consequences of a posture of absolute spectatorial detachment. He also associates the compulsive and impersonal spectatorship of Wakefield with a modern metropolitan environment. In the tales and sketches he was to write during the remainder of his career, Hawthorne would demonstrate a consistent interest in the consequences of spectatorial and imaginative detachment. Most of Hawthorne's detached artist figures are not urban or in any significant way modern, although as Millicent Bell has demonstrated, they may all express Hawthorne's understanding of the peculiar position of the "modern" artist. Yet the association that Hawthorne began to explore in his sketches, between spectatorial detachment as a mode of social being and the conditions of modern urban life, resurfaces in the romances that Hawthorne wrote in the early 1850s. In these romances, Hawthorne explores this association much more fully than he does in his sketches, and he conducts this exploration in the context of the rapid urbanization of America in the 1830s and 1840s and the concomitant development of a diverse and interconnected cosmopolitan culture.

Chapter 7

The Blithedale Romance *and* the Culture of Modernity

When "Wakefield" was published in 1836, most of Hawthorne's audience, like Hawthorne himself, would only have known of the conditions of urban life treated in the sketch by having read about them. Hawthorne takes advantage of the exoticism of a European metropolitan setting, just as Poe was to have done a few years later in "The Man of the Crowd" and "The Murders in the Rue Morgue." Yet by 1852, when *The Blithedale Romance* was published, the urbanization of America was no longer an abstract possibility; it was, thanks to economic growth, industrial development, and large-scale immigration, an increasingly insistent reality. The intellectual and social movements represented by the Blithedale community were, in large measure, a response to these historical changes. The process of urbanization is therefore never entirely out of sight in *The Blithedale Romance*. Expressing the ideas implicit in the agrarian experiment, Coverdale offers several standard Transcendentalist criticisms of urban life. Driving through the streets of Boston, he describes "how the buildings, on either side, seemed to press too closely upon us, insomuch that our mighty hearts found barely room enough to throb between them" (3:11). Observing how the snow falling upon the city is blackened by smoke, and molded by boots, Coverdale makes it into a metaphor for the way in which human nature is corrupted by the "falsehood, formality, and error" (3:11) of city life. In addition, Coverdale identifies cities as the sources of the "selfish competition," which powers the "weary treadmill of established society" (3:19). Yet although Coverdale will occasionally express the Juvenalian and Thoreauvian ideology of Blithedale, he implicitly recognizes, late in the book, that it may be futile to attempt to arrest the advance of urban civilization. When he observes a crowd at a village lyceum, it seems to him to be "rather suburban than rural" (3:197). The decline of authentic rusticity has been implied earlier when we learn that Blithedale, in spite of its Edenic pretensions, is located in an area of market gardens catering to the needs of the expanding "New England metropolis." From the very beginning of *The Blithedale Romance*, we know that the utopian experiment has failed and that Coverdale has returned to the urban existence he originally fled.

Most criticism that has dealt with the urban theme in Blithedale has restricted itself to a consideration of Coverdale's very conventional observations. Because Hawthorne has never been considered an advocate of urban life, several critics have felt justified in associating Coverdale's observations with Hawthorne himself. But considering that it is so clearly a satire of an explicitly antiurban social experiment, *The Blithedale Romance* poses problems for those who would view it as a conventional indictment of urban life. It is much more than that. In *The Blithedale Romance*, Hawthorne represents an urban civilization that is on the point of becoming ubiquitous. For Hawthorne, the meaning of this is not that buildings and smokestacks are rapidly replacing the countryside so much as that the characteristically cosmopolitan modes of interacting with reality that he represents in "Wakefield," "Sights from a Steeple," "The Old Apple Dealer," and in brief portions of *The House of the Seven Gables*, are replacing older modes of interaction. An important agent of this change is the village lyceum, and in a chapter of *The Blithedale Romance* entitled "A Village Hall," Hawthorne gathers together many of the components of the cosmopolitan culture he represents throughout the book.

In the opening section of "A Village Hall," Coverdale, in an effort to solve the personal mysteries that elude him, goes to a lyceum to see a performance of The Veiled Lady. Before the performance begins, he provides a lengthy and apparently gratuitous catalog of the amusements that may be seen in the lyceum in the course of the year. Villagers in this New England town may hear lectures on a wide variety of topics. They may attend exhibitions of a "diorama of Moscow or Bunker Hill" or a "moving panorama of the Chinese wall." In addition to these actual panoramas and dioramas, they may see such panoramic entertainments as a "museum of wax figures, illustrating the wide catholicism of earthly renown by mixing up heroes and statesmen, the Pope and the Mormon Prophet, kings, queens, murderers, and beautiful ladies" (3:196). They can see models of their internal organs and, at mesmeric demonstrations, they can hear communications from a world of spirits.

In Coverdale's catalog, Hawthorne shows that villagers in formerly rustic rural New England may now entertain themselves by viewing images of everything in the world. Everything is available, if only in the form of a representation. This historically novel acquaintance with a great diversity of images, often presented in panoramic form, has had a profound effect on their consciousness. The crowd that strikes him as "rather suburban than rural" suggests to Coverdale that "in these days, there is absolutely no rusticity, except when the actual labor of the soil leaves its earth-mould on the person" (3:197). Coverdale discerns that the villagers, by attending such exhibitions, have become, to however limited a degree, cosmopolitans. Within the village hall, they enjoy an experience that had formerly been an exclusive privilege of the urban educated classes: the sense of spectatorial power associated with the reduction of the world to a panorama of images.[1]

The crowd in the Village Hall differs significantly from another crowd of spectators Hawthorne had represented in a sketch written a few years before *The Blithedale Romance*. In "Main Street" (1849) an itinerant showman exhibits a "shifting panorama" (11:49) of the history of Salem to residents of that town. As the showman turns the crank that makes the panorama move forward, his audience persistently objects to the magnitude of the discrepancy between the showman's rhetoric and his "wretchedly bedaubed sheet of canvas" and his "pasteboard slips that hitch and jerk along the front" (11:63). In "Main Street," the conflict observable in "Sights from a Steeple," between the panoramist's rhetorical ambition and his practical achievement, is given concrete form in the interaction between the contemptuous audience and the frustrated entertainer. Even if their criticisms have merit, this audience is excessively literal-minded. Like the villagers who mock the crudeness of the Jew's diorama in "Ethan Brand," they have an inbred mistrust of the simplest conventions of representation. Entreated by the showman to use their imaginations, the audience responds that to do so would be a violation of their principle of "see(ing) things precisely as they are" (11:52). Descendants of the Puritans, living in a naively empiricist nation and age, they do not merely object to the crudeness of the pasteboard figures, they object to the presumptuousness of an artist who gathers together, in a single scene, individuals who are unlikely to have ever been in Salem at the same time.

The crowd in the village hall, having an extensive acquaintance with images, does not share the naiveté of the Salem audience with respect to the conventions of representation. They represent a new breed of American, a breed that would become and is still dominant. These Americans are a Jeffersonian nightmare. Yet they are the natural product of the most successful capitalist society of the nineteenth century. They have an insatiable appetite for images. They have discarded, along with their provinciality, any Puritan suspicion of images and their power. Coverdale's "suburban" New England villagers are consumers of experience. The shape and structure of their consciousness has changed so that like the village lyceum itself, they may contain the massive amount of images they encounter without feeling the need or obligation to choose among them and to structure an identity by means of such choices. Although they are not yet quite comparable, in this respect, to the inhabitants of such capitals of the nineteenth century as Paris, London, or even New York, they are moving in that direction. Representing this movement, Hawthorne represents, as few other authors have, one of the most important developments in nineteenth-century American history.

In *The House of the Seven Gables*, the book that he wrote immediately before *The Blithedale Romance*, Hawthorne had begun to consider the effect of modernity upon consciousness. He did this most openly in the chapter in which Clifford Pyncheon, fleeing with Hepzibah, takes his first ride in a railway carriage. Clifford, whose sensibility and situation have made him into a natural consumer of lived moments, marvels at the opportunities the railroad creates for the kind of consciousness he represents. As he observes to the ticket taker: "Transition being so facile, what can be any man's inducement to tarry in one spot?" (2:260). For Clifford, the appeal of the world created by the railroad is that it can perpetually offer the sensation of novelty, as one image supersedes another, for an observer seated within the mobile vantage point. Clifford understands that, in such a world, he could preserve the sense of protected speculative dominion he enjoys at his arched window, while being able to observe so much more than he can see from that window.

Excited by the railroad, Clifford's mind moves on to a delighted recognition that other new technologies and sciences, like electricity and mesmerism, also offer unprecedented opportunities for omnivorous spectatorship. When the old man he addresses in the railway carriage dismisses mesmerism as humbug and showmanship, Clifford urges him to consider its more philosophical aspects. He describes the mesmeric conception of electricity, the notion, fundamental to the science of mesmerism, that electricity was "the demon, the angel, the mighty physical power, the all-pervading intelligence!" "By means of electricity," Clifford has heard, "the world of matter has become a great nerve, vibrating thousands of miles in a breathless point of time . . . the round globe is a vast head, a brain, instinct with intelligence" (2:260). When the old man assumes that Clifford is talking about the telegraph,[2] Clifford is able to draw an analogy between the mesmeric ideal and the possibilities offered by the telegraph for the establishment of connections between dispersed and individuated consciousnesses. By offering the possibility of such unity of consciousness, mesmerism offers the prospect of gaining access to and becoming one with the minds of all others. In his ravings, Clifford sees a unity of purpose in the innovations of the modern world. Commenting on its new sciences and technologies, and the new ways of life they make possible, he recognizes that the ultimate consequence of modernity will be a universal cosmopolitanism, in which everyone will be able to exist "everywhere and nowhere" (2:260), perpetually satisfying a compulsive curiosity.

After his brief expression of enthusiasm for a world for which he would have been suited, but which it is too late for him to enjoy, Clifford returns to his passivity. His outburst has no significant effect on the narrative. Yet Clifford's monologues address many of the issues that are also raised in *The House of the Seven Gables* by the character and career of Holgrave. Perpetually changing homes and professions, Holgrave actually enjoys the freedom that, as Clifford perceives, the railroad makes available to everyone. In the course of his wanderings, Holgrave has been an itinerant showman, a mesmerist, a Fourierist, and a daguerrotypist. He achieves the absolute freedom from identity that Wakefield aspires to, and that is implicit in all of the avant-garde activities in which he has engaged. In all of his distinctly modern professions, Holgrave has been able to fix and read others without himself being fixed and read. As a daguerrotypist, he makes images and boasts that his images "bring out the secret character" of an individual "with a truth that no painter would ever venture upon, even could he detect it" (2:91). As a mesmerist, he also sought to gain access to the consciousness of others. As a Fourierist, he adhered to a belief in the possibility of redesigning communities and, in the process, the consciousness of those who would inhabit them. All of these quintessentially modern activities offer, to their practitioners, a utopian sense of the malleability and accessibility of the human world. The character of all of Holgrave's activities is expressed in his remark to Hepzibah Pyncheon that "I find nothing so singular as that everything appears to lose its substance, the instant one actually grapples with it" (2:269).

In *The House of the Seven Gables*, Hawthorne does not attempt a full-scale treatment of the modern world that impinges so tantalizingly upon his narrative. Holgrave ultimately repudiates the culture with which he is identified and he does not therefore become the "grave" of the "whole." Conceiving a sudden fondness for stone houses, he marries Phoebe and settles down. His modern enthusiasms appear, in retrospect, to have only been means to the end of regaining what was rightfully his. However, by collectively introducing and associating such cultural phenomena as mesmerism, daguerrotypy, utopian socialism, and the technological innovations that shrink the world and grant access to it, Hawthorne defines the culture that would be the subject of his next book. He brings together a series of social and technological processes that have in common the fact that they call into question the solidity and permanence of an older understanding of reality; his purpose is to redesign the world so as to make it better suited to the requirements of a consciousness that seeks to reduce everything to an accessible and consumable image. The village hall where Coverdale observes the emerging culture of modernity is a recapitulation of Clifford's meditations and of Holgrave's résumé. Yet it is central to *The Blithdale Romance* in ways in which these aspects of *The House of the Seven Gables* are not as central to the romance in which they appear.

In *The Blithedale Romance*, Hawthorne examines the culture that is spreading to the village lyceums and he examines the consciousness that such a culture produces. Miles Coverdale's subjectivity is a radical development of Holgrave's and it fulfills several of Clifford Pyncheon's prophecies. It is also in many ways an expansion and generalization of the subjectivities of Wakefield and the narrator of "Sights from a Steeple." It is where the New England villagers are headed. Many critics have questioned Hawthorne's wisdom in entrusting the treatment of such important historical issues as urbanization and agrarian socialism to a narrator as idiosyncratic as Coverdale.[3] Others, unwilling to believe that Hawthorne could have made so mammoth a technical mistake, have argued that Coverdale's consciousness is in fact the center of the romance, and that the interesting historical issues raised in *Blithedale* are less important than the issue of how Coverdale watches them.[4] I think that these two most important aspects of the *The Blithedale Romance* may be brought together if one assumes that, in the context of the book, Coverdale's limitations as a narrator are not merely personal idiosyncrasies. They reflect the configuration of the culture he represents. *The Blithedale Romance* is the culmination of Hawthorne's critique of the culture of modernity. It is a portrait, with both a general and an individual focus, of a civilization whose representative subjectivity is that of the flaneur.[5]

Like many of the most important figures in the history of the flaneur, Miles Coverdale is an idle bachelor of independent means. When he becomes ill at Blithedale, he recalls his earlier mode of life with a bitter nostalgia:

> My pleasant bachelor-parlor, sunny and shadowy, curtained and carpeted, with the bedchamber adjoining; my centre-table, strewn with books and periodicals; my writing-desk with a half-finished poem, in a stanza of my own contrivance; my morning lounge at the reading-room or picture-gallery; my noontide walk along the cheery pavement, with the suggestive succession of human faces, and the brisk throb of human life, in which I shared; my dinner at the Albion, where I had a hundred dishes at command . . . my evening at the billiard-club, the concert, the theatre, or at somebody's party, if I pleased, – what could be better than all this? (3:40)

Boston, Coverdale remembers, was not only more comfortable than Blithedale. It also offered a variety of urban distractions, not least of which was the activity of walking along the pavement, watching the "suggestive succession of human faces" and "shar[ing]" in the "brisk throb of human life." The interpretative and empathic pleasures of the flaneur were prominent among Coverdale's activities in Boston. No moralist, he found the pavement cheery, and he has no qualms about inserting the observation of other people into a catalog of a bachelor's urban recreations, interchangeable with going to the theater or playing billiards. Coverdale's bachelorhood, emblematic of his freedom from human attachments, recalls that of Burton, the Spectator, and Geoffrey Crayon. Like these other speculative bachelors, and like Wakefield and the narrator of "Sights from a Steeple," Coverdale is detached and idle, with few apparent responsibilities or ambitions.

Abstracted from the world of the living, without having taken his place among the dead, Coverdale lives the life of a classic cosmopolitan.[6] Financially secure and socially invisible, with a personality assembled from the personae of a variety of urban and urbane essayists of the eighteenth and early nineteenth centuries, Coverdale – like Elia, the Spectator, and others – is able to suspend all choices, to be at home in all possible ideas and situations. As he sees it, to commit himself to any particular idea is to close off the option of appreciating another. This is the substance of his criticism of Hollingsworth's reformatory project. Coverdale complains that Hollingsworth "had taught his benevolence to pour its warm tide exclusively through one channel. . . . Such prolonged fiddling upon one string, – such multiform presentation of one idea!" (3:55–6).

Coverdale's distaste for the narrowness of commitment is evident in the freedom with which he will contradict himself and assume the ideas and attitudes of whomever he happens to be with. He tries, for example, to interest Hollingsworth in the system of Fourier. When Hollingsworth expresses his disgust for Fourier, Coverdale cheerfully contributes a witticism in support of Hollingsworth's attack on his current intellectual idol. Coverdale is similarly accommodating to his "former acquaintances, who showed themselves inclined to ridicule [his] heroic devotion to the cause of human welfare." To these, Coverdale acknowledges, he "spoke of the recent phase of [his] life as indeed a fair matter for jest" (3:195). Coverdale is not only willing to modify his opinions, he can also modify his tone, and his mode of expression, depending upon the person he is addressing. When he encounters Westervelt in the woods, he is so susceptible to his influence that he joins the mesmerist in his cynical ridicule of Hollingsworth. At one point, speaking to Priscilla, Coverdale even finds himself falling into an "Orphic" (143) mode of expression. In order to remain free to engage all possibilities for existence, Coverdale avoids the consistency of orientation and attachment that, for others, constitutes an identity.

Detached from all human possibilities and close human contacts, liberated from social identity in order to observe the spectacle of human life, Coverdale's situation is very much like that which Wakefield chooses. Wakefield's action, however, differs from Coverdale's in that by choosing to exchange his identity for the advantages of invisible spectatorship, he betrays an important human bond. Coverdale cannot betray such a bond because he has none. Yet although and because Coverdale's isolation is less freely chosen than Wakefield's, it has a broader social meaning. In the class of urban cosmopolitans represented by Coverdale, Wakefield's pathology has become congenital.

Not having chosen the isolation and detachment that are a consequence of his cosmopolitan style of life, Coverdale believes that he can transcend them. He imagines that by joining the Blithedale community, he will be able to enjoy authentic social intercourse because the number of people with whom he will interact will be limited, and he will automatically share a bond with all of them. His expectation resembles that of the Blithedale community as a whole. Blithedale, like most agrarian utopian experiments, is an effort to go against the grain of urban modernity. It is an expression of nostalgia for premodern experience, for the intimacy with things and with the activities of daily life that is presumed to have existed before modern civilization made people aware of so many things and so many possible activities. By limiting the range of their experience, while increasing its depth, Coverdale and Blithedale expect to cure the malaise and isolation endemic to modern cosmopolitan life.

Although Coverdale goes to Blithedale in order to transcend the limitations of his cosmopolitan existence, when he arrives there, he is unable to discard his cosmopolitan habits of social interaction. Meeting his fellow communitarians, Coverdale's response to them is not "familiar love" but a compulsive and often inordinate curiosity. In a rural, communitarian setting, he becomes an urban spectator, absorbed in the observation of others, and trying to gain access to their "mysteries."

It is only because of his own habits that Coverdale is inclined to treat his fellow communitarians as "indices of a problem which it was my business to solve" (3:69). No one he meets is really committed to the community's goal of universal openness. Everyone Coverdale encounters preserves their private secrets, protecting themselves, in a characteristically urban manner, from the surveillance of those they live among. Even if he had more of an inclination to become intimate with his fellow communitarians, Coverdale would have no opportunity to do so. In fact, his desire to satisfy his curiosity creates barriers to the attainment of whatever intimacy he might have had.[7] Zenobia excludes him from her confidence after she intuits and he admits that his incessant observation of her is motivated by curiosity about the "mystery of [her] life" (3:47). Shortly after this, Coverdale reflects that Priscilla, "though she appeared to like me tolerably well" (3:50), does not like him well enough to tell him her secrets. They are further estranged when, immediately after this, Priscilla becomes angry with him for his characteristic activity of "fancy[ing] such odd things in [her]" (3:52). Hollingsworth, of course, with his hostile intentions toward the Blithedale community, does not let Coverdale into his confidence. By the time he has recovered from his illness, Coverdale recognizes that he has not achieved one of the most important goals of his coming to Blithedale. He is as isolated and detached as he had ever been in the city. He sadly acknowledges that "it was impossible not to be sensible, that, while these three characters figured so largely on my private theatre, I – though probably reckoned as a friend by all – was at best but a secondary or tertiary personage with either of them" (3:70).

Surprised and wounded by his exclusion from intimacy with others, Coverdale becomes increasingly absorbed in the act of trying to read those who exclude him.[8] The rhetoric of communal love and intimacy disappears entirely from his prose and he becomes almost exclusively engaged by the effort to solve his various human puzzles. Meeting with little success, encountering new situations that appear to make everything more complicated, Coverdale reaches a point of epistemological crisis. After discovering that there is a relationship between Priscilla and Moodie and after Hollingsworth leads Moodie away to see Priscilla, Coverdale is left standing "under a tuft of maples, doing [his] utmost to draw an inference from the scene that had just passed" (3:87). Unable to read what is around him, feeling isolated and excluded, Coverdale begins to feel the "irksomeness" of the "settled routine" (3:89) at Blithedale. He decides to take a "holiday" (89), secluding himself at a short distance from the community. In a mood of "drowsy pleasure" (3:89) shared by all of Hawthorne's panoramic spectators, Coverdale climbs up into a tree-top hermitage. From this vantage, he tries to restore his faltering sense that he can have access to the mysteries around him. He does this by replicating, in a rural setting, the conditions of urban spectatorship typical of the flaneur. Invisible and distanced, viewing Blithedale as if it were a panorama or diorama, Coverdale hopes to restore a distinctively urban mastery over a world that has become opaque to him.

Coverdale's hermitage is enclosed by a sphere of foliage that, like the type of diorama featured in "Ethan Brand," has several peepholes. Through the peepholes, Blithedale appears to be a reduced-scale representation of itself, in which details have been suppressed in order to convey a greater impression of the whole. Coverdale sees the farm, on which several of his fellow communitarians are working, and he sees the river enclosing it. The details Coverdale does observe are, like those in a panorama or diorama, representative and significant. Reading them, Coverdale illustrates the degree to which his assumption of a panoramic relation to reality is essentially a semiological activity. Reduced by distance and framed by the peephole, the inhabitants of Blithedale are removed from their individual contexts and inscribed with the meanings Coverdale gives them. Through one peephole, Hollingsworth is visible shouting at some oxen that are pulling some stones for a fence. In this image, Coverdale "reads" his own conception of Hollingsworth as a frustrated and domineering philanthropist. Through another peephole, Priscilla is visible, sewing beneath Zenobia's window. In this image, Coverdale reads his conception of Priscilla as a seamstress and as Zenobia's acolyte. Coverdale enjoys, in his treetop hermitage, a feeling of omniscience as great as that of the flaneur narrator of "The Man of the Crowd" when he observes the crowd passing by the coffee-shop window.

The ease with which he can read everything around him encourages Coverdale to believe that everything he could possibly know about the world he is watching is in fact accessible to him. When Zenobia and Westervelt come walking by, Coverdale marvels "at how aptly matters had chanced thus far, I began to think it the design of fate to let me into all Zenobia's secrets" (3:103). As in "Sights from a Steeple," however, there is, in Coverdale's panoramic moment, an almost ludicrous contrast between what an observer aspires to and what he achieves. Although he is serenely confident of his power to gain access to Zenobia's secrets, Coverdale must ruefully report that Zenobia and Westervelt do not in fact sit down beneath his tree. Also: "Zenobia's utterance was so hasty and broken, and Westervelt's so cool and low, that I hardly could make out an intelligible sentence, on either side" (3:104). "What I seem to remember," he admits, "I yet suspect may have been patched together by my fancy, in brooding over the matter afterwards" (104). In spite of these disclaimers, Coverdale offers a highly detailed and revealing transcription of the conversation. His sensation of power, apparently, has prepared him for a creative assertion of power that, although undercut at the very moment it is presented, reduces an opaque situation to coherence.

Coverdale's imposition of coherence in an act of spectatorship is, in the context of the romance, a characteristically urban process.[9] This is not what he has come to Blithedale to do. As when he was in the city, Coverdale, in the classic manner of the flaneur, understands someone by making up a story about a "suggestive" trace. The urban quality of

Coverdale's panoramic subjectivity is brought into clearer focus a few chapters later when the main features of the moment in the hermitage are reproduced in an urban setting. As with his removal to the hermitage, Coverdale's removal to a panoramic vantage at the rear window of a Boston hotel is precipitated by a sense of personal exclusion and epistemological incapacity. Hollingsworth has just rejected him and he continues to be unable to understand what is going on around him. He therefore feels a need to "remove [him]self to a little distance, and take an exterior view of what we had all been about" (3:140). Just as, from the hermitage, Coverdale was struck by the absurdity and insubstantiality of the Blithedale project, so in the Boston hotel room, he experiences, as he did in his hermitage, a "mood that . . . robbed the world of its solidity" (3:146). In such a mood, Coverdale finds that objects are suddenly pliant to his reformulation. Abandoning himself to his earlier stated enthusiasm for the "suggestiveness" of urban sights and sounds, he observes:

> Whatever had been my taste for solitude and natural scenery, yet the thick, foggy, stifled element of cities, the entangled life of many men together, sordid as it was, and empty of the beautiful, took quite as strenuous a hold upon my mind. I felt as if there could never be enough of it. Each characteristic sound was too suggestive to be passed over unnoticed. Beneath and around me, I heard the stir of the hotel; the loud voices of guests, landlord, or bar-keeper; steps echoing on the staircase; the ringing of a bell, announcing arrivals or departures; the porter lumbering past my door with baggage, which he thumped down upon the floors of neighboring chambers; the lighter feet of chambermaids scudding along the passages; it is ridiculous to think what an interest they had for me! From the street came the tumult of the pavements, pervading the whole house with a continual uproar, so broad and deep that only an unaccustomed ear would dwell upon it. A company of the city soldiery, with a full military band, marched in front of the hotel, invisible to me, but stirringly audible both by its foot-tramp and the clangor of its instruments. Once or twice all the city bells jangled together, announcing a fire, which brought out the engine-men and their machines, like an army with its artillery rushing to battle. Hour by hour the clocks in many steeples responded one to another. In some public hall, not a great way off, there seemed to be an exhibition of a mechanical diorama; for three times during the day occurred a repetition of obstreperous music, winding up with the rattle of imitative canon and musketry, and a huge final explosion. Then ensued the applause of the spectators, with clap of hands and

thump of sticks, and the energetic pounding of their heels. All this was just as valuable, in its way, as the sighing of the breeze among the birch-trees that overshadowed Eliot's pulpit. (3:146–7)

Rediscovering the sights and sounds of urban life, Coverdale displays the characteristically obsessive yet indolent curiosity of Wakefield and the traditional flaneur. Here, as in the "Hermitage" chapter, Coverdale blends together the particulars of a scene and creates a totalizing harmony. In this passage, Hawthorne makes the association between Coverdale's view of the world and a diorama explicit. There is a regular, repetitive, and essentially mechanical quality to the city he listens to. The sounds of the hotel and street crowds are regular and recognizable. As in "Sights from a Steeple" a military procession creates a sense of order in the streets. Bells ring periodically to bring out the firemen, who are themselves compared with "an army with its artillery rushing to battle" (3:147). "Hour by hour the clocks in many steeples responded to one another" (3:147). By concluding his description with an actual diorama, with its own cycle of largely military sounds, and with its series of equally regular audience responses, Coverdale unselfconsciously reveals the clockwork and pasteboard nature of the city he has created for himself.

Having reduced the sounds of the city to understandable and predictable patterns, Coverdale expresses his intention to "linger on the brink or hover in the air above . . . the muddy tide of human activity and pastime" (3:147). He sinks into a pleasant lethargy, putting his feet up, reading, and smoking fine cigars. Like many flaneurs before him, Coverdale becomes tired of a book. Placing it aside, he looks out his rear window and just as he reduces what he has heard to a panoramic harmony, he begins to reduce what he sees to a panoramic representation of the human world of the city. After cataloging the flora and fauna of the urban backyards, and after conveniently and lazily deciding that his view of the rear of the houses is in fact a privileged perspective, Coverdale concludes, even before he has observed a single human inhabitant, that the people who live in the houses across the way are as mechanical and predictable as the sounds he has been listening to.

> Together with a due contemplation of the fruit-trees, the grape vines, the buttonwood-tree, the cat, the birds, and many other particulars, I failed not to study the row of fashionable dwellings to which all these appertained. Here, it must be confessed, there was a general sameness. From the upper story to the first floor, they were all so much alike, that I could only conceive of the inhabitants as cut out on one identical pattern, like little wooden toy-people of German manufacture. One long, united roof, with its thousands of slates glittering in the rain, extended over the

whole. After the distinctness of separate characters, to which I had recently been accustomed, it perplexed and annoyed me not to be able to resolve this combination of human interests into well-defined elements. It seemed hardly worth while for more than one of those families to be in existence, since they all had the same glimpse of the sky, all looked into the same area, all received just their equal share of sunshine through the front windows, and all listened to precisely the same noises of the street on which they boarded. Men are so much alike in their nature, that they grow intolerable unless varied by their circumstances. (3:150)

Other Hawthorne narrators have encountered similarly opaque roofs and bosoms. Coverdale, however, comes up with a novel solution to the problem of opacity. Without any conceivable justification, he assumes that people in the city, whom he cannot see, are as identical as the exterior of their houses, which he can see. Thanks to this metonymic sleight of hand, he is able to resolve the epistemological crisis that causes so much frustration to the narrators of "Sights from a Steeple" and "The Old Apple Dealer." The subjectivities of strangers, according to this assumption, are either uniform or easily accessible. Coverdale does not seem to doubt his ability to generalize about the consciousness of urban strangers any more than he doubts that "the design of fate" (3:103) is to reveal to him all of Zenobia's secrets. For the moment at least, Coverdale is able to reduce the population of Boston to "toy-people of German manufacture," suitable inhabitants of the mechanical diorama to which he has reduced the city itself.

Although numerous critics have taken Coverdale's observations in this episode as a perceptive reading, from a privileged rear perspective, of the uniformity produced by modern urban life,[10] Hawthorne's distance from Coverdale's overreductive reading is evident in the difference between these passages from the romance and the passage from Hawthorne's journals that are the basis of them. The description of what can be seen and heard from the rear window of Coverdale's hotel is an adaptation of several journal entries made by Hawthorne after visits to Boston. Revising passages from his own journal in order to make them characteristic of Coverdale, Hawthorne infuses them with a panoramic quality missing in the original entries.[11] From his vantage at the back window of a house in Boston, Hawthorne records hearing a variety of city sounds, including those produced by a dioramic exposition. The journal entry that forms the basis for the passage in the book does not include, however, the military procession and the periodical bell-ringings that give the passage its dioramic regularity. Although the passages in which Coverdale describes what he sees from his rear window are in large part copied verbatim from Hawthorne's journals, nowhere in these journal entries is there any suggestion that people are as uniform as the architecture of their dwellings or that any of the various people observed resemble "toy-people of German manufacture." Adapting his journal entries to Coverdale's consciousness, Hawthorne revises them in such a way as to recall the phenomenological situation of the Hermitage chapter. The characteristic process of Coverdale's consciousness, as Hawthorne appears to have conceived of it, is to reduce diversity and complexity to a condition of unnatural transparency, simplicity, and abstraction.

As the placement of "The Hermitage" and "The Hotel" chapters clearly illustrate, Coverdale's panoramic moments are defensive retrenchments. In them, he experiences interpretative power and emotional security after having recently been deprived of both. Yet even as he is complacently experiencing this power, Coverdale seems to be aware that he is not reading but writing. Immediately after "reading" Hollingsworth and Priscilla from his treetop hermitage, Coverdale pulls a bird out of the air and uses it to convey a message to Priscilla. He instructs the bird to tell her "that if any mortal really cares for her, it is myself; and not even I, for her realities, – poor little seamstress, as Zenobia rightly called her! – but the fancy-work with which I have idly decked her out!" (3:100). Here, as throughout the romance, Coverdale's creation and use of signs is completely self-enclosed. Priscilla will never receive any message he sends. Nor will anyone else. Coverdale does not love Priscilla. He has simply embroidered the seamstress. Yet as quickly as Coverdale can sew, Hawthorne seems intent upon pulling out the threads. In *The Blithedale Romance*, as in his earlier sketches, Hawthorne systematically dismantles the presumptuous interpretations his spectatorial narrator has imposed upon the world he observes.

In both the "Hermitage" chapter and in the section of the book involved with Coverdale's observations from his rear window, it is clear that Coverdale, in spite of his claims, is an unsuccessful reader and spy. When he first begins to observe the human inhabitants of the houses across the backyards, Coverdale does not see anything to contradict his original decision that they are toy-people. In spite of his assurance that there is "vastly greater suggestiveness in the back view of a residence, than in its front" (3:149), in spite of his conviction that "realities keep in the rear" (3:149), Coverdale is no more able to prove the superiority of his perspective than is the narrator of "Sights from a Steeple." He watches a dandy get ready for dinner, he observes a touching though rather ordinary domestic scene, and he watches some housemaids at work. Yet, of course, Coverdale is soon surprised to find himself a witness to the same drama he had observed from his other panoramic perspective. He also finds that he is subject to many of the same spectatorial limitations. Just as he cannot really hear, in his treetop, what Zenobia and Westervelt are saying to each other, all he can see, from his back window, are people moving from room to room. He can base his conjectures only on "fancy and prejudice. . . . The distance was so great as to obliterate any play of feature by which I might otherwise have been made a partaker of their counsels" (3:156). After he has been detected and Zenobia has let down the curtain, Coverdale is in the same situation. Watching the forms against the curtain, he reports that: "The shadow of a passing figure was now and then cast upon this medium, but with too vague an outline for even my adventurous conjectures to read the hieroglyphic that it presented" (3:161). In these parallel scenes, as in "Sights from a Steeple," the narrator's inability to see what he claims he is in a position to see becomes ludicrously comic.[12]

Frustrated by his inability to read the hieroglyphics, Coverdale leaves his niche to call on the principals in the drama across the courtyard. They, of course, do not let him into their confidence and his frustration becomes even more acute. Deciding to see if he can learn anything by consulting Moodie, Coverdale goes to a saloon frequented by the old man. Before their actual interview, Coverdale offers a peculiarly lengthy, and apparently gratuitous description of the saloon where it is to take place. This description is the second urban re-creation of the phenomenological situation of the "Hermitage" chapter and, like that earlier re-creation, it is an adaptation, to fit the consciousness of Coverdale, of entries from Hawthorne's own journals. In the saloon, Coverdale, as he did in the hotel room, imposes an artificial uniformity of consciousness upon all of the individuals he watches. In the journal entry that is the basis of this passage, the crowd in Parker's saloon is fairly diverse and it is this diversity that particularly attracts Hawthorne's interest. In Coverdale's account, however, all of the "good fellows" in the saloon are described as drinking with the same deportment and motivations. There is no distracting particularity among these men whose eyes all twinkle and who all rub their bellies in the same way.

Among such simplified individuals, Coverdale finds it easy to indulge in the empathic spectatorship characteristic of the flaneur. He says that he takes "by sympathy, a boozy kind of pleasure in the customary life that was going forward" (3:175). Just as Hawthorne suggested the artificial nature of an earlier panoramic reduction by mentioning an actual panorama, he represents the distanced, panoramic nature of Coverdale's perception here by describing the paintings that hang on the wall of the saloon. Everything that might be found in the saloon itself, from food and drink to revelers and drunks, is represented in a painting. Hawthorne suggests, in this way, that Coverdale has reduced the three-dimensional reality of the saloon to a harmonious set of legible and picturesque images.

This is, in a sense, exactly what he has done, since most of what Coverdale sees in the paintings are things that Hawthorne, in his journal entry, describes himself as seeing in three dimensions. Coverdale's reduction culminates in a rapturous description of a fountain, in which goldfish swim in a little pool, the bottom of which is strewn with coral and rockwork. Coverdale notes that the fish move in intriguing yet predictable ways. Freely speculating about and empathizing with them, Coverdale approaches the fish in the pool as he approached the men in the saloon. In both instances, as in all of his panoramic moments, Coverdale observes a simplified and enclosed space of which he is the sole and invisible observer. Assuming the creative privileges of such a situation, Coverdale enjoys a fantasy of panoramic omniscience that temporarily compensates for his inability to observe freely and interpret the more complex human interaction he is attempting to understand.

The panoramic moment in the bar is, like the panoramic moment in the treetop, a preparation for the exercise of Coverdale's imagination in order to solve part of the mystery. Here, as in that earlier moment, Coverdale emerges from the security of his panorama into a highly self-conscious creative act of representation, the veracity of which is undercut at the same moment as it is presented. Coverdale meets Moodie at the bar and hears his story. Yet, he is anxious to inform the reader that the story he is about to tell is not the story Moodie told him. Moodie's narrative "referred exclusively to a long past and more fortunate period of his life" (181). Coverdale's narrative tells us virtually nothing about the period with which Moodie's narrative is exclusively concerned. What Coverdale relates has its source in his "subsequent researches" (3:181) and he cannot forbear telling the reader, as he did in the earlier instance, that "my pen has perhaps allowed itself a trifle of romantic and legendary license, worthier of a small poet than of a grave biographer" (3:181).

By undercutting his own account in this way, Coverdale makes it clear that although the panoramic moments may arrest the narrative, they are what enables the narrative to move forward. They are the basis of the structure of the romance, which appears to consist of progressive accumulations of illegible details followed by panoramic restorations of creative power, each of which then produces a narrative that retrospectively reduces the details to coherence.[13] As the source of Coverdale's creativity, the panoramic moments resemble other moments in urban texts in which a writer's imagination stops the potentially overwhelming stream of urban phenomena in order to create the distance necessary to give it form.[14] In all of them, Coverdale, as the artist of his own narrative, enjoys a sense of mastering reality by replacing it with a model.

Imposing coherence in this way, Coverdale replicates the goals of the Blithedale experiment. The community conceives of itself as an ideal model of society, simpler and more harmonious than what exists. The similarity between the utopian experiment and Coverdale's utopian moments is suggested by the similarity of their names. This can hardly be a coincidence. The shared syllable, a "dale," is a small valley, a space that is generally visible in its entirety from any of the hills that enclose it. In his panoramic moments, Coverdale "covers" a "dale," he experiences a sense of dominion over an enclosed space. In Coverdale's few physical descriptions of it, Blithedale is always viewed in its entirety as a landscape of "pleasantly swelling slopes" (3:84) completely encircled by the Charles River. With its "breezy swells" and "sheltered nooks," it offers a variety of ideal potential dwelling places, so long as one's "taste leans towards" either "snugness or the picturesque" (3:128). In these descriptions of its physical setting, Blithedale appears to be pleasant, yet artificial and schematic. Graspable, innocuous, and uniform, it conforms to the requirements of Coverdale's subjectivity as well as any of the landscapes he creates in his panoramic moments.

The sense that Coverdale conveys of the enclosed quality of the Blithedale community is reminiscent of the virtual obsession with enclosure that is present in Charles Fourier's *Design for Utopia*, which Hawthorne had read in preparation for writing *The Blithedale Romance*, and which Coverdale himself reads within the romance. Describing the architecture of the phalanstery, the communal units of his utopian society, Fourier emphasizes the importance of remaining indoors. As he proudly projects:

> The most poverty-stricken of the Harmonians, a man who hasn't a farthing, gets into a vehicle in a portico well-heated and inclosed; he goes from the Palace to the stables through paved and gravelled underground passages; he passes from his dwelling to the public halls and the workshops through the galleried streets which are heated in winter and ventilated in summer. (146)

Although Fourier represents himself as primarily concerned about protecting the inhabitants of his community from the elements, the degree of his concern seems to be out of proportion to the discomfort of the climate of all but a few places on earth. Fourier's dream of an enclosed community appears to be more truly motivated by the kind of enthusiasm he betrays in the following observation:

> One is dazzled by lingering a few moments over a picture of the enormous benefits which would be derived from the union of three hundred households, in a single edifice. (148)

Like Hollingsworth's socioarchitectural daydreams, Fourier's utopia resembles the flaneur's traditional project of bringing society indoors, of creating, as an arcade does, a physical sense of a world that is entirely encompassed by what "covers" it. This indoor utopia, like the domesticated city of the flaneur, resembles a panorama or diorama. Like the consciousness of the flaneur, it is a diorama in which legible types interact in a coherent fashion within an enclosed space.

The utopian quality of Coverdale's consciousness, the congruence between his consciousness and the Blithedale community, is not only evident in the panoramic description of its setting. It is also apparent in Coverdale's account of Blithedale's ideology. Although both Blithedale and Coverdale hope to cure urban malaise by narrowing and focusing experience, the Blithedale community is no more able to accomplish this successfully than is Coverdale. The seeds of its failure are evident in its ideology as much as the seeds of Coverdale's are evident in his personality. For all that they are committed to the idea of narrowing the scope of human experience, the cosmopolitans who formulate the ideology of Blithedale are much more sincerely attached to the values of fluid identity and perpetual freedom of choice. By attempting to construct a society in which there is no division of labor, and in which everyone takes part in all kinds of work, the Blithedale community is an effort to bring about an absolute freedom from constricting roles that is, within existing culture, only the prerogative of wealthy cosmopolitans like Coverdale. While conceiving of itself as a cure for them, Blithedale, if successful, would intensify the conditions of cosmopolitanism. This proves to be an unresolvable contradiction and Blithedale degenerates into pagaents and masquerades that express the impatience of the communitarians with their discovery that if they were to become farmers, they would be unable to be all of the other things they had hoped to be.

The similarity between the way in which Coverdale tries to view the world and the way in which the Blithedale community tries to remake it is also evident in the way in which the community eventually degenerates into a sort of theater workshop, a series of masquerades, pagaents, and tableaux vivants. Just as Coverdale can never transcend his habits of urban spectatorship when he becomes part of the community, so too the Blithedale community, as a whole, cannot transcend its accustomed fluid and theatrical modes of urban self-presentation. In both instances, the conditions of urban modernity are inescapable. This congruence is particularly evident in the chapter entitled "The Masqueraders," which is significantly placed immediately after "The Village Hall" chapter. After observing a paradigm of a culture in which the only realities are images, Coverdale embarks upon a walk from Boston to Blithedale. On the way, the main actors in the drama to which he is trying to be a spectator appear to his mind's eye repeatedly as a "spectral throng" (3:206), "glid(ing) mistily" (3:205) before him. After making an obligatory stop at his hermitage, the paradigm of his consciousness, Coverdale soon encounters the inhabitants of Blithedale who, engaging in a masquerade, appear, like "Comus and his crew" (3:209), to be no less like spectral images than he has imagined them. Even he is struck by the way in which they have willingly assumed the stylized and legible forms to which a mind like his is likely to have tried to reduce them. As "the whole fantastic rabble forthwith streamed off in pursuit" of him, he feels as if he "was like a mad poet hunted by chimeras" (3:211), as if he were, as he has been throughout the romance, trapped within his own mind.

In this way, Blithedale reflects one of the central social meanings of the flaneur. Like a flaneur, and indeed like Coverdale, Blithedale embodies a fantasy that it is possible to be free of the restrictions of society and a fixed identity without having to expose oneself to the dangers, or even to the potential pleasures, that would actually be involved in this freedom. Like the flaneur, Blithedale represents a kind of cleaning up of carnival, in which the bourgeoisie can indulge itself in an orgy of empathy with a great variety of pastoral figures, without really having to become any of them, any more than the flaneur, identifying himself with urban types, has to become anyone he sees. Here, as in every aspect of the culture of modernity with which Hawthorne appears to be concerned, consciousness is free to dissociate itself from identity. In the culture that results, identity is, like everything else, merely a series of images. Although aspects of its ideology suggest that the Blithedale experiment is an effort to eschew the advantages of cosmopolitan consciousness and recapture the experience of fixed identity, in reality the community is at odds with the goals of any such nostalgia. It is a product of the Village Hall and it represents an effort to turn the phenomenology of the Village Hall into a principle of social organization.

There is another important sense in which the ideology of the Blithedale experiment resembles the dynamic of Coverdale's panoramic moments. As Coverdale articulates it, one of the main purposes of Blithedale is to establish something very much like the uniformity and predictability that he imposes upon the inhabitants of Boston from his back window. Coverdale's city dwellers are identical because they live in identical houses, and do, see, and hear identical things. By doing the same work in the same place, if Blithedale were to succeed, everyone in it would have identical interests and desires. In such a harmonious and homogeneous society, everyone would be as transparent and innocuous as Coverdale imagines the inhabitants of Boston to be. Everyone would also be able to experience the centrality Coverdale experiences in his panoramic moments since each individual consciousness would be a model for the consciousness of the entire community. In addition to incorporating an ideal of absolute cosmopolitanism, Blithedale is a fantasy of universal access to the minds of others. It is a dream of a society without strangers and without opacity, in which one only needs to read oneself in order to read others. It is, to return to Leigh Hunt's formulation, a crowd as the reduplication of oneself.

If the utopian socialism represented in *The Blithedale Romance* resembles, both in structure and intention, the utopian moments Coverdale enjoys in his various niches, so too does the other modern cultural phenomenon represented in detail in the romance. Mesmerism, as it is represented in *The Blithedale Romance*, has several similarities, in its goals and techniques, with the utopianism of the Blithedale community, and with the urban spectatorship of the flaneur. This is evident in the very similar ways in which the ideologies of Blithedale and of mesmerism are described, in the romance, by their adherents. Outlining the fundamental ideals of the Blithedale experiment, Coverdale writes:

> And first of all, we had divorced ourselves from Pride, and were striving to supply its place with familiar love. We meant to lessen the laboring man's great burthen of toil, by performing our due share of it at the cost of our own thews and sinews. We sought our profit by mutual aid, instead of wresting it by the strong hand from an enemy, or filching it craftily from those less shrewd than ourselves . . . or winning it by selfish competition with a neighbor; in one or another fashions, every son of woman both perpetrates and suffers his share of the common evil, whether he chooses it or no. And, as the basis of our institution, we purposed to offer up the earnest toil of our bodies, as a prayer, no less than an effort, for the advancement of our race. (3:19)

Describing Westervelt's explanatory introduction to his mesmeric exhibition, Coverdale writes:

> [The Professor] spoke of a new era that was dawning upon the world; an era that would link soul to soul, and the present life to what we call futurity, with a closeness that should finally convert both worlds into one great, mutually conscious brotherhood. He described (in a strange philosophical guise, with terms of art, as if it were a matter of chemical discovery) the agency by which this mighty result was to be effected; nor would it have surprised me, had he pretended to hold up a portion of his universally pervasive fluid, as he affirmed it to be, in a glass phial. (3:200)

As Coverdale represents them, both mesmerism and utopian socialism are millennial reform movements whose goal is the establishment of a unified community.[15] In each case, this unification is to be achieved through the weakening of the processes of individuation. Mesmerists dream that the apparent gulf between individual subjectivities may be bridged if each becomes conscious of and connected to a "universally pervasive" spiritual "fluid." Utopians imagine that the gulf between individuals in society may be overcome if people become more alike in their occupations, if, that is, the more comfortable classes were to perform their "due share" of "man's burthen of toil" and if the laboring classes were, in this way, able to develop more of their intellectual, aesthetic, and spiritual potential. The relative uniformity of individual consciousness produced by the uniformity of occupations will enable, or so the Blithedalers hope, the diffusion of "familiar love" as a universally pervasive connecting fluid, much like mesmeric electricity, overcoming the atomization of modern life.

As Hawthorne represents them, the blind spot of each of these universal systems seems to be that, in an atomized society like the one represented in the romance, a thrilling sense of universal connection to the consciousness of others can only be attained by reducing other individuals to a falsely coherent homogeneous mass, over which one exercises power. Imagining liberation from self-consciousness, a thoroughly self-conscious bourgeois intellectual like Coverdale cannot imagine that his own consciousness would not be diffused throughout the entire structure. This is an inherent problem in the form of individualism Coverdale represents. He always seeks the power of a vantage point and avoids the constriction of a role, just as a utopian theorist, imagining his ideal social structure, does not imagine himself as an occupant of a small restricted space within it. The mesmerist too is a theoretician of universal community and brotherhood but, in practice, his activity epitomizes the exercise of power over others by a single central consciousness. Hawthorne illustrates these troubling power dynamics, in Coverdale's relation to reality, by developing several analogies between Coverdale and the book's chief mesmerist.

When Coverdale climbs to his hermitage and observes Blithedale, he "suddenly" finds himself "possessed by a mood of disbelief in moral beauty or heroism, and a conviction of the folly of attempting to benefit the world. Our especial scheme of reform, which, from my observatory, I could take in with my bodily eye, looked so ridiculous that it was impossible not to laugh aloud" (3:101). The serious solidities of human character are similarly insubstantial to the mesmerist. In the Village Hall, Coverdale overhears a man say of the mesmerist that "Human character was but soft wax in his hands; and guilt, or virtue, only the forms into which he should see fit to mould it" (3:198). This sense of insubstantiality, shared by Coverdale and Westervelt, and produced by their respective senses of personal power over and distance from the worlds they observe, recalls Holgrave's observation in *The House of the Seven Gables* that "I find nothing so singular as that everything appears to lose its substance the instant one actually grapples with it" (2:269). Just as Holgrave reduces the world to photographs and Westervelt controls the consciousness of his clairvoyant, Coverdale repeatedly refers to the characters of his narrative as shadowy and ghostlike forms. Describing his first sight of Zenobia, Coverdale says that her "aspect . . . impressed itself so distinctly, that I can now summon her up like a ghost, a little wanner than the life but otherwise identical with it" (3:15). This being the case, Coverdale finds it especially easy to characterize Zenobia as Eve, or Pandora, or as anyone else he chooses. Moodie is described as characteristically "glid[ing] about like a spirit, assuming visibility close to your elbow" (3:179). Even someone as unquestionably substantial as Silas Foster is described at one point as "vaporous and spectre-like" (3:18) when steam is seen rising from his wet garments in a warm house. These descriptions reflect the fact that for a consciousness like Coverdale's, reality consists of a sequence of images, of representations that reflect the power of a central consciousness.

Each of these men conceives of himself as living in a world of insubstantial forms he can easily control. In Westervelt, this sense of control produces a supercilious cynicism.[16] When Coverdale expresses his sense of how absurd Blithedale looks from his hermitage, he blames his "sceptical and sneering" mood on the influence of Westervelt. In doing this, he illuminates, first of all, the kinship between his own cosmopolitanism and Westervelt's cynicism. Both perspectives on reality reduce the world to a kind of insubstantial homogeneity in which one can remain free of limiting attachments to particulars. At the same time, by acknowledging Westervelt's influence, Coverdale suggests that Westervelt's ability to influence him is not solely due to the power of the man's personality. Westervelt also represents an important, in fact dominant feature of his own personality. As Coverdale observes, Westervelt's tone "represented that of worldly society at large, where a cold scepticism smothers what it can of our spiritual aspirations, and makes the rest ridiculous. I detested this kind of man; and all the more because a part of my own nature showed itself responsive to him" (3:101–2).

Identifying Westervelt with the spiritual tone of "worldly society at large," Coverdale makes an association that Hawthorne has made by naming the character Westervelt. Westervelt is associated with the subjective condition of the "Western world" in the mid-nineteenth century. As a thoroughly contaminated product of this increasingly urban and socially atomized civilization, Coverdale, unsurprisingly, finds himself "responsive" to Westervelt. He is responsive to him throughout the romance. Each of Coverdale's three major encounters with Westervelt has the same structure. In the woods, in Boston, and at Zenobia's funeral, an initial revulsion toward the mesmerist for his arrogant manner or cold, reductive world view yields to a grudging expression of admiration for his personal qualities and his acumen. For Coverdale, each encounter with Westervelt involves an experience of recognition of a personal ideal. Exceptionally handsome, urbane, and well dressed, comfortable and superior in all situations, with an uncanny ability to become "acquainted with whatever it suited him to discover" (3:158), Westervelt is the epitome of everything Coverdale the cosmopolitan aspires to be and everything Coverdale the communitarian is unconvincingly attempting to transcend.

The kinship between Coverdale and Westervelt is further illustrated by the profusion of mesmeric metaphors in Coverdale's descriptions of his own mental processes. Seeking to explain his own ability to intuit that Zenobia has been in love, Coverdale writes:

> There is a species of intuition, – either a spiritual life, or the subtile recognition of a fact, – which comes to us in a reduced state of the corporeal system. The soul gets the better of the body, after wasting illness, or when a vegetable diet may have mingled too much ether in the blood. Vapors then rise up to the brain, and take shapes that often image falsehood, but sometimes truth. The spheres of our companions have, at such periods, a vastly greater influence upon our own than when robust health gives us a repellent and self-defensive energy. Zenobia's sphere, I imagine, impressed itself powerfully on mine, and transformed me, during this period of my weakness, into something like a mesmerical clairvoyant. (3:46–7)

At another point, describing Hollingsworth's efforts to appropriate him, Coverdale writes that: "Had I but touched his extended hand, Hollingsworth's magnetism would perhaps have penetrated me with his own conception of all these matters" (3:134).

In these instances, and throughout the book, Coverdale uses a mesmeric vocabulary to describe the dynamics of human relations. With extraordinary frequency, Coverdale speaks of individuals as having "spheres," in which they are central and in which others may become absorbed, as they are "penetrated" by someone else's magnetism. When Coverdale observes Zenobia and Westervelt turn away from each other, he speculates that "perchance, they mutually repelled each other, by some incompatibility of their spheres" (3:156). Elsewhere Coverdale asks Zenobia if it is "safe" that Priscilla "should be so constantly within the sphere of a man like Hollingsworth" (3:167). After he leaves Blithedale, Coverdale says of his friends that he felt a "stubborn reluctance to come again within their sphere" (3:194). In the process of dissociating himself from Westervelt's cynicism after noting how ridiculous Blithedale looks from his niche, Coverdale observes that: "There are some spheres the contact with which inevitably degrades the high, debases the pure, deforms the beautiful" (3:101). The word *sphere* appears at least twenty-three times (according to my own count) in *The Blithedale Romance* and Coverdale uses the term in a sense that was quite common among the Swedenborgian adherents of mesmerism, at the time the romance was written.

In an article published in the *American Phrenological Journal* in 1853, William Fishbough explained the concept of "spheres" as follows:

> The idea, I believe, was first distinctly set forth by Swedenborg that all forms and existences, whether inorganic or organic, or whether in the natural or spiritual world, respectively send forth their own peculiar emanations, by which is formed around each an enveloping sphere or atmosphere. (Cited in Stovall, 155)

In the third volume of *The Great Harmonia*, published in 1852, Andrew Jackson Davis, America's most important mesmeric theoretician and a major influence on Whitman, used the Swedenborgian concept of spheres to explain the process of mesmerism.

> Everything hath its own magnetic atmosphere; its own medium of sympathetic relationship. And Man, particularly and pre-eminently, possesses this sphere of mind, so to speak, constantly surrounding his body; which sphere is negative or positive, attractive or repulsive, gross or refined, passive or active, and less or great in magnitude, just in proportion to his general refinement and intrinsic development of mind. This atmosphere, surrounding man, can not be detected by the material organs of sense; but to the spiritual senses of the soul, it is very visible, and its manifestations are familiar to you all. (3:125)

When, according to Davis, the positively charged sphere of the mesmerist encounters the negatively charged sphere of the clairvoyant, the two spheres may join, with the mesmerist's in control. This notion seems to explain Coverdale's fear of the "magnetism" of Hollingsworth and Westervelt. He wishes to remain in control of his own sphere. He does not wish to be drawn into that of another.

Implicit both in the mesmeric meaning of "sphere," and in the geometric metaphor embedded in it, is a conception of the self as a circumscribed province of power. Coverdale sees in others an analogy to the mental process exemplified by his panoramic moments. From the centers of their respective spheres, each of the "cosmopolitan" selves of Blithedale seeks panoramic dominion, a sense of being in control of and at home in everything that can be taken in by a circular glance. Coverdale's panoramic paradigm is reflected in Westervelt's establishment of mesmeric dominion, as he claims to subject the will of others to his own by penetrating and usurping their centrality within their spheres. It is also reflected in Hollingsworth's incessant drawing and model building. Like Coverdale, Hollingsworth imagines a circumscribed space, an externalization of his own consciousness, in which he may alter and, in essence, reimagine the recalcitrant subjectivities of others.

By illuminating the same basic spherical structure in all of the identifiably modern consciousnesses and philosophical movements with which *The Blithedale Romance* is concerned, Hawthorne proposes a model for the analysis of the culture of modernity. Although what he identifies is a form of what is traditionally referred to as pride or egoism, it is nevertheless a specifically modern form of pride and egoism, a form that reflects the increasing prevalence, in modern civilization, of cognate cultural processes that have restructured subjectivity as a storehouse of images. A modern cosmopolitan like Coverdale, Hawthorne suggests, may exult in the way in which his self, his world, his "sphere," resembles a panorama, a department store, or a world exposition. It is loosely organized and cozily domesticated, pleasantly various, tolerant, and expansive. Yet the Coverdalian model of consciousness, like Westervelt's mesmerism or Hollingsworth's reformatory project, depends upon the exercise of power. This is, as Hawthorne represents it, the flip side of the culture of modernity, the point at which the flaneur's genial aestheticism is poisoned by its complicity with powerful engines of coercive and reifying interpretation.

By demonstrating the similarity between Coverdale's consciousness and other forms of "spherical" encompassment, and by illuminating the way in which these systems work, Hawthorne offers an analysis of modern bourgeois culture that is interestingly similar to Foucault's. Hawthorne's paradigms (panoramas, mesmeric "spheres," utopian social models, reformatories) are all related to Foucault's model of the Panopticon. Like Foucault, Hawthorne uses these paradigms as metaphors to show how there are structures of domination at the core of modern efforts to impose coherence on the complexity of social reality. Throughout *The Blithedale Romance*, as in his sketches, Hawthorne demonstrates the impotence of systems that attempt this. He also elucidates the power relations embedded in them. Much of the latter project is achieved by the way in which Hawthorne positions the two main female characters of the romance, in relation to the systems that are used to interpret them. In *The Blithedale Romance*, the impotence and for Hawthorne the moral character of these systems is most clearly represented by the way in which the two most prominent female characters in the book elude the various systems that are used to interpret them.

The character most often subject to the interpreting systems of others is, of course, Priscilla. Repeatedly characterized as "wraithlike," "pale," "insubstantial," and "silent," her most characteristic function in the romance is to be interpreted. Her first appearance is emblematic of what is to happen to her throughout the romance. She knocks on the door of the house at Blithedale, and the communitarians respond to her knock as something to be interpreted rather than as something to be answered. After Hollingsworth finally brings her in out of the snowstorm, she becomes, for the next several pages, the focus of several new efforts of interpretation. Coverdale speculates that she might be "some desolate kind of creature, doomed to wander in snowstorms" (3:27). Less fantastically, he wonders if she is someone whom Hawthorne is trying to reform. Hollingsworth suggests that she is sent by Providence as a sign and test for their new venture. Soon after, Zenobia suggests that Priscilla is a seamstress with "no more transcendental purpose than to do my miscellaneous sewing" (3:33). Even after she begins to show some signs of physical vigor and independent spirit, Priscilla continues to exist primarily as an object to be interpreted. Perceiving this, she remarks at one point, in exasperation, that she wishes "people would not fancy such odd things in me!" (3:52).

The nature and significance of Priscilla's situation is most clearly represented by the fact that she is a mesmerist's clairvoyant. As the Veiled Lady, her very opacity makes her available as an object to be read. Everything about her, in this role, suggests the quality of having no substance other than that which can be created by acts of interpretation. Her "Sybilline" utterances have meaning only insofar as they are interpreted. They are "nonsensical in [their] first aspect, yet, on closer study, unfolding a variety of interpretations, one of which has certainly accorded with the event" (3:6). Her physical form is similarly fluid and subject to external control. Coverdale speaks of a legend that "affirmed that there was no single and unchangeable set of features beneath the veil; but that whosoever should be bold enough to lift it would behold the features of that person, in all the world, who was destined to be his fate" (3:110). Coverdale's own tendency to love Priscilla, not for herself but for "the fancy work" with which he has "idly decked her out," has the same form as the response of audiences to the Veiled Lady.

At all times an object of interpretation and at all times remaining opaque, Priscilla is emblematic of those groups within society who are conventionally reduced and inscribed by the panoramic processes exemplified by Coverdale. She is clearly identified, first of all, with the urban proletariat. Not only does Zenobia peg her as an urban seamstress, but Coverdale, as soon as he sees her, speculates that "She had been bred up, no doubt, in some close nook, some inauspiciously sheltered court of the city (3:35). There, he concludes, she grew like "plants that one sometimes observes doing their best to vegetate among the bricks of an enclosed court, where there is scanty soil, and never any sunshine" (50–1).

As Nina Baym has pointed out, Priscilla may be understood as "represent[ing] the whole range of exploited female roles in society" (*Hawthorne's Career*, 196).[17] Priscilla is controlled and exploited by a mesmerist and a father, each of whom sells the fruit of her labor. At several points in the book, there are implications that Priscilla may be or may have been a member of a profession specifically associated with the female urban proletariat.[18] When Coverdale reconstructs her story and describes how Westervelt began to visit Priscilla after discovering her psychic powers, he acknowledges that it would be possible for some to find "rich food for scandal in such visits" (3:188). The Veiled Lady is represented as a kind of virginal prostitute, offering herself to the imaginative appropriation of anyone. There is also a sexual voyeurism implicit in the form of entertainment she provides, in which a man demonstrates complete control over the mind of a passive woman. In Zenobia's story of the Veiled Lady, the Veiled Lady's plea to Theodore to love her in order to free her from "a bondage" to the mesmerist, which she characterizes as "worse . . . than death," resembles the plea of a prostitute (particularly in nineteenth-century fiction) to be freed from a pimp. Such an association would by no means have been farfetched for Hawthorne's audience. In several popular novels of the day, most notably George Lippard's *Quaker City*, white slavers used mesmeric powers to enslave and control young women.

When Priscilla is given over to a group of utopian socialists, she is not exploited as overtly as she is in Boston. Still, she is subject to a form of exploitation that, though subtler, is equally a denial of her independent identity. As an image, repeatedly recreated by the interpretations of cosmopolitan spectators, Priscilla is emblematic of each of the various classes of individuals, most notably women and the working class, who are reduced to subjection as much by the inscribing, interpretative gaze of those who have power as by concrete conditions of exploitation. As the inscrutable yet subjected "other," she exists to be turned into a text. As Coverdale exemplifies the mode of consciousness whose characteristic process is the reduction of the world to the most innocuous form of textuality, Priscilla exemplifies the individuals who are most often reduced by means of such processes.

Yet just as Hawthorne repeatedly undermines Coverdale's fantasies of dominion, Priscilla, everyone's dominated object, is always slipping out from under the interpretations that others impose on her. In viewing Priscilla as a pliant, completely dominated individual, I believe many critics have made a mistake similar to that which they have made by remarking upon the success of the narrator's enterprises in "Sights from a Steeple" or "The Old Apple Dealer." They have taken pronouncements of ambition by self-deceiving characters as statements of what these characters have actually accomplished.[19]

As might be expected, Zenobia is the first to perceive the "obtuseness of masculine perception" (3:34) of Priscilla. As she correctly points out, the qualities that make Priscilla appear to be "spiritual" can be accounted for by poor nutrition, hard work, and bad air. Zenobia's undermining of this particular interpretation of Priscilla is the first instance of what becomes her perpetual mocking of Coverdale's tendency to turn his imagination into an "opera-glass through which to view women." But it is not only the feminist Zenobia who disagrees with Coverdale's reading of Priscilla. Priscilla herself expresses annoyance when Coverdale sees Margaret Fuller in her and when, in Boston, he comments, as he often does, on her dreamlike insubstantiality. "Oh, there is substance in these fingers of mine!" she protests. "Why do you call me a dream? Zenobia is much more like one than I" (3:169).

Throughout *The Blithedale Romance*, Coverdale discovers for himself that the "fancy-work" with which he decks her does not accurately represent Priscilla. In fact, virtually every time Coverdale sees Priscilla responding to something, she responds differently from what he would have supposed. At one point, Coverdale observes that "while she seemed as impressible as wax, the girl often showed a persistency in her own ideas, as stubborn as it was gentle" (3:78). Elsewhere, he observes that "with all her delicacy of nerves, there was a singular self-possession in Priscilla, and her sensibilities seemed to lie sheltered from ordinary commotion" (3:142). When Priscilla orders him to leave her, after he has sadistically commented upon Hollingsworth's apparent affection for Zenobia, Coverdale marvels at Priscilla's "true feminine imperiousness, which heretofore I had never seen her exercise" (3:126). At Zenobia's funeral, Coverdale "look[s] often towards Priscilla, dreading to see her wholly overcome with grief" (3:241). He then finds himself having to explain why she very clearly is not.

Priscilla is not only more stable, substantial, and resistant to the control of others than Coverdale's superficial reading of her would suggest, there are also strong indications, throughout the romance, that she has a will to power, a "sphere," of her own. The first scene at Eliot's Pulpit, generally read as establishing Priscilla's character as "gentle parasite," can be read with equal coherence as a struggle between two women for the affection of a man who, although a would-be despot, is so obtusely self-centered that he is easy prey to their stratagems. If we assume that Priscilla is intentionally seeking to attract Hollingsworth, which is certainly plausible considering her reaction to Zenobia and Hollingsworth a few pages later, it is clever of her to ask Hollingsworth's opinion of what Coverdale and Zenobia have been saying. When she beams at him, she is therefore able to signify not only her acceptance of his views, but that she is dependent upon him in order to know anything at all. Unlike Zenobia, she is a blank slate, and the surest way to win Hollingsworth's heart, she may reasonably imagine, is to give him the impression that her mind is wax in his hands.

Zenobia, of course, understands her relationship with Priscilla as a power struggle. In her final scene, she calls her sister "the victorious one!" (3:219). In spite of what he has seen, Coverdale still cannot imagine this. When Priscilla, in response to Zenobia's acknowledgment of her victory, gasps: "We are sisters!" Coverdale says "I fancied that I understood the word and action; it meant the offering of herself, and all she had, to be at Zenobia's disposal. But the latter would not take it such" (3:219). Zenobia will not take it such because that is not what it means. As Coverdale's own understanding of Priscilla by this point makes clear, Priscilla would do anything rather than give up her hold on Hollingsworth. That Coverdale knows this is evident, just a few pages later, when he uses Priscilla's exclusive preoccupation with Hollingsworth to explain her suspicious lack of grief at Zenobia's funeral.

At the end of the book, Coverdale describes his final encounter with Hollingsworth and Priscilla. The powerful, self-absorbed Hollingsworth has been reduced to a "self-distrustful weakness, and a childlike or childish tendency to press close" (3:242) to Priscilla, about whom there is "a protective and watchful quality, as if she felt herself the guardian of her companion" (3:242). As Coverdale approaches, she makes a proprietary gesture, entreating him not to make himself known to Hollingsworth, and she is protectively angry when Coverdale ignores her and begins his needling. Observing Priscilla, Coverdale perceives "a deep, submissive, unquestioning reverence, and also a veiled happiness in her fair and quiet countenance" (3:242). For all that she gives her life to Hollingsworth, Priscilla does not share his unhappiness. Her happiness is veiled because it is indecorous. Whatever Hollingsworth may be experiencing, Priscilla is happy because she possesses him entirely. As throughout the book, Priscilla is anything but a leaf. Although she needed quite a bit of outside help in order to get it, at the end of the book Priscilla is the only character who has gotten what she wanted and what she fought for.

Priscilla's irreducible independence demonstrates the inefficacy of each of the systems that would reduce her. Zenobia cannot dispose of her, Hollingsworth cannot use her, Westervelt cannot enslave her, and Coverdale cannot understand her. Just as her apparent malleability makes her emblematic of all human beings reduced by such systems, the fact that she cannot be "moulded" or grasped demonstrates how unsuccessful these systems are at achieving what they are designed to accomplish. Yet if Priscilla may adequately represent the opacity of the other, she is nevertheless not equipped to analyze the culture that thinks it can read and define her.[20] Zenobia is a far more articulate critic of this culture. However, since Zenobia aspires to the actual possession of the type of power the men in the novel assume they possess, her resistance to this culture takes a very different form than Priscilla's, and it produces a very different result.

Zenobia's specific misery consists in the fact that she aspires to exercise the freedom and power of Coverdale and yet she is inscribed at all times as a woman. The dynamic of this is illustrated when she is expected to assume responsibility for Priscilla. Although Coverdale reserves the right to be annoyed when anyone asks a favor of him that might entail any degree of inconvenience, he "never thoroughly forg[ives]" (3:28) Zenobia when she does not respond warmly to Priscilla when the girl throws herself at her feet. Rebuked by Hollingsworth, and feeling the weight of his "stern and reproachful" (3:28) gaze, Zenobia accepts what would be for anyone the onerous responsibility of, in Priscilla's words, "shelter[ing]" Priscilla and allowing her to "be always near her" (3:29). After she does this, Coverdale and Hollingsworth, in turn, proceed to poeticize the girl as a "poor, shivering . . . friendless" (3:30) object of sympathy. A few pages later, responding scornfully to this "poetical" (3:33) tendency of the masculine nature, Zenobia suggests to Coverdale how annoyed she is that she is expected to let Priscilla into her heart when it is not she but Hollingsworth and Coverdale who "take so much interest in this odd creature" (3:34). Zenobia's characteristically cosmopolitan dilemma is defined in Coverdale's humorous perception of the discomfort Priscilla causes when she arrives at Blithedale. For the communitarians, but preeminently for Zenobia, Priscilla is an "unknown and unaccountable calamity" into which they have been "entrapped, without the liberty of choosing whether to sympathize or no" (3:29). What defines the cosmopolitan mode of life is such a liberty of choice, and this is a privilege that Hollingsworth and Coverdale claim for themselves as men but are unwilling to grant to Zenobia.

Trapped in a role, when she wishes to enjoy the intellectual freedom of a vantage, Zenobia formulates her feminism in terms of what she feels she is being excluded from. Trying to convince Coverdale of the universal unhappiness of women, she gives special attention to the fact that they are not permitted to have the type of consciousness and relationship to the world that Coverdale so purely exemplifies. She asks him: "How can [a woman] be happy, after discovering that fate has assigned her but one single event, which she must contrive to make the substance of her whole life? A man has his choice of innumerable events" (3:60). Not recognizing that she has exactly defined the nature of his own freedom, Coverdale stupidly remarks that "A woman . . . by constant repetition of her one event, may compensate for a lack of variety" (3:60). Zenobia contemptuously dismisses this suggestion and later, in Boston, she reiterates her belief that the most desirable form of existence is that in which one never loses one's sense of having "a choice of innumerable events." When Coverdale, seeing her in an urban setting, observes that he can hardly imagine her at Blithedale, she responds by saying: "Those ideas have their time and place. . . . But I fancy it must be a very circumscribed mind that can find room for no other" (3:164). Although, once again, Zenobia has expressed the central principle of his existence, Coverdale is "bewildered" (3:164) by this response. He presses her and asks if she has given up Blithedale forever. Once again she asserts: "I should think it a poor and meagre nature, that is capable of but one set of forms. . . . Why should we be content with our homely life of a few months past, to the exclusion of all other modes?" (3:165). At this point, although she has merely repeated his own explanation, to his fellow communitarians, of his decision to take a vacation from Blithedale, Coverdale is outraged. "It irritated me," he writes, "this self-complacent, condescending, qualified approval and criticism of a system to which many individuals – perhaps as highly endowed as our gorgeous Zenobia – had contributed their all of earthly endeavor, and their loftiest aspirations" (3:165). As she defines it here, the goal of Zenobia's feminism is to permit women to enjoy Miles Coverdale's freedom to stand outside of fixed roles, moving between them freely. As Coverdale's response makes clear, this is precisely what she cannot be permitted to enjoy.

Zenobia, as much as Westervelt, is a kind of double of Coverdale. Yet unlike Westervelt, she does not represent an ideal, or an extreme or potential tendency of Coverdale's consciousness. Rather, as she throws his own arguments and self-justifications back to him, she represents what he represses about himself. As a man who claims to be something of a feminist, Coverdale is not theoretically opposed to a woman enjoying the freedoms he enjoys. Yet when a woman voices a desire for such freedom, he suddenly becomes aware of the socially destructive consequences of such a cosmopolitan freedom from commitment. Although he is never able to turn his disapproval on himself, he can appreciate the problem when he sees it in a woman. It does not occur to him that, as much as a woman, he too might be expected to fulfill a role in society.

Excluded from masculine modes of power, Zenobia understands their functioning in ways that the men in the book do not. She understands that the basic instrument of male power, in the romance at least, is the distanced gaze from the center that reduces everything within a circumference to subjection. Zenobia actually knows, in other words, what Coverdale's vocabulary implies. Her understanding of the structure and nature of the masculine assertion of power is evident in her perpetual consciousness of Coverdale's gaze. When she first becomes aware of his prying glances, she characterizes them, with a striking and appropriate metaphor, as a new form of the "eye-shot" she has always been exposed to. Throughout the book, Coverdale appears, at each of the important moments of Zenobia's drama, to represent the intrusiveness of the inscribing male order. Zenobia is vividly aware of him in this role. When she gives Priscilla to Westervelt she recognizes him as "the only spectator of my poor tragedy" (3:163). After the climactic scene at Eliot's Pulpit, she perceives him again and asks if he is "turning this whole affair into a ballad" (223). She expects, apparently, that he is viewing her through the "opera glasses" through which she has earlier accused him of viewing women.

At the climax of the final scene at Eliot's Pulpit, Zenobia demonstrates her understanding of the static self-sufficiency of masculine egotism. She asserts that Hollingsworth is a "self-beginning and self-ending piece of mechanism" (3:218). Entirely self-contained in his spherical system of order, he needs no one and reduces everyone. "It is all self!" she cries. "Nothing else; nothing but self, self, self! . . . I see it now! I am awake, disenchanted, disenthralled! Self, self, self! You have embodied yourself in a project" (3:218). Defining panoptic egotism in this way, Zenobia's analysis illuminates the contradiction that will ultimately destroy her. The "self-beginning and self-ending" personality she criticizes is the personality she claims a right to have. Yet, as Hawthorne apparently believes, as a woman, she can never be as self-sufficient as Wakefield, Coverdale, or Hollingsworth. She has a natural tendency to love. This is what will put her in the pond. In Hawthorne's conception, her feminine nature makes it impossible to sustain the self-absorption a man might be capable of. Throughout all of Hawthorne's work, it is women who are represented as having the greatest attachment to stability and continuity, while it is men who are the most enamored of the opportunities offered by modernity.

In her final gesture, Zenobia's body resists all efforts to lay it out flat. Even in death, she is intransigent. Although, like Priscilla, she never attains freedom from the strictures imposed upon her by society and her femininity, she is also never successfully understood by any of the men around her. The opacity and itnractability of Zenobia and Priscilla are as significant as that of the old apple dealer or the town in "Sights from a Steeple." Unfree, they are nevertheless unfathomed and unreduced.

The Blithedale Romance ends as "The Man of the Crowd" ends, with a narrator, teetering on the brink of a void, drawing back with a final, unconvincing pronouncement that seems to explain everything but in fact explains nothing. Coverdale declares that he loves and has always loved Priscilla, even though there's absolutely no evidence in his narrative that this is so. In each of these texts, the culminating assertion enables the narrator to avoid the implications of his narrative. The narrator of "The Man of the Crowd" preserves himself from the terrifying realization that he has, in fact, no understanding of the crowd. Coverdale preserves himself from the realization that the universal detachment that he hoped would give him access to everything has in fact given him nothing. Desperate for a role in a drama he has not been able to understand from his vantage, Coverdale retrospectively inserts himself into the drama in the role of Priscilla's secret admirer. The pathetic way in which Coverdale clings to his confession as that which explains his entire life suggests that at the end of his long narrative, Coverdale has nothing more to show than "Wakefield" after his twenty years of surveillance, the narrator of "Sights from a Steeple" after his presumptuous climb, or the narrator of "The Old Apple Dealer" after his painstaking reading.

Unraveling the social postures and interpretive presumptions of these urban spectators, Hawthorne, like Poe, unravels the flaneur. He does so, however, not in order to create a new form of urban consumption but in order to provide an analysis of the cosmopolitan assumptions that underlie the modern civilization of which the flaneur is merely a representative. Miles Coverdale, with his insistence on social invisibility, his presumption of interpretive power, his complacement enjoyment of a world he has reduced to an unnatural degree of coherence, and his claim of access to the minds of others, represents such quintessentially modern cultural phenomena as utopian socialism, mesmerism, panoramas, and physiognomy. Modern metropolitan society, as Hawthorne represents it, offers the same contradictory promise as the tradition of the flaneur. It suggests that the complexity of social life can be reduced to an order that is visible to a specially gifted and positioned observer who is himself free from the forces that maintain the order. Throughout his work, Hawthorne demonstrates that the attainment of such a privileged perspective is impossible and he suggests that, even if it were possible, it would create enormous problems for the construction of identity and would involve an unacceptable degree of personal isolation.

Although Hawthorne, in *The Blithedale Romance*, presents what is in many respects a conservative critique of the culture of modernity, his book is far too complex to be reduced to what the narrator of "Wakefield" would call a "moral . . . done up neatly" and "condensed into the final sentence" (9:131). *The Blithedale Romance*, like the sketches that precede it, appears to be written by someone with a certain degree of sympathy for the flaneur and for the culture of modernity. Hawthorne himself loved to explore cities and to read the literature of the flaneur. Through-out his career, Hawthorne was absorbed with the issue of what it meant to approach experience as something to be consumed, rather than as something of permanent substance and resonance, irradiated by meaning. His work also demonstrates his fascination with the culture of panoramas and dioramas, and he briefly joined the Brook Farm utopian community. The evidence of all of Hawthorne's work suggests that he was as excited as Clifford Pyncheon by the opportunities presented by modernity, even if in his romances and sketches, he consistently demonstrates, regretfully, dutifully, that no cosmopolitan dream of freedom, whether it is Cov-erdale's or Hester Prynne's, is as accessible or desirable as it may seem in an ecstatic moment of power.

However ambivalent Hawthorne may have been toward what he would have understood as modernity, there can be no question but that he was interested in it, and that in *The Blithedale Romance* and *The House of the Seven Gables*, he tried to write about it. Like several of his characters, Hawthorne may even have wanted to write a panoramic modern novel, a novel that, in the words of the narrator of "Sights from a Steeple," would encompass "the new-born, the aged, the dying, the strong in life, and the recent dead . . . the full of hope, the happy, the miserable, and the desperate [who] dwell together within the circle of my glance" (9:196). Hawthorne's unwillingness to use modern fictional techniques to deal with modern issues, a reluctance that seems to have derived from a lack of comfort with their philosophical and moral implications, may have prevented him from writing a novel in the manner of Dickens or Balzac. This particular failure to embrace modernity may be, in some way, behind all of the others. An ambivalent modern, a conscience-stricken flaneur, a skeptical utopian, Hawthorne was unable to be the "painter of modern life" that part of him clearly wanted to be.

One of Hawthorne's contemporaries, Walt Whitman, did not share these inhibitions. Whitman celebrated the panoramic urban spectatorship and universal cosmopolitan openness that, for Hawthorne, was the root of Coverdale's problem. In his urban poetry, Whitman proposed new forms of being, new ideas of community, and new forms of spirituality that accepted virtually everything that Hawthorne, in *The Blithedale Romance*, had, however ambivalently, rejected.

Chapter 8

"Immense Phantom Concourse": Whitman and the Urban Crowd

William James's remark that Whitman "felt the human crowd as rapturously as Wordsworth felt the mountains" (272) is one of the unquestioned commonplaces of Whitman criticism. Scholars in a variety of disciplines have acknowledged Whitman's urbanism, which has generally been considered unique in American literature in the middle of the nineteenth century.[1] Yet although Whitman's enthusiasm for New York is universally acknowledged, and although his position as America's first significant poet of urban life is unquestioned, there has been surprisingly little discussion of the nature and contexts of Whitman's imaginative interaction with the city.

If this subject has been neglected by critics, it is not because it has been perceived as unimportant. Whitman insisted that his life in New York was the foundation of his poetry. He wrote the first three editions of *Leaves of Grass* (1855, 1856, and 1860) while a resident of New York and it was in New York that he underwent his miraculous transformation from printer to journalist to poet. Unlike the two other authors I have dealt with – a Virginian who never felt at home in New York or Philadelphia and a New Englander who was attracted to yet profoundly suspicious of great cities – Walt Whitman thought of himself as a man of the city. He was, as he wrote in the "Song of Myself": "Walt Whitman, a kosmos, of Manhattan the son" (52).

Whitman's family moved to Brooklyn from Huntington, Long Island by the time he was four and his childhood was spent in what was, at that time, the rapidly growing suburban city across the East River from New York. Running errands as an office boy and later, as a printer's apprentice, Whitman had ample opportunity, even as a child, to become familiar with both of the cities on the East River. At the age of fifteen, having lost his printer's job in an employment squeeze that followed New York's great fire of 1835, Whitman moved back to Long Island and taught school in several rural communities. When employment opportunities for printers improved, Whitman returned to New York in 1841 to work in the pressroom of Park Benjamin's *New World*. From this time until 1863, when he settled in Washington, Whitman was a continuous resident of New York and Brooklyn. During this period, as New York grew from a promising port town of about 300,000 into a metropolis of over a million, the third largest city in the Western world, Whitman was actively involved in the life of the city as a printer, editor, and writer for several New York newspapers and magazines.

By the time Whitman wrote "Crossing Brooklyn Ferry," New York was no longer the city that the narrator of "The Man of the Crowd" Poe contemptuously referred to as small and uncrowded by European standards. America's undisputed leader in commerce, industry, and banking, the port of entry for millions of immigrants, New York had become, by the middle of the 1850s, a city of crowds, rapidly spreading northward on Manhattan Island. As American journalists had marveled at the innumerable streets and immense crowds of the metropolises of Europe in the 1820s and 1830s, European journalists had begun to do the same with the American metropolis. Bayard Still writes, of the European journalism of this period:

> Gone was the condescension with which British travellers had viewed Broadway a generation earlier. By the fifties they were willing to admit that London could not provide its equal. Not even the cluttered and dirty condition of many of the city's streets and pavements, which most of the foreign visitors continued to criticize, or the obstructing festoons of telegraph wires overhead checked their admiration for a city whose "monster hotels," handsome shops, and "stately mansions" equaled if not surpassed Old World standards. (125–6)

Since his own growth, into a kosmos, and into the poet of *Leaves of Grass*, was parallel to that of New York, Whitman may have felt a particularly close identification with his native city. In any case, he suggests, in *Specimen Days*, that the amplitude of the new New York, a "kosmos" in its own right, played an important role in the development of his poetic imagination.

In *Specimen Days*, while acknowledging that "critics will laugh heartily" at such an unconventional assertion, Whitman affirms that such urban experiences as his "Broadway omnibus jaunts and drivers and declamations and escapades undoubtedly entered into the gestation of *Leaves of Grass*." In his account, in *Specimen Days*, of the "formative stamps" to his "character and its subsequent literary and other outgrowth" (*Prose Works*, 1:22–3), Whitman reduced his two decades in New York to four "specimens" entitled "My Passion for Ferries,"

"Broadway Sights," "Omnibus Jaunts and Drivers," and "Plays and
Operas Too."] The dynamic in each of these "specimens" is the same.
In each of them, Whitman places himself in a position, relative to the
city, from which he can observe, as he writes in "My Passion for Ferries,"
"a full sweep, absorbing shows, accompaniments, surroundings" (*Prose
Works*, 1:16). Whitman's "formative stamps" are all experiences of panoramic spectatorship, in which he grasps an entire world in a glance,
from a central and invisible vantage.

The panoramic and spectatorial quality of Whitman's interaction with
the city is evident in all of his poetic descriptions of New York. In
Whitman's poetry, New York is virtually always represented as it would
appear from the center of the East River or from the center of Broadway.
The importance of these perspectives is obvious, of course, in "Crossing
Brooklyn Ferry" and "Broadway." It is also evident in poems that do
not specifically deal with these thoroughfares. In "Mannahatta," for example, Whitman's characteristic emphasis on the "Tides swift and ample
. . . The flowing sea-currents, the little islands, larger adjoining islands,
the heights, the villas, / The countless masts, the white shore-steamers,
the lighters, the ferry-boats" (475) imply an observer in the pilothouse
of a ferryboat. It is from such a perspective that New York would most
dramatically appear to be a "City of hurried and sparkling waters! city
of spires and masts!" The brief glimpse of New York in "When Lilacs
Last in the Dooryard Bloom'd" is an image of a city of spires and ships.
In "A Broadway Pageant," though the perspective is from the sidewalk,
the focus of Whitman's rapt attention is a procession moving up the
center of Broadway. The city scene in the eighth section of "Song of
Myself" with its "blab of the pave," "promenaders," and "heavy omnibus" (36) with driver, is also apparently a Broadway scene.

Viewed at all times in "full sweeps," Whitman's New York is strikingly impressionistic.[2] Sense impressions are rarely unique, particular,
or extensively described. They are experienced in clusters, subsumed
under general categories. In the eighth section of "Song of Myself"
Whitman sees and hears "The blab of the pave, tires of carts, sluff of
boot-soles, talk of the promenaders, . . . The snow-sleighs, clinking,
shouted jokes, pelts of snowballs, / The hurrahs for popular favorites,
the fury of rous'd mobs" (36). All individual "sluffs" and "clinks" are
brought together into a single general impression. All of the general
impressions are brought together into a single "full sweep," in which
none is given special prominence. This technique is also evident in
"Broadway" in which "glints of love" and "glances" are disembodied
and made to swim, with "endless sliding, mincing, shuffling feet" in the
"hurrying human tides" (521). As in an Impressionist painting of a city
scene, individual objects are dissolved into broad general impressions

that combine to produce an overall sense of distanced motion and diversity. When Whitman does isolate a figure in one of his crowd "sweeps," it is generally in order to provide a focal point for a general urban motion, mood, or texture. All we see of the driver of the omnibus moving up Broadway in the eighth section of "Song of Myself" is his interrogating thumb. An "excited crowd" is given a specific texture by "the policeman with his star quickly working" (36) his way to its center.

The panoramic and impressionistic nature of Whitman's apprehension of the city does not lend itself to concrete and particularized representation. In such urban poems as "Mannahatta," "Broadway," "City of Ships," "A Broadway Pagaent," or "Give Me the Splendid Silent Sun," it is impossible to find even the degree of particularity one finds at the opening of "The Man of the Crowd." This lack of particularity may help to explain why critics have found it so hard to discuss these poems. Because they represent only general motions and tones, Whitman's city poems often appear to be excessively abstract and distanced. They seem to blend everything together, and, to a large degree, they are indistinguishable from each other. Reading Whitman's descriptions of New York, some readers have reluctantly concluded that, however much enthusiasm Whitman may have had for the city, he had little of substance to say about it.

Yet if it is difficult to say more about Whitman's descriptions of New York than that they are panoramic and impressionistic, one thing that can certainly be said, in the context of this discussion, is that Whitman's representations of New York have some interesting similarities with Coverdale's descriptions of Boston. Part of the reason for this is that both Coverdale and Whitman have roots in the same English and American tradition of urban spectatorial essays. Whitman was a friend and certainly a reader of Willis. As a New York journalist, he was undoubtedly familiar with the work of the New York flaneurs, in the *Knickerbocker*, *Tribune*, *Mirror*, and other New York publications. Whitman was also familiar with the work of English urban spectators. To judge from his reviews, he was a great admirer of Lamb (*Uncollected Poetry and Prose*, 133) and the early Dickens (See "Boz and Democracy"). It is clear from Whitman's clippings, cataloged by Bucke, that he was a regular reader of the *Westminster Review*, *North British Review*, *Edinburgh Review*, *Blackwood's Edinburgh Magazine*, and the *Quarterly Review*, and it can therefore be assumed that he was familiar with the horde of minor flaneurs who appeared in these and other English magazines.[3]

More than any of the other authors I have dealt with in this discussion, however, Whitman not only knew the flaneur; he was a flaneur. For the various newspapers and magazines that employed him during his journalistic career, Whitman wrote dozens of urban essays in the complacent style characteristic of the flaneur.[4] When Mr. Walter Whitman, the extravagantly dressed young editor of one of the city's most fashionable newspapers,[5] describes himself as "saunter[ing] forth" with his "heavy, dark beautifully polished" walking stick to explore "Gotham's glorious promenade" (*Walt Whitman of the "New York Aurora,"* 44), it is difficult to imagine that he is likely to see or experience anything substantially different from what Coverdale sees and experiences when he leaves his "pleasant bachelor-parlor . . . reading room or picture gallery" to take his "noontide walk along the cheery pavement, with the suggestive succession of human faces, and the brisk throb of human life" (9:40). To judge from Whitman's newspaper accounts of his own *flaneries*, he does not.

The following Coverdalian passage is typical of many in Whitman's journalistic sketches of New York life in the 1840s:

> We did think we had exhausted all the superlatives in praise of the aspect of Broadway of a pleasant afternoon. Yesterday, however, was too fine not to receive a passing notice.
>
> We took a stroll down to the Battery, about four P.M. The crowds and the jam were tremendous. Hundreds of splendid women and fashionable men filled the pave; and between the curbstones whirled one incessant clang of omnibuses, carriages, and other vehicles. (*Aurora*, 54)

Elsewhere in the *Aurora* sketches, Whitman writes:

> As we sauntered out of the west gate of the Park, feeling in an observative mood, we recollected an old custom of ours, long since disused – we went up the stairs of the American Museum, entered the first room, took a chair, placed it in a roomy niche made by the settling in one of the front windows – and in that chair ensconced we ourself. Out before us was the busiest spectacle this busy city may present. One mighty rush of men, business, carts, carriages, and clang. (26)

As a flaneur, Whitman tampers with none of the conventions of the genre. His city is always bland and amusing, suggestive at most of a moral platitude. While Dickens's *Sketches by Boz* contains some interesting anticipations of his mature style and reflects his very productive struggle with the limitations of the genre in which he is working, Whitman's pieces are, as Paul Zweig has lamented (3), pure hackwork, offering virtually no indication that their author could ever develop into any kind of genius. In the early years of his journalistic career, it appears that Whitman was simply one of a legion of imitators of Nathaniel Parker Willis writing in the New York press. The early Whitman's resemblance to Willis, however, neither explains nor excuses the fact that at many points in his mature poetry, Whitman's urban descriptions continue to sound as if they could have been written by the most superficial of Hawthorne's spectatorial narrators. When Whitman responds to Broadway, in the following lines from the poem that bears its name:

> What hurrying human tides, or day or night!
> What passions, winnings, losses, ardors, swim thy waters!
> What whirls of evil, bliss and sorrow, stem thee!
> What curious questioning glances – glints of love!
> Leer, envy, scorn, contempt, hope, aspiration!
> Thou portal – thou arena . . . (521)

he sounds very much like the narrator of "Sights from a Steeple" who writes:

> How various are the situations of the people covered by the roofs beneath me, and how diversified are the events at this moment befalling them! The new-born, the aged, the dying, the strong in life, and the recent dead, are in the chambers of these many mansions. The full of hope, the happy, the miserable, and the desperate, dwell together within the circle of my glance. (9:196)

Coverdale's catalog of the sounds heard from his hotel room is also not strikingly different in effect from Whitman's catalog of urban sights and sounds in his poetry. It is even somewhat more particularized. In all of Coverdale's and Whitman's descriptions of the city, there is the same flaunted laziness, a paralyzed gaping working to a pitch of ecstatic appreciation at the apparently unencompassable yet, by panoramic means, entirely encompassed, multiplicity of the city.

The panoramic harmony of Whitman's representations of the city also may not be accounted for by the suggestion that it reflects the way in which Whitman actually perceived New York. Whitman understood, every bit as much as Hawthorne, that the panoramic "full sweep" was in fact a denial of the complexity of what was taken in by it. He demonstrates this vividly in *Democratic Vistas* where he offers one of the most characteristic of his urban descriptions:

> The splendor, picturesqueness, and oceanic amplitude and rush of these great cities, the unsurpass'd situation, rivers, and bay, sparkling sea-tides, costly and lofty new buildings, facades of marble and iron, of original grandeur and elegance of design, with the masses of gay color, the preponderance of white and blue, the flags flying, the endless ships, the tumultuous streets, Broadway . . . the assemblages of citizens in their groups, conversations, trades, eve-

ning amusements, or along the by-quarters – these I say, and the like of these completely satisfy my senses of power, fulness, motion, &c. and give me, through such senses and appetites, and through my aesthetic conscience, a continued exaltation and absolute fulfillment. (*Prose Works*, 2:371)

Immediately after this passage, Whitman undercuts his own apparent complacency. He writes: "But sternly discarding, shutting our eyes to the general superficial effect, coming down to what is of the only real importance, Personalities, and examining minutely, we question, we ask, Are there, indeed, *men* worthy of the name?" (2:371). Turning a "moral microscope" onto this crowd, Whitman finds "a sort of dry and flat Sahara appears." "These cities," he writes, are:

crowded with petty grotesques, malformations, phantoms, playing meaningless antics. Confess that everywhere, in shop, street, church, theatre, barroom, official chair, are pervading flippancy and vulgarity, low cunning, infidelity – ... everywhere an abnormal libidinousness, unhealthy forms, male, female, painted, padded, dyed, chignon'd, muddy complexions, bad blood, ... shallow notions of beauty, with a range of manners, or rather lack of manners, (considering the advantages enjoy'd,) probably the meanest to be seen in the world. (*Prose Works*, 2:372)

Even in the earliest stages of his career, Whitman was aware that much of the reality of nineteenth-century urban life was not visible from the physical and imaginative vantages he preferred.[6] Yet if Whitman was as aware as Hawthorne of the limitations of the panoramic vantage, he does not appear to have been as concerned as Hawthorne with undermining the specious sense of comprehension afforded by such vantages.

The resemblances between Coverdale and Whitman reflect the fact that in addition to being formed by the tradition of the flaneur, they were both formed by the entire civilization with which the flaneur is associated. As an avid frequenter of the museums, panoramas, dioramas, lectures, and exhibitions of New York, as well as an enthusiastic and well-informed adherent of phrenology and mesmerism, Whitman was as pure a representative of what Coverdale exemplified as Coverdale himself.[7] His "self," as he characteristically describes it, is a veritable Village Hall, and in "Pictures," the long, diffuse poem Whitman wrote before the first edition of *Leaves of Grass*, he even compares his mind to an exhibition hall filled with "pictures," images of everything in the world. In addition, the persona Whitman created for himself as the poet of *Leaves of Grass* is a more successful fulfillment of Coverdale's utopian plans for his own personality than anything Coverdale was able to

achieve. An avowedly lazy, yet physically robust container of all possibilities for human existence, on confidently intimate terms with everyone, with a penchant for panoramic perspectives and a dream of himself
as the poet the age has been waiting for, Whitman is the paradigm of
what Coverdale hoped to become. He is the ultimate cosmopolitan personality, the pure product and reflection of the culture of modernity.

What makes Whitman different from Coverdale is that he actually
develops a voice. Coverdale's inability to express himself may reflect
Hawthorne's Wordsworthian conviction that the cosmopolitan civilization of his day could not produce a true poet. If Whitman had remained
an imitator of Willis and a cousin of Coverdale, such a conviction would
have been vindicated. Yet Whitman made a serious effort to transform
the lazy, yet compulsively curious, all-containing personality, associated
with the flaneur and typified by Coverdale, into a new form of poetic
consciousness. He also attempted to adapt the characteristic environment
of this consciousness, the modern city, for use as a poetic landscape. This
double project is a crucial aspect of the first three editions of *Leaves of
Grass*, which were written in the middle and late 1850s, when Whitman
was resident in New York. In several of the poems of this period, Whitman establishes himself as the true poet of the Village Hall, as the poet
not only of the city, but of modernity, of the new urban culture of
spectacle and image.

The process by which the Coverdalian Walter Whitman transformed
himself into Walt Whitman, poet of urban modernity, is obscure, and
in large part unknowable. Critics and biographers like Allen, Stovall,
Kaplan, and Zweig have done an excellent job of listing the ingredients,
while respectfully backing away from the presumptuous project of providing the recipe. What I am about to suggest only supplements what
they have done, although I intend to be somewhat more presumptuous.
In the following discussion, I wish to propose a possible way of understanding how various features of Whitman's emotional and intellectual
life were drawn together to the point where he could begin to produce
the kind of urban poetry he was ultimately able to write. One way to
begin to observe Whitman's development of an urban poetic voice is to
consider the relation between "Crossing Brooklyn Ferry," Whitman's
greatest urban poem, and an article Whitman wrote nine years earlier
about a visit to a gallery of photographs.

Whitman's fascination with photography is well known and well documented.[8] Whitman often visited photographic exhibitions and he often
used photography as a metaphor for his journalism and his poetry. His
fullest consideration of photography's appeal may be found in an article
he wrote entitled "A Visit to Plumbe's Gallery," which appeared in the
Brooklyn Daily Eagle of July 2, 1846. This article is of particular historical

interest because it is one of the earliest accounts, by someone who would become a major author, of the phenomenology of looking at a photograph. Although this journalistic piece does not offer any extensive analysis of the historically novel experience it describes, the vocabulary of the article anticipates the vocabulary as well as the conceptual foundations of Whitman's exploration of the poetic and spiritual dimensions of modernity in his poetry.

At the opening of "A Visit to Plumbe's Gallery," Whitman describes the strange effect produced by looking at "the great legion of human faces" on Plumbe's wall of photographs. A visitor to the gallery, he writes, may observe "human eyes gazing silently but fixedly upon you, and creating the impression of an immense Phantom concourse – speechless and motionless, but yet realities. You are indeed in a new world – a peopled world, though mute as the grave" (*The Gathering of the Forces*, 2:116).[9] Returning what he calls the "gaze" (2:116) of the photographs with his own "peering gaze" (2:114), Whitman reflects upon the "strange fascination" (2:116) of highly realistic representations of the human face.

> We love to dwell long upon them – to infer many things, from the text they preach – to pursue the current of thoughts running riot about them. It is singular what a peculiar influence is possessed by the eye of a well-painted miniature or portrait. – It has a sort of magnetism. We have miniatures in our possession, which we have often held, and gazed upon the eyes in them for the half-hour! An electric chain seems to vibrate, as it were, between our brain and him or her preserved there so well by the limner's cunning. Time, space, both are annihilated, and we identify the semblance with the reality. – And even more than that. For the strange fascination of looking at the eyes of a portrait, sometimes goes beyond what comes from the real orbs themselves. (2:116–7)[10]

In "Crossing Brooklyn Ferry," Whitman experiences a comparable sense of the annihilation of time and space. Addressing the crowds that will cross between Manhattan and Brooklyn in the future, he asks: "What is it then between us? . . . time nor place – distance avails not." Feeling a profound yet indefinite sense of connection to the crowds of the future as well as to the crowds of silent faces that cross with him on the ferry, Whitman asks, in the poem: "What is more subtle than this which ties me to the woman or man that looks into my face?" (164). The subtle cord that "ties" him to these others is anticipated by the "electric chain" that he describes as connecting him to the images of faces in "A Visit to Plumbe's Gallery." At Plumbe's, Whitman feels that the silence of the "Phantom concourse" provides him with an opportunity for speculation. He feels free to "pursue the current of [his] thoughts running riot" around these gazing images. He has the same sentiment of power in relation to the gazing faces on the ferryboat. He asks: "What is more subtle than this . . . Which fuses me into you now, and pours my meaning into you?" (164). At the end of "Crossing Brooklyn Ferry," the "speechless," "mute," yet "beautiful and multifarious" daguerrotypes of "A Visit to Plumbe's Gallery" seem to have become transformed into the "dumb, beautiful ministers" who are "receive[d] with free sense at last" (165) and are "plant[ed] . . . permanently" (165) inside the poet's "soul."

The similarity of the language used in the article and in the poem, as well as the similar structure, outlined in each, for the mechanism of interacting with silent faces, suggests that, for Whitman, there was a significant analogy between the experience of looking at photographs and the experience of the urban crowd. The general parallel between photography and urban spectatorship was already clear to flaneurs writing at about this time. Nathaniel Parker Willis had written an urban essay series, "Daguerrotypes of the Present," and Whitman himself, shortly after, wrote a series of sketches called "City Photographs." Willis, Whitman, and others no doubt saw in photography a metaphor that served their purposes even better than "sketch," the two-dimensional metaphor that had previously been the most popular illustration of their activity. The flaneur and the photographer each offer a collection of images that, because of the way in which they are selected, arrested, and posed, appear to be as accessible to an interpreting consciousness as the images in a painting, print, or drawing. Yet because the photographer and the flaneur claim to be offering a relatively unmediated image of the actual surface of reality, and because their production traditionally presents itself as prosaic, to be evaluated in terms of its fidelity, their images lay claim to a greater authority than art. They are more "real," because they are supposed to be less determined by a representing consciousness. They have been encountered, rather than created.

Yet for all that flaneurs may have attempted to appropriate the authority of photography to themselves, there is still a fundamental difference between looking at a photograph and reading a flaneur's sketch. One is a visual image, with a certain claim to immediacy, the other is a highly mediated interpretation and rendering, in language, of something that is not immediately visible to the reader. The appeal of the flaneur's sketch traditionally derives from what the flaneur is able to make out of what he has purportedly seen. Yet in both his article and his poem, as in all of his urban sketches, Whitman is unable to do what Dickens could do so easily. Although he claims that the silence of the faces is an opportunity for him to "infuse," and "pour in" his own meanings, his infusions are uniformly diffident and vague. There are no interesting interpretations and there are no narratives. Whitman wonders if a couple pictured in a wedding photo is still married; he is impressed by the "calm serene bearing" of "an aged matron" (*The Gathering of the Forces*, 2:114). In "A Visit to Plumbe's Gallery," Whitman is once again a failure as a flaneur. Yet Whitman's failure does not appear to involve the epistemological scruple that in large part accounts for the failure of the flaneurs in Hawthorne and Poe. His bold claims of spectatorial dominion are convincing enough. So too are his assertions that he is profoundly moved by what he observes, even if he cannot describe what he sees in any detail. It appears that, gazing at silent faces or encountering what he calls "the strange fascination of photographs," Whitman sees and feels something that cannot be adequately expressed in the language of the flaneur.

The nature of Whitman's paralysis is to a certain degree represented by the fact that the word he consistently uses, in the article and the poem, to characterize his interaction with silent faces is the word "gaze." It is the spectator's "peering gaze" (*The Gathering of the Forces*, 2:114) that surveys the wall of faces. The "human eyes" of the photographs are described as "gazing silently but fixedly upon you" (2:116). The word *gazing*, also figures prominently in "Crossing Brooklyn Ferry." Near the end of the poem, Whitman writes: "Gaze, loving and thirsting eyes, in the house or street or public assembly!" (164). The word *gaze* differs from the word *observe* or *look* in that it is less definite and more comprehensive. Like taking a photograph, gazing, as Whitman describes it, does not necessarily privilege any portion of the field of vision nor does it imply that the gazer is having any definable response to or understanding of what he or she observes. The eye that gazes, in a photograph or in an urban crowd, does not surrender its mystery or allow itself to be read. Yet this increases its fascination. As Benjamin writes, discussing the eyes of city dwellers in Baudelaire's poetry, "Baudelaire describes eyes of which one is inclined to say that they have lost their ability to look. Yet this lends them a charm. . . . The deeper the remoteness which a glance has to overcome, the stronger will be the spell that is apt to emanate from the gaze. In eyes that look at us with a mirrorlike blankness the remoteness remains complete" ("Some Motifs in Baudelaire," 149–50).

Whitman, it appears, made an independent discovery of this same phenomenon, at about the same time as Baudelaire, in the decade after the invention of photography. What he repeatedly calls, in the article on Plumbe's gallery, the "strange fascination" (*The Gathering of the Forces*, (2:116, 117) of photographs, a fascination that "goes beyond what comes from the real orbs themselves" (2:117), is clearly related to what he finds to be the strange fascination of faces in an urban crowd in "Crossing Brooklyn Ferry." This fascination, which, as Whitman writes in "A Visit to Plumbe's Gallery," is profound precisely because it is indefinite, is an experience for which the flaneur has no discourse, for which Whitman, when he wrote his article, had no discourse. By the time Whitman wrote "Crossing Brooklyn Ferry," however, he had developed the rudiments of a discourse. Although it did not make him any more competent as a flaneur, it opened up new possibilities for the poetic representation of modern urban objects. The development of this discourse is Whitman's development as an urban poet. Though no one can ever know, of course, how this development was experienced or how long it took, my hypothesis is that it can be imagined to have taken place as a result of Whitman's internal exploration of his emotion of arrest before the silence of photographs and faces in crowds. In tracing the line between "A Visit to Plumbe's Gallery" and "Crossing Brooklyn Ferry," I see a process that can be most clearly conceptualized in relationship to the theory of photographic response that is developed by Roland Barthes in his final book, *Camera Lucida.*

According to Barthes, the *noeme* (115) of photography, its essence, is its ability to produce precisely the "arrest of interpretation" that Whitman experiences, in which, Barthes writes: "I exhaust myself realizing that *this-has-been*" (107). "The *noeme* of Photography," which "is simple, banal; no depth: 'that has been'" (115), is nevertheless also certain and "it is in proportion to its certainty that I can say nothing about [a] photograph" (107). A photograph provides a "certificate of presence" (87). It certifies, simply, that the photographed object or person has existed, and has existed in a specific place, and in relation to the specific objects with which it is photographed. In this way, it offers proof of the reality of time while enabling a sense that it is possible to see across time. The authority of the image permits a viewer to feel a sense of connection to the certainty of something as it existed in the past. The power and poignance of this sense of connection, according to Barthes, overwhelms and preempts any effort the viewer might make to interpret or say anything about the image. All that is experienced is what Whitman would call "an electric chain" that "vibrate[s], as it were, between our brain and him or her preserved" as an image, or as Barthes wrote: "A sort of umbilical cord" that "links the body of the photographed thing to my gaze" (81).

In "A Visit to Plumbe's Gallery," Whitman clearly feels the silent power of his "phantom concourse," he experiences the "arrest of interpretation," and he records the sense that photography gives him of being able to see across time. To judge from his language, and to judge from the poetic use he was eventually able to make of this experience, Whitman also seems to have experienced another significant effect of photography, as Barthes describes it. Gazing at a wall of photographed faces, Whitman describes how the "immense Phantom concourse" seems to be "a peopled world, yet mute as the grave." This, and the mesmeric language he uses throughout the article, his references to the "magnetic attraction" of the faces, the "electric" chain that connects him to them, with all that this metaphor implies about contacting minds that cannot be contacted in the physical world, suggest that in the photographs Whitman encountered what Roland Barthes refers to as "that terrible thing which is there in every photograph, the return of the dead" (9). The "strange fascination" that Whitman finds in photographed faces appears to be related to the effect that, according to Barthes, is shared by a variety of ancient theatrical forms that make use of the mysterious power and authority of a "phantom concourse." Like the made-up or masked faces of ancient Greek, Indian, Chinese, and Japanese theater, photography is, in Barthes words, "a kind of Tableau Vivant, a figuration of the motionless and made-up face beneath which we see the dead" (31–2).

Whitman's positioning of himself as speaker in "Crossing Brooklyn Ferry" offers as clear an example as can be found of the opportunities for self-conception that, according to Barthes, photography made possible. The invention of the photograph, Barthes writes, "is the advent of myself as other: a cunning dissociation of consciousness from identity" (12). It creates the possibility of "see[ing] oneself . . . on the scale of History" (12) because, until the invention of photography, the possession of images of oneself was a rare and limited privilege. Producing a profound revolution in the relationship of the individual to his or her own identity within time, as well as to time itself, photography could induce the sort of speculation that is the premise of "Crossing Brooklyn Ferry." As Barthes writes: "The Photograph . . . represents that very subtle moment when to tell the truth, I am neither subject nor object but a subject who feels he is becoming an object: I then experience a micro-version of death (of parenthesis): I am truly becoming a specter" (14). In "Crossing Brooklyn Ferry," Whitman, as it were, takes a photograph of New York harbor, with himself in its midst. He imagines what it would be like to be in the future, looking at the photograph he has made of everything that surrounded him at a specific moment in time. His self-consciousness about the gaze of invisible future generations resembles nothing so much as the self-consciousness of someone being photographed. In "Crossing Brooklyn Ferry," Whitman represents himself as both subject and object, both living and dead. In his account of the ferry passage, Whitman represents himself as the only living person in the midst of a crowd of phantoms, of people who will be dead when the audience addressed in the poem actually reads it. Yet in addressing the crowds of men and women "a generation hence and ever so many generations hence," Whitman simultaneously assumes the posture of the

only dead person in the midst of a crowd of the living. In his consciousness of the moment, looking at the faces around him and imagining them
as dead, imagining himself as dead, Whitman experiences the death, or
the promise of death that is contained in the photograph.

Imagining himself as dead, as photographed, Whitman, in effect, dou-
bles himself. What he does has a significant structural similarity to what
Hawthorne's "Wakefield" does. He becomes invisible in order to look
back on himself, and on his Here and Now, as an image. Yet what
motivates Wakefield is the defining emotion of the flaneur, curiosity.
Whitman's emotion in "Crossing Brooklyn Ferry" is something quite
different, something suggested in "A Visit to Plumbe's Gallery" but only
finally expressed in "Crossing Brooklyn Ferry." The effort to define this
emotion, in relation to photography, occupies Barthes for most of *Camera
Lucida*. Near the end of the book, Barthes formulates his emotion as
clearly as he can. The fruit of Barthes's meditation is a discovery: "There
was a sort of link (or knot) between Photography, madness, and something whose name I did not know. I began by calling it: the pangs of
love. . . . It was a broader current than a lover's sentiment. In the love
stirred by photography . . . another music is heard, its name oddly old-
fashioned: Pity. . . . I passed beyond the unreality of the thing represented,
I entered crazily into the spectacle, into the image, taking into my arms
what is dead, what is going to die" (*The Gathering of the Forces*, 2:116,117).
This emotion of inexpressible wonder and compassion, the product of
the intensity of the moment of arrest as one gazes at a photograph, is,
in the end, what Barthes calls "the photographic ecstasy" (*Camera Lucida*,
119), a quintessentially modern emotion, born of the imaginative contact
with the mortality signified in the mechanically produced images of other
human beings.

The emotion that Whitman experiences and that Barthes describes as
"the photographic ecstasy" is clearly related to an emotion that, as I
considered earlier, becomes prominent within the tradition of the flaneur
shortly before the invention of photography, and in conjunction with
the ascendancy of the culture of the panoramas. What Whitman describes
himself as experiencing on the Fulton Ferry is analogous to the apprehension of the ephemerality of the crowd that is part of the phenomenological effect of viewing a frozen panoramic image of it. The
paradoxical melancholy of the panoramic moment, which appears in the
flâneries of Dickens and Murray, and which James Grant in *The Great
Metropolis* compares with the emotion of Xerxes "survey[ing] his fine
army of a million men from an eminence" (1:18), is a crucial aspect of
what is transforming the flaneur at this time. It is part of what impels
Dickens, in the *Sketches by Boz*, toward narrative as a principle of urban

representation. The photographic ecstasy, or the melancholy of the panoramas, also impels Whitman to explore new ways to represent cities, ways that come out of, yet transcend what the flaneur makes available.

Whitman's development of a new kind of urban poetry is worked out within "Crossing Brooklyn Ferry." Although this poem is not explicitly concerned with photography, it takes as its starting point "the photographic ecstasy" that Whitman experiences when he gazes at faces in an urban crowd as if they were photographs on the walls of Plumbe's gallery. It is just such an emotion, as impersonal as the gaze of the flaneur yet much more deeply involved with the object of the gaze, that may have enabled Whitman to transcend his speechless fascination. "Crossing Brooklyn Ferry," I suggest, is a meditative account of a process, an exploration of the way in which an arrested gaze may lead to a compassionate, empathic encounter with the dead, opening into a vision of the poet himself as dead, and viewed, as in a photograph, by future generations gazing across time. Although this meditation, in my view, does indeed have the form of Roland Barthes's own account of his emotional and philosophical progress as he meditated upon his response to photography, Whitman, like any other poet of the nineteenth century, would hardly have needed Roland Barthes to define for him the connection between the gaze of the dead, the experience of "pity," and the writing of poetry. Whitman had read, and was significantly influenced by the poetry of Wordsworth. Although there are certainly other sources that Whitman could have drawn on to make these connections, I think that it is significant that "Crossing Brooklyn Ferry" consistently reads as if it were a step-by-step rewriting of Wordsworth's "Ode: Intimations of Immortality from Recollections of Early Childhood." Each of these poems is an effort to transcend paralysis, to convert an emotionally charged "arrest of interpretation" into language, through encountering and coming to terms with the signification of death and loss in the external world. Both poems, in addition, make use of the affective energy of the encounter with death to transform conventionally unpoetic objects into subject matter suitable for poetry. While Wordsworth uses this energy to bring the rural commonplace into the purview of poetry, Whitman uses the same emotional structure to establish an imaginative foundation for urban poetry.

Whitman was not an admirer of Wordsworth as a man and he was only a grudging admirer of Wordsworth as a poet.[11] Nevertheless, as Roger Asselineau has demonstrated, Whitman appears to have identified with Wordsworth as a poetic revolutionary, self-consciously bringing poetry closer to common speech and ordinary things.[12] Whitman also perceived, in Wordsworth's poetry and his own, a similar preoccupation with the issues of death, immortality, and human limitation, although he was proudly aware of the fundamentally different ways in which they treated these issues. In a fragment, found among his papers after his death, which, Richard Bucke speculates, was "probably written as a note to be used by some friend who was writing about *Leaves of Grass* – possibly as part of a notice to be given by himself to some periodical" (*Notes and Fragments*, 14), Whitman expressed his view of these parallels and differences. Written around July 1876, the fragment, the only extant reference by Whitman to a specific Wordsworth poem, reads as follows:

> July, by the Pond. The same thoughts and themes – unfulfilled aspirations, the enthusiasms of youth, ideal dreams, the mysteries and failures and broken hopes of life, and then death the common fate of all, and the impenetrable uncertainty of the Afterwards – which Wordsworth treats [in] his Intimations of Immortality, Bryant in his Thanatopsis and in the Flood of Years, and Whittier in his pieces W. W. also treats in Leaves of Grass. But how different the treatment! Instead of the gloom and hopelessness and spirit of wailing and reproach, or bowed down submission as to some grim destiny, which is the basis and background of those fine poems. Instead of Life and Nature growing stale – instead of Death coming like a blight and end-all . . . (*Notes and Fragments*, 14)

The quoted fragment indicates that, twenty-one years after he wrote "Crossing Brooklyn Ferry," Whitman understood that his own poetry radically revised a Romantic tradition of conceiving of death and immortality exemplified by the "Immortality Ode" and extended by two of the American poets Whitman admired most. Yet neither here nor elsewhere does Whitman give any indication of having been conscious of this when he began to write the *Leaves of Grass*. Even if it is impossible to conclusively determine whether Whitman had the "Immortality Ode" in mind as he was writing "Crossing Brooklyn Ferry," the two poems are remarkably similar in their structure, diction, changes in tone and voice, and in their thematic concern with the problems of death, immortality, the reality of the phenomenal world, and the possible role of conventionally unpoetic objects in poetry and spiritual experience.

The parallel between the two poems is immediately evident from their opening sections. Each poet invokes a catalog of objects that will reappear at the end of the poem, and which are examples of the kind of objects that each poet intends to make into suitable subject matter for poetry.[13] As Wordsworth's objects are natural, Whitman's are urban. They are cataloged in the context of an address to an ostensible audience that is represented as enjoying a privileged and vivid relation to the objects that the poet himself can no longer enjoy. Yet though Wordsworth can never again enjoy nature as unselfconsciously as the birds, lambs, and shepherd boy, and although Whitman, when the audience he addresses is reading the poem, is no longer alive, each poet asserts that he experiences an imaginative empathy with his distanced listeners. Wordsworth declares that he hears the calls they make to each other, he sees the heavens laughing with them at their jubilee, his heart is at their festival, his "head hath its coronal." "I feel" he claims, "I feel it all" (*Poetical Works*, 4:280). Whitman, in his analogous identifications, writes: "I am with you" (160). Just as his future audience feels, looking at the river and sky, so he felt. "I too," he tells them, "watched . . . saw . . . look'd . . . loved . . . lived . . . walk'd . . . felt . . . knew" (161–3) what they do. At a point in this opening address exactly analogous to that in Wordsworth's, Whitman asserts that his head too hath its coronal: "The fine centrifugal spokes of light round the shape of my head in the sunlit water" (161).

At the end of their respective four-stanza openings, each poet suggests that despite the intimacy they profess with their auditors, a distance yet remains. The distance consists of an ultimately insurmountable difference of perception. Wordsworth asks: "Whither is fled the visionary gleam?" (*Poetical Works*, 4:280). Unable to restore the sense he had in his childhood that the world was "apparelled in celestial light" (4:279), he is aware that although he may be present at the "festivals" of the birds, lambs, and shepherd boy, he cannot fully participate in them. His loss of the vivid consciousness of childhood distinguishes him from these creatures who can still experience it, and since that vividness was, in his conception, a proof and trace of his immortal being, he looks upon his loss as a form of alienation, not only from them, but from his conception of eternity, what he believes to be the source of the "celestial light."

At the parallel point in his poem, addressing those who will cross the East River in the distant future, Whitman asks "What is it then between us?" (162). Although he has asserted that he is "with" and "among" the "men and women of a generation, or ever so many generations hence," he too knows that a distance remains. Just as Wordsworth cannot be content merely to experience empathy with the animals and children, Whitman also wishes to be brought closer to the consciousness of those who will read him in the future.

By asking these questions, asserting these identifications, and acknowledging the distances that remain, each poet announces the project of his poem. The purpose of their poetic meditations will be to determine the degree to which the distances may be overcome. By doing this, and by examining the way in which they may be overcome, or compensated for, each seeks to establish a new, fallen relation with things, a relation in which the immediacy of childhood is replaced by a relationship to time and eternity that can be mediated by the commonplace objects formerly experienced in their immediacy.

In the second and central section of the "Immortality Ode," Wordsworth meditates upon the aspects of human experience that produce and intensify the alienation the poem is being written to overcome. In his treatment of the causes of the fading into the light of common day, he gives particular prominence to the loss of innocence and originality brought about by the inauthenticity of social life. Describing the child, as he learns, in essence, to be an adult, Wordsworth writes:

> The little actor cons another part;
> Filling from time to time his "humorous stage"
> With all the Versions down to palsied Age,
> That Life brings with her in her equipage;
> As if his whole vocation
> Were endless imitation.
> (*Poetical Works*, 4:282)

Burdened by the customs, conventions, and habits they assume as a result of their propensity to imitate, human beings are ultimately, Wordsworth writes, "In darkness lost, the darkness of the grave." What offers hope for an emergence from this darkness, what Wordsworth raises his "song of thanks and praise" for, are the "obstinate questionings / Of sense and outward things" (4:283) that provoke his own realization that there is more to reality than he can perceive with his senses. These questionings, which come upon him "in a season of calm weather" (4:283), lead him to an oceanic vision of a primordial unity behind appearances. The "questionings" permit him to have a glimpse of "that immortal sea / Which brought us hither" (4:284). "In a moment" of calm and questioning, the soul can "travel thither, / And see the Children sport upon the shore / And hear the mighty waters rolling ever more" (4:284). It is this metaphysical apprehension that enables Wordsworth to move into his triumphant concluding stanzas.

In the central section of his poem, Whitman echoes Wordsworth's formulations and concerns, and sometimes his actual language as well. Whitman also deals with the apparent limitations of human experience and consciousness, which, like Wordsworth, he figuratively represents as a darkness contrasting with the plentiful light imagery of the opening and concluding stanzas. He writes: "It is not upon you alone the dark patches fall. / The dark threw its patches down upon me also" (162).

As Wordsworth expresses gratitude for the "obstinate questionings of sense and outward things" that come upon him "in a season of calm weather," Whitman writes of "curious abrupt questionings" that "stir within" him at unanticipated moments, in the midst of crowds, or on walks through the city, or in bed late at night. Using the *same* word, Whitman finds that his "questionings" serve the same purpose as Wordsworth's. They prompt him to suspect the ultimate reality of the phenomenal world and to wonder about his own relation to a cosmic whole.[14] Like Wordsworth also, Whitman is led by his "questionings" to a conviction that his existence is only a temporary separation from a primordial oceanic unity. As Wordsworth feels separated from "the immortal sea / Which brought us hither," Whitman senses, in his moments of "questioning," that he has been "struck from the float forever held in solution" (162) from which he came and to which he will return.

Although the metaphysical questionings of each poet are similar in character and function, they are positioned at significantly different points in the resolution of the problem of their respective poems. Wordsworth places his questionings, and his vision of the "immortal sea," after his meditations on the "darkness" of human experience. Whitman places his questionings, and his vision of the cosmic "float," *before* his meditations on human imperfection. Wordsworth's vision of heavenly unity is therefore presented as a contradiction and redemption of human existence. Whitman, by contrast, is able to use his vision of unity as a framework in which to assimilate the imperfections cataloged in the subsequent stanza. Believing that he has only temporarily been separated from a unity to which all human beings belong, Whitman uses his affirmation that he too "was wayward, vain, greedy, shallow, sly, cowardly, malignant" (163) as a bridge between himself and the temporally distant yet nevertheless human audience he addresses.

The very different use each poet makes of his metaphysical questionings, in relation to the problem of human limitation, illuminates a central difference between the poems that is also evident in the different way in which Whitman expresses his understanding of the nature of role playing. In his meditation on darkness, echoing Wordsworth's description of the "little actor con[ning] another part," Whitman describes how he:

Play'd the part that still looks back on the actor or actress,
The same old role, the role that is what we make it, as great as we
    like,
Or as small as we like, or both great and small. (163)

For Wordsworth, learning to play parts puts you under the yoke of the world, reducing existence to a form of imitation in which one is controlled by what one imitates. Whitman, on the other hand, describes role playing as a form of self-expression, as something one controls. It "is what we make it, as great as we like, / Or as small as we like, or both great and small" (163). Viewing roles in this way, Whitman rebuts Wordsworth's suggestion that role playing, an important part of social and particularly urban life, is an activity that alienates human beings from their essential humanity. In this way, he affirms a crucial component of modern, cosmopolitan existence. To be human, Whitman suggests, is to be fluid. It is to accept discontinuity, to be capable of imaginative empathy, and the sort of personal change that involves the appropriation of the personal traits one sees in others.

Whitman rebuts Wordsworth's notion that the authentic self is prior to experience, and is obscured by complex social interaction. The structure of this rebuttal, and the nature of his negative personal observations about Wordsworth, suggest that he is likely to have understood Wordsworth's apprehension of the "immortal sea" in "Crossing Brooklyn Ferry" as an asocial, mystic vision of something that precedes and transcends human existence. Whitman's own concept of primordial oceanic unity, while undeniably mystical and abstract, is nevertheless a concept that joins him with the crowds he sees crossing on the Fulton Ferry and those that he imagines will cross centuries after he is dead. The "float forever held in solution" is an explicitly human entity, and Whitman's conception of immortality is, consequently, a human one as well. Whitman anticipates survival in the consciousness of others, who share his humanity, his city, and his river.

In the final section of their poems, Whitman and Wordsworth triumphantly describe a sunset. The passage of time has not been arrested and the distance between the poet and his ostensible audience has not been overcome. Yet each poet looks out upon a world of "splendor" and "glory," in which the sun, however, may be expected to set. In the final section of each poem, the acceptance of the world of transient phenomena is expressed in the form of a recapitulation of the catalog of objects originally presented in the third section of each poem. In this recapitulation, however, the poet's verbal relation to the objects has been altered to reflect what has been accomplished in the course of the meditation. The birds and lambs mentioned in the third section of the "Immortality Ode" are addressed by Wordsworth at his poem's conclusion in the following lines: "Then sing, ye Birds, sing, sing a joyous song! / And let the young Lambs bound / as to the tabor's sound!" (4,284). The river, clouds, crowds, and cities described in the third section of "Crossing Brooklyn Ferry" are addressed by Whitman in the following way:

> Flow on, river! flow with the flood-tide, and ebb with the ebb-tide!
> Frolic on, crested and scallop'd-edg'd waves!
> Gorgeous clouds of the sunset! drench with your splendor me, or the men and women generations after me!
> Cross from shore to shore, countless crowds of passengers!
> Stand up tall masts of Manhattan! stand up, beautiful hills of Brooklyn! (164)

In each poem, the tone has shifted from meditative observation to enthusiastic exhortation. The reasons for these shifts are similar. Each poet
believes that the meditative process represented in his poem has enabled
him to view certain ephemeral objects as conduits to eternity. Each poem
ends with a dramatic assertion of this realization, which, in each case, is
a revolutionary challenge to the hierarchical understanding of objects
prevalent in the culture and poetry of their time. Wordsworth writes:
"To me the meanest flower that blows can give / Thoughts that do often
lie too deep for tears." Whitman, addressing his "dumb, beautiful ministers" writes: "You furnish your parts toward eternity, / Great or small,
you furnish your parts toward the soul" (165).

Whitman concludes "Crossing Brooklyn Ferry" with an abstract recapitulation of his accomplishment. The objects are greeted at the end
of a long wait. Having been treated with contempt for so long, they
may now be received with free, presumably unprejudiced sense. Asserting that the objects will no longer be able to foil those who would
receive them, Whitman claims to have found a way of establishing intimacy with that which has always been thought to withhold itself. This
claim of the possibility of intimacy becomes the basis of his assertion,
near the end of the poem, that urban life is intrinsically the most spiritual
form of life. In his concluding exhortation, he writes:

> Thrive, cities – bring your freight, bring your shows, ample and
>   sufficient rivers,
> Expand, being than which none else is perhaps more spiritual,
> Keep your places, objects than which none else is more lasting. (165)

In these lines, the poet urges the cities to thrive. He tells the rivers to
bring its freight and shows, feeding the cities with substance so that they
may respond to his next exhortation, to "expand." Expanding and thriving, the cities are that "than which none else is perhaps more spiritual."[15]
The objects that fill them, conventionally scorned by poets, are that "than
which none else is more lasting."

Laying the groundwork for a conception of urban spirituality, Whitman accepts precisely those qualities of urban life that, according to the
romantic poets, made it antithetical to poetic or spiritual experience.
Unlike Wordsworth, who felt that the incomprehensible multiplicity and
transience of urban impressions caused the city to appear to be terrifyingly
unreal, a "second-sight procession," Whitman imaginatively embraces
crowds that are explicitly referred to as consisting of fleeting and "un-
fathomed" surfaces. In fact, Whitman's sense of the world as a "necessary
film" of "appearances" is an important component of his ecstasy and
power at the end of the poem. As he writes in "Song of the Open Road,"
the "certainty of the reality and immortality of things," the goal of

"Crossing Brooklyn Ferry," is not something immediately visible in reality but something "provoke[d] . . . out of the soul" by "the float of the sight of things" (152). His language, in these assertions, specifically stresses the sufficiency of the insubstantial. The modern world of un-fathomed and fleeting images is sufficient, because consciousness can provide what it lacks. As Whitman asserts at the conclusion of "Crossing Brooklyn Ferry," the objects of the harbor are not themselves lasting, but they may be "used." They are not eternal but may "furnish their parts towards eternity."

When Whitman, in the final lines of "Crossing Brooklyn Ferry" ad-dresses his "dumb, beautiful ministers," and expresses his intention to "plant you permanently within us," acknowledging that "We fathom you not – we love you" (165), he expresses the same tongue-tied fas-cination he experienced in Plumbe's gallery. In "Crossing Brooklyn Ferry," as in a photograph, everything has been taken in and nothing has been "fathomed." As ı unified spectacle of sequential images – "glo-ries strung like beads on my smallest sights and hearings" (160) – crowd and the surrounding objects in this poem recall Lamb's "multitudinous moving picture" or what Pierce Egan sees with his "camera obscura," or Dickens with his "magic lantern." Like these and other flaneurs, Whitman sees the very insubstantiality of objects, as they are experienced in a modern city, as an opportunity rather than as a reason to experience a mystified alienation. His urban epiphany is therefore related to the general tendency of the culture of modernity to suggest that one does not need to understand something in order to bond with it, that art and experience do not have to be coherent.

Yet in the way in which he emphasizes the sufficiency of the image, Whitman is moving toward something very different from the flaneur's traditional celebration of the fecundity of images. Whitman's formulation of modernity preserves the notion of depth behind things, of time as a poignant reality rather than the self-destroying medium through which the pageant of late capitalism moves. By describing the process by which he has come to "love" what he plants inside him, he moves beyond the arrest of interpretation. He is coaxed by the silence of faces into an intimation of mortality that eventually expands into an emotion of com-passionate empathy with everything that is transient.

In this way, Whitman swerves from an acceptance of the full conse-quences of postmodern discontinuity and freedom from signification, possibilities that still remain present in his entire enterprise. In his swerve, he resists the modern phenomenology Barthes associates with photog-raphy, the phenomenology of "no depth." He preserves the concept of an identity in the midst of a spectacle that threatens to overwhelm it. His new phenomenology of urban experience still posits a distance between the observing consciousness and what is observed, except that the process that structures this distance, and the distance that is preserved within the object as sign, is no longer the process of interpretation. It is an indefinite emotional charge, not the definite, yet unconvincing illusion of a reading. It is a link, an "electric cord that vibrates" between transient consciousness and transient extension, between the living and the dead, between the unfathoming and the unfathomed. Ultimately Whitman replaces the spectatorship of the flaneur with the undiscriminating gaze of a camera endowed with an ability to love what it cannot gain access to.

In "Crossing Brooklyn Ferry," Whitman is not so much concerned with representing the city as he is with representing what might be done with it. He appears to have had great plans for the "spiritual" urban spectatorship he describes in the poem. The paradigm of visual interaction with crowds developed in this poem appears also in the utopian poems Whitman wrote shortly after "Crossing Brooklyn Ferry." In several of the "Calamus" poems, and in some of the "Drum-Taps" poems as well,[16] Whitman explores the possibility of using what he had worked out in "Crossing Brooklyn Ferry" as the basis of a comprehensive poetic, spiritual, political, and erotic system suited to the conditions of modern urban life.

In the 1876 preface to the centennial edition of *Leaves of Grass* and *Two Rivulets*, Whitman offers an explanation of a strand that runs through his poetry.

> The special meaning of the "Calamus" cluster of *Leaves of Grass* (and more or less running through that book, and cropping out in "Drum-Taps,") mainly resides in its political significance. In my opinion it is a fervent, accepted development of comradeship, the beautiful and sane affection of man for man, latent in all the young fellows, north and south, east and west – it is by this, I say, and by what goes directly and indirectly along with it, that the United States of the future, (I cannot too often repeat,) are to be most effectually welded together, intercalated, anneal'd into a living Union. (*Prose Works*, 2:471)

In this and in other passages in his prose, Whitman claims to have adapted the phrenological concept of "adhesiveness" in such a way that it can provide the emotional and spiritual basis that democracy appears to lack. This elaborate justification for the "Calamus" series has usually been ignored in the twentieth century as a cover for the homoeroticism of the poems. While I certainly do not deny that his justifications may have served this purpose, I wish to refocus attention on Whitman's insistence that "Calamus" love is spiritual, and that it has great potential usefulness for a democratic community.[17] Whitman, I suggest, tried to use the energy of his sexuality to formulate a utopian image of social harmony that would have many of the same virtues as the panoramic image of the city in the writings of the flaneur, but would not involve some of the limitations of the flaneur's city. The "City of Friends" projected in the "Calamus" poems would be as much of a friendly spectacle as the city of the flaneur, and it would achieve certain of the utopian and mesmeric goals of characters in *The Blithedale Romance*, but it would not involve the personal isolation associated with these imaginative projects, nor would it involve the denial of time and mortality that requires the flaneur to assume a tone of genial superficiality. Whitman's theoretical formulation of the "Calamus" love in the 1876 preface offers a retrospective description of a project that begins at least as early as the "Sun-Down Poem" of the first edition and that continues through the "Calamus" poems of the third edition and into the "Drum-Taps" series: the project of turning the power of the experience of observing crowds into the emotional and phenomenological basis of a specifically urban form of spirituality, a specifically urban form of poetry, and a specifically urban concept of community.

In Whitman's plan for the 1860 edition of *Leaves of Grass*, in which both series of poems first appeared, the "Calamus" poems are paired with the "Children of Adam" poems. The main ostensible distinction between these series is that the former is a celebration of the love of man and the latter is a celebration of the love of woman. There are, however, several other consistent distinctions. As Whitman affirms in "Scented Herbage of My Breast," the "Calamus" sensibility and "Calamus" love, like the imaginative strategies of "Crossing Brooklyn Ferry," are a response to an awareness of time, death, and loss. Whitman writes: "Oh I think it is not for life I am chanting here my chant, of lovers / I think it must be for death" (114). Chanting for death, Whitman is aware of doing so in a way different from that of the Romantic poets he refers to in the fragment quoted earlier. "Through me," he writes, "shall the words be said to make death exhilarating" (115).

The effort to make death exhilarating is appropriate to the "Calamus" poems because the experience of "Calamus" love is generally characterized as an experience of loss. The moment of the expression of love in the "Calamus" sequence is often an encounter with a stranger that is simultaneously a parting from him. This experience, which is particularly characteristic of an urban environment, is what forces the "Calamus" sensibility to question the reality of the phenomenal world and to seek something more permanent behind it. Several of the "Calamus" poems are expressions of the sort of "questionings" that lead, in "Crossing Brooklyn Ferry," to an intimation of unity behind the world of transient phenomena. In "Scented Herbage of My Breast," Whitman addresses death as a possible transcendental unity, expressing his curiosity about the "purports essential / That you hide in these shifting forms of life, for reasons, and that they are mainly for you, / That you beyond them come forth to remain, the real reality, / That behind the mask of materials you patiently wait, no matter how long . . . that you will perhaps dissipate this entire show of appearance" (115). Several of the poems in the "Calamus" sequence, notably "Of the Terrible Doubt of Appearances," "The Base of All Metaphysics," and "Are You the New Person Drawn toward Me," also deal with, even if they resolve, a questioning of the ontological nature of the phenomenal world.

In the "Children of Adam" poems, there is no such metaphysical questioning. On the contrary, at several points in "Children of Adam," Whitman asserts the absolute sufficiency of the phenomenal world while celebrating the form of sexuality that enables its continuance. As he writes in "I Sing the Body Electric": "I have perceived that to be with those I like is enough, / To stop in company with the rest at evening is enough, / To be surrounded by beautiful, curious, breathing, laughing flesh is enough" (96). Although there is a similar assertion of sufficiency in "Of the Terrible Doubt of Appearances," that assertion is presented in the context of "questionings." In the unabashedly physical "Children of Adam" poems, these questionings and doubts never arise. Because of this unfallen rather than redeemed sense of sufficiency, the "Children of Adam" poems never lead to the intimation of unity that, in "Crossing Brooklyn Ferry" and the "Calamus" poems, recontextualizes the recognition of mortality and loss.

Less involved with death and transience, the "amative" love celebrated in the "Children of Adam" poems is intrinsically less spiritual than the "adhesive" love celebrated in the "Calamus" sequence. It has its basis in what is represented as a natural instinct leading directly to the continuation of life. It does not involve, as "Calamus" love does, intellectual or spiritual perceptions that are responses to the encounter with death and absence. This distinction between the two forms of love is expressed in its most condensed form in a poem in the "Calamus" sequence entitled "Fast Anchor'd Eternal O Love!" (135). In this brief poem, the love of woman is described as "anchor'd, eternal . . . resistless," and in the original version, "primeval." A "resistless" form of love, characterized at several points in the sequence as "gnawing," amative love is an appetite, which, being "primeval," must be satisfied. It is, as Whitman makes clear throughout the sequence, physical in nature and procreative in function. "Separate" from this sort of love is the "love of man," which Whitman, following the *Symposium*, considers to be more "ethereal."

The love of man is not "anchor'd" or "eternal" but "roving." It involves an "ascent" to "float in regions" figuratively situated above those of the love of woman.

As Whitman represents them, these different forms of love are necessarily suited to different milieus. The settings of the "Children of Adam" poems are virtually always rural. Although it is impossible to determine the nature of the setting of most of the "Calamus" poems, most of those that do have an identifiable setting are urban – for example, "City of Orgies," "Behold This Swarthy Face," "I Dream'd in a Dream," "What Think You I Take My Pen in Hand?," "A Glimpse," "A Leaf for Hand in Hand," and "Among the Multitude." In the "Drum-Taps" poem, "Give Me the Splendid Silent Sun," in which he offers his most explicit statement of the distinctions between adhesive love and amative love, he subsumes all of these distinctions under a larger distinction, between urban and rural life.

In the first section of "Give Me the Splendid Silent Sun," Whitman celebrates the fecundity of the natural world, with its fruits and grains, flowers and animals. The form of love appropriate to such a world is expressed in the following lines:

> Give me for marriage a sweet-breath'd woman of whom I
>   should never tire,
> Give me a perfect child, give me away from the noise of the
>   world a perfect domestic life,
> Give me to warble spontaneous songs recluse by myself, for my
>   own ears only,
> Give me solitude, give me Nature, give me again O Nature
>   your primal sanities! (312)

Here is the "anchor'd eternal" love of "Children of Adam," an isolated family homestead, and a creativity that thrives, not on the mesmeric pleasures of imaginative contact with crowds of phantoms, but on solitude and the "primal sanities" of Nature.

As soon as he presents this rural idyll, however, Whitman rejects it for himself. "Still," he says, "I adhere to my city," because the city alone has the capacity not to satisfy the body, but "to make me glutted, enrich'd of soul." Only the city gives him "forever faces." In the urban section of the poem, Whitman asks the city to provide the things he apparently values it for:

> Give me faces and streets – give me these phantoms incessant
>   and endless along the trottoirs!
> Give me interminable eyes – give me women – give me comrades

and lovers by the thousand!
Let me see new ones every day – let me hold new ones by the
   hand every day!
Give me such shows–give me the streets of Manhattan! (313)

At the end of the poem, after having conjured an image of his beloved
city at a pitch of war enthusiasm it probably never experienced, Whitman
offers his final celebration:

Manhattan crowds, with their turbulent musical chorus!
Manhattan faces and eyes forever for me. (314)

In "Give Me the Splendid, Silent Sun," as in the "Calamus" poems,
and as in "Crossing Brooklyn Ferry," the objects of the poet's love are
the faces and eyes of a crowd of swiftly passing strangers. In the "Children
of Adam" poems, all body parts can be used to express a supremely
physical love. The chief organs of adhesive love, however, are eyes.
Whitman formulates this connection between eyes and adhesive love as
early as "Song of the Open Road," published in the second (1856) edition.
In that poem, he writes:

Here is adhesiveness, it is not previously fashioned, it is apropos;
Do you know what it is as you pass to be loved by strangers?
Do you know the talk of those turning eyeballs? (153)

In several of the "Calamus" poems, particularly "City of Orgies," "To
a Stranger," and "Among the Multitude," the most characteristic experience of love is an act of silent gazing into the eyes of an unparticu-
larized stranger with whom one is somehow mysteriously and
magnetically intimate. As Whitman represents his conception of this
intimacy, it appears to be closely related to and presumably has developed
out of the specular and photographic model of interaction with crowds
presented in "Crossing Brooklyn Ferry."

In "City of Orgies," Whitman asserts that what he values most about
his beloved Manhattan is its "frequent and swift flash of eyes offering
me love, / Offering response to my own" (126). The eyes of lovers are
explicitly preferred, in the poem, to the "pageants," "tableaus," "spectacles," and "processions" of city life. This assertion, and the rural setting
of "In Paths Untrodden," have caused many readers to understand the
"Calamus" sequence as a kind of rejection of urban life, as a mature
recognition that individual intimacy is preferable to the attractive, yet
comparatively superficial pleasures of urban spectatorship.[18] It seems to
me, however, that Whitman, in his poems about eyes in the midst of
crowds, is not talking about intimacy in any sense in which we conventionally understand it. Whitman's lovers are never particularized. They

are undifferentiated "eyes," encountered in "frequent and swift" flashes. When he expresses love for someone, it is not because he has at last freed himself from the crowd and can retreat from the world to experience true intimacy, but because he has reduced the crowd to a synechdoche, to an impersonal individual who is almost always described as having been abstracted from the crowd. Such an individual, as Whitman unfailingly describes him, differs from a Whitmanian crowd only in that he is an individual rather than a collectivity. As a representative of that collectivity, such a lover is the temporary focus of a love that is actually directed toward the entire collectivity. Whitman therefore refers to this form of love as "roving," as experienced in "frequent and swift" visual "flash[es]." "Roving," not "anchored," it can be transferred rapidly and easily from one phantom gaze to another. Because of its nonexclusive nature, "Calamus" love is a cosmopolitan love. It is directed toward a city of lovers or, as Whitman refers to it in "I Dream'd in a Dream," a "new city of Friends" (133). As comprehensive as the faculty of sight, "Calamus" love is a more emotionally charged version of the classic gaze of the flaneur. It is urban spectatorship magnified with affective energy. It is, in other words, the new form of emotional, noninterpretive urban spectatorship that emerges from "Crossing Brooklyn Ferry."

When "Calamus" lovers do have some form of physical contact, as in such poems as "These I Singing in Spring," "For You O Democracy," and "A Leaf for Hand in Hand," they generally hold hands or place arms around each others' necks. These forms of contact, which are entirely different from the forms of physical joining described in the "Children of Adam" series, may also have a fundamentally visual relevance. To place an arm around the neck of a lover, or to walk hand in hand with him, is to join gazes, to look out at the world from a joined perspective. Even if such contact differs from gazing into the eyes of the lover, it is still a form of love experienced in a shared gaze. The eyes of the lover are not a mirror in such an interaction, but they are imagined to be seeing what the other lover sees as well. There is therefore a similar, if not identical, unification.

In the "Calamus" poems, lovers do not speak to each other. Their love does not require speech and could even be thwarted by it. Whitman never addresses the eyes he encounters. In the poem "To a Stranger" (127), for example, Whitman and a "passing" stranger "flit by each other," swiftly exchanging a glance. In spite of the brevity and superficiality of their contact, Whitman is convinced that they share a profound spiritual affinity, an intimacy of such intensity that speech would mar it. It can only be imagined. "I am not to speak to you," he writes. Rather he turns the lover's face into an image that can be summoned in solitude: "I am to think of you when I sit alone or wake at night alone, / I am to wait, I do not doubt I am to meet you again, / I am to see to it that I do not lose you." This insistence upon silence, as part of the process by which the lover is reduced to an image, recalls Whitman's characteristic description of crowds as consisting of "mute" "phantoms."

By not particularizing his lovers, and by asserting that intimacy can be attained without speech and in the space of a moment, Whitman imagines a form of love suited to the conditions of urban life, a form of love that can be enjoyed with strangers who emerge "out of the rolling ocean the crowd" (106).[19] The interaction that originates in a brief exchange of glances is, like the taking of a photograph, the origin of a more permanent interaction with an "ethereal" image. The power of this intimacy, however, depends upon the fact that what is appropriated in this way has no definable content that would resist the infusion of the appropriating gaze. Encountering "mute" "phantoms" lacking an ability to resist his infusion, Whitman experiences the existential satisfaction of "fathoming" what he sees without claiming to have actually "fathomed" it. What he takes in with his gaze is not read because its potential otherness is not even acknowledged. Unlike the sort of flaneur who controls a highly differentiated multiplicity by organizing it with a typology, Whitman dreams of reducing a crowd to coherence by imagining that it consists of unified and undifferentiated comrades. His goal is utopian, as he acknowledges in the 1876 preface and in such "Calamus" poems as "I Hear It Was Charged Against Me," "The Prairie-Grass Dividing," "A Promise to California," "A Leaf for Hand in Hand," "I Dream'd in a Dream," "To the East and to the West," and the discarded poem "States!" In this respect, it resembles the goal of the Blithedale community, which also attempted to create unity by obliterating individual differences. As was the case with the utopian ideals of Blithedale, there is a disturbing resemblance between Whitman's utopian ideal and Coverdale's complacent assumption of intimacy with an urban population he has reduced to "toy-people of German manufacture."

In a strand of his poetry beginning with "Crossing Brooklyn Ferry" and extending through a number of poems in the "Calamus" and "Drum Taps" series, Whitman tried to convert a kind of freedom and power experienced by a detached spectator in a populous city into a new form of spiritual experience. In a quasi-mystical moment of union with crowds, or with lovers abstracted from their midst, he believed that it was possible to enjoy a preeminently visual form of love that could be the basis of a new social bond appropriate to the conditions of urban life. What makes it difficult to accept Whitman's effort to turn some traditional features of urban spectatorship into a viable basis for new forms of community and spirituality is his apparent innocence of the degree to which his ideal visual love retains the narcissistic characteristics of panoptic spectatorship. Whitman's gaze, as much as that of any flaneur, is an inscribing one. It is powerful; it is unique within its "sphere"; and it reduces everything in sight to subjection. Satisfied with the order he observes in his "vast" panoramic "sweeps," satisfied with the receptiveness of "phantom" faces to whatever meanings he chooses to "pour" into them, satisfied with his freedom and detachment in the midst of so much life, Whitman's poetic persona combines all of the traditional poses of the flaneur.

The failure of Whitman's urban poetry may suggest the degree to which, for all of his originality, Whitman could not transcend the limitations of what was in mid-nineteenth-century America the most familiar mode of favorable urban representation. For all that he was able to see more to value in urban life than his contemporaries, Whitman, like others of his time, was unable to turn toward the crowd a gaze that could accept the reality of its otherness, that desired to reduce it to neither insubstantiality nor coherence. The inability of nineteenth-century spectators to look at crowds with a questioning rather than an imperial gaze is one of the many human tragedies of that century. Of the authors I have considered, only Hawthorne seriously attempted to elucidate the dehumanizing structures of power embedded in such gazes. Yet Hawthorne was unable to offer an alternate mode of urbanism to a civilization that, as he himself recognized, could not "return" to a pastoral ideal. Whitman at least tried to offer a theory of how it might be possible to live in the midst of crowds of strangers. He sought to provide an alternative to the reactionary and fastidious disgust that so many of his contemporaries felt in the metropolis. This effort is laudable and much of Whitman's urban poetry is unquestionably impressive. His urbanism is, however, marred by the panopticism of his age.

Chapter 9

Conclusion

In the works of three of the most important American writers of the nineteenth century, there are spectators who look out upon an urban space and respond to it as if it were a coherent and infinitely entertaining spectacle. At some point in the texts in which they appear, each of these spectators is serenely confident of his ability to interpret everything he sees and to gain access to the consciousness of everyone he observes. Bathing in a stream of benign impressions, preserving at all times a sense of power and inviolability, each of these observers resembles a social type who figures prominently, even if he is only elliptically defined, in some of the writings of Charles Baudelaire and his twentieth-century critic, Walter Benjamin. They are flaneurs, American versions of a Parisian figure in whom Baudelaire and Benjamin found a paradigm for the consciousness produced by the experience of "modernity."

The preceding discussion has its foundation in the conception of the flaneur that is implicit in Baudelaire writings and Benjamin's critical treatment of them. Like these authors, I have assumed that the flaneur represents a historically significant accommodation of the bourgeoisie to the urban, cosmopolitan world they were creating. I have also assumed a relation between the consciousness of the flaneur and the cultural forms with which nineteenth-century capitalist society represented itself to itself, in panoramas, arcades, department stores, and world expositions. Finally, I have assumed that, as a spectator of a rapid succession of diverse signs and images, the flaneur is an early anticipation of a form of consciousness that is often considered characteristic of the twentieth century.

Although I have based my discussion upon Benjamin's understanding of the flaneur as a historical figure, I have tried to expand, modify, and contextualize this understanding. I have taken issue with Benjamin's representation of the flaneur's influence as extremely local and extremely brief. For if the flaneur is understood in the way Benjamin himself suggests, then his origins can be found long before the 1830s and his influence

186

can be found in many places other than Paris. This urban spectator, this paradigm of "modernity," was at least as influential in England as he was in France. What is more, the process of his development begins as early as the turn of the seventeenth century and is intimately associated with the progress of the historical forces that are generally understood to have produced modernity: urbanization, the development of consumer society, the cultural ascendancy of the bourgeoisie, and the development of modern techniques of image production.

As early as the beginning of the seventeenth century, London was able to support a thriving embryonic consumer culture, as well as a diverse literature of urban spectatorship, possibly stimulated by the existence of spaces for the viewing and display of people and goods. By the early eighteenth century, London's literature of urban spectatorship included works written with all of what Benjamin identifies as the most prominent features of the literature of the flaneur. As a development of typological and panoramic strands in earlier urban literature, and as a gentlemanly reaction against contemporary genres that presented the city as a chaotic and illegible carnival, the flaneur was an important component of the eighteenth-century periodical essay tradition. By the beginning of the nineteenth century, the flaneur's genial, consumer's aestheticism had largely displaced the moralism with which it had coexisted in the writings of the periodical essayists. Reflecting a particular accommodation of the bourgeoisie to the world they were creating, the posture and strategies of the flaneur had become the dominant framework for the representation of London in the most prominent English periodicals. As such, they became a crucial part of the context in which new forms of urban representation developed in the nineteenth century. New genres, like the detective story and "mysteries" serial, and new urban literary perspectives, like those of Dickens, Baudelaire, and Balzac, developed in relation and response to the flaneur and what he was understood to represent.

Because the flaneur was ubiquitous in the periodicals of England and France in the early and middle nineteenth century, he was, inevitably, an important presence in the highly derivative metropolitan culture of the United States in this period. Although America, before the Civil War, did not yet have a metropolis comparable with those of Europe, it was, culturally speaking, very much a part of the civilization that produced the flaneur. As their own cities grew and as their own metropolitan culture began to develop, Americans read the writings of European, and particularly English flaneurs. By the late 1830s, and certainly by the 1840s, the United States had produced flaneurs of its own, urban journalists who expressed the cosmopolitan aspirations of a committedly commercial and rapidly urbanizing nation. Each of the three major authors I have treated in this discussion were familiar with the English and American tradition of the flaneur. In the works of all three, there are significant encounters with the flaneur and his characteristic ways of looking at and representing cities. By engaging the assumptions that were common in the urban spectatorial literature of their time, these authors dealt with issues that American authors are not generally thought to have confronted before the Civil War. Representing the act of urban spectatorship, Poe, Hawthorne, and Whitman explored the question of what cities do to consciousness and what consciousness may in turn do with the city. Each offers a different analysis of the process of urban spectatorship and each has a different understanding of the opportunities created by such spectatorship for consciousness and art. In the case of all three authors, the encounter with the spectatorial processes associated with the flaneur reveals a great deal about their understanding of modern urban civilization and the type of literature that can be created in it.

In his story "The Man of the Crowd," Poe's encounter with the flaneur takes the form of a complex critique that leads to his invention of a new kind of urban observer. By transforming the flaneur into the detective, Poe expanded the possible scope of urban literary consumption in response to changes that were taking place in the public's understanding of the nature of the city. Hawthorne's encounter with the flaneur gave intellectual form to several of his most enigmatic sketches and romances. In these, it is possible to trace a sophisticated examination of the assumptions of cosmopolitan urban culture, an examination whose ambivalence and contradictions reflect those of Hawthorne's own relation to the life of his time. Whitman, who had himself been one of the most active flaneurs in the New York press, tried to adapt the flaneur's spectatorial posture for poetic use. By adding an emotional dimension and a consciousness of time to the flaneur's panoramic arrest of time, he self-consciously set out to develop a new kind of urban poetry, a new kind of urban spirituality, and ultimately a new kind of urban love suited to serve as the glue of democracy.

In their encounters with the dominant mode of literary urban spectatorship in the magazines they read and in some cases wrote, each of these authors confronted the problems involved in representing urban modernity. Each of them illuminates, depending upon his particular emphasis, the complacency, shallowness, and obtuse selectivity of the flaneur. The texts produced by these critical encounters are impressive literary works, as well as fascinating and significant cultural documents. Yet as I review their accomplishments, and contemplate the extraordinary spectacle and subject the nineteenth-century city must have presented to those who saw and lived in it, I cannot help but feel a certain disappointment that American authors in the first half of the nineteenth century could not have come up with something more than they did.

Although it is true that Poe's encounter with urban modernity enables him to invent what would become an extraordinary popular urban literary form, he really accomplishes little more than the joining together of a journalistic fiction about the perpetual menace of urban life with a rehabilitation of a preposterous illusion of its legibility. Hawthorne offers a challenging critique of cosmopolitanism, but as someone committed to cosmopolitanism as a valuable modern perspective, I find myself, like Henry James, lamenting the fact that the part of Hawthorne that could assemble this critique was in the end stronger than the part of him that was drawn to what he was criticizing. Of these three authors, Whitman is the one who appears to be most openly committed to the imaginative embrace of urban life. He did indeed write a maddeningly small amount of moving and generous urban poetry. Yet because, like many in his century, he could only imagine being reconciled to an "other" if its otherness were in some way reduced, the man who is considered America's greatest nineteenth-century urban poet often wrote about his glorious Mannahatta as a sort of puree: swirling, indefinite, and easy to digest. Impressive as their work is, none of these authors, I feel, provides a literature that rises to the challenges or takes advantage of the opportunities presented by the experience of the American city in the first half of the nineteenth century.

I recognize, of course, that the assumptions that underly my disappointment are entirely subjective. Still, I would love to open a book written by a nineteenth-century American and find an exploration of what Hawthorne said he loved: "all of the nooks and crannies of cities." I would love to encounter a catalog and pageant of all of the glorious junk that filled the nineteenth century and that one now stumbles over in a flea market. I would love to find the volume of rich urban particularity that one feels one should find in Whitman's poetry, but that only emerges in a few sections of a few poems. I would love to read a mid-nineteenth-century American panorama of city life, one that did justice to the complexity and density of that life as it was lived by all kinds of people, as it can now be reconstructed from historical, journalistic, and popular cultural records. I find that I am moved by what I imagine of this lost world, as I am rarely moved by what survives to record it, and I cannot conclude this discussion without confessing to my disappointment.

Part of what I feel, I acknowledge, is the inevitable disappointment of one age with another. Authors in the nineteenth century record what they think is important, not what I would find important looking back at them. What puzzles me in this case is the fact that many, particularly in the journalism of the early nineteenth century, were calling for a literature that would have represented what I want to see. In France, Baudelaire celebrated the possibility of painters of "modernity," of the ephemeral moment, artists sensitive to the qualities of modern urban daily life that distinguished it from the daily life of earlier periods and would distinguish it from the daily life of later ones. Cornelius Mathews, Nathaniel Parker Willis, George Foster, and a few of the writers in the *Knickerbocker* called for an American version of this literature. France, in the mid-nineteenth century, produced numerous "painters of modern life" who are still of interest today. Yet where are the American artists of modernity? Did they exist and simply not end up in the canon? From what I have been able to find, there were quite a few writers, Mathews, Willis, and Foster among them, who tried to provide an American literature of urban modernity. In my judgment, however, they failed, through sheer lack of literary talent, to write anything that modern readers are likely to want to read for any reason other than historical curiosity. Even if they were better than they are, these urban writers would have difficulty leaping from the microfilm into the canon because, as flaneurs, the conventions that shape their work would make them appear bizarre and implausible to most modern readers. Most of the Americans, then, who attempted to write a self-consciously urban and urbane literature in this period remain buried in the journalistic records, where the ephemerality of what they represent, the ephemerality of their genre, and the ephemerality of the medium in which they wrote consign them to a triple oblivion.

In France, Benjamin suggests, the attention to urban ephemera in the *flaneries* of the *feuilletons* helped to stimulate Baudelaire's poetic explorations of Paris. In England, as I argue in Chapter 2, the tradition of the flaneur provided a similar seedbed out of which could grow the panoramic urban narratives of Dickens. In America, as my book tries to establish, there was a similar process through which fascinating responses to urban modernity developed out of encounters with the urbanism of the flaneurs. In America, however, although we do have Whitman, we do not have a Dickens or a Baudelaire, a Balzac or a Dostoievsky. Furthermore, Whitman stands alone. Unlike his European contemporaries, he is not a part of a thick tradition of literary urbanism. Of course, it is possible that our lack of an impressive urban literary tradition before 1860 is simply due to the accidents and vagaries of literary production. It is never possible to fully account for the absence of a certain kind of literature. It is possible, however, that what I have been considering in this discussion may help to explain the absence, in mid-nineteenth-century America, of the kind of literature I would like to find.

As I try to account for what I feel is the failure of American writers in the mid-nineteenth century to rise to the occasion of representing the nineteenth-century city, I find myself grudgingly acknowledging the validity, up to a point, of one of the assumptions I have been trying to challenge. Although, as I continue to maintain, American culture as a whole has never been as hostile or as indifferent to cities as has often been assumed, the strength of antiurban traditions in America, in the city and in the country, has hampered the development of the kind of literature I am looking for. What America lacks, to a greater degree than other urbanized nations, is a discourse of urbanism, a permanent and ongoing tradition of valuing cities, as places to live or as objects of contemplation. For all of his drawbacks, the flaneur provided a possible foundation for such a discourse. He existed in America and he was popular in America. To a limited degree, he still survives, in the happy weekend window-shopper's tone of certain travel books and in the parts of newspapers and magazines devoted to facilitating the consumption of the city. Yet when the interactions described in this book took place, when the flaneur's mode of observing and representing cities was revised by writers looking for new modes, the flaneur's urbanism was discarded along with his inadequacies. No alternate mode of urbanism developed to take its place. Whitman attempted to provide a new urbanism, but his influence was virtually nonexistent until the twentieth century, and even in the twentieth century, it can hardly be said to be a dominant American mode of looking at cities. Lacking an urbanism, what Americans produced in the nineteenth century is a body of urban literature that either tries to exploit the spectacle of urban misery for the purposes of consumption or that tries to squeeze the richness of modern urban experience into tired and simple biblical and classical formulas or newer, though equally tired and simple Romantic truisms. In spite of some wonderful, brief splashes of twentieth-century urbanism, in poets like Hart Crane and Frank O'Hara, and in a substantial number of autobiographical memoirs and (interestingly) autobiographical novels, these principles continue to have a preponderant influence on American urban literature. This has been a misfortune, for our literature, for our national culture, and for our cities.

It is beyond the scope of this book to deal with the causes and products of what I consider to be a tremendous failure of the imagination. I can only, in conclusion, register my own fatigue with what seem to me to be the reigning assumptions that have, since the mid-nineteenth century, prevented the development of an American discourse of urbanism. We are, first of all, still stuck with the conception of everyday urban life in response to which Poe invented the detective, a conception that – as much as the conception contained within the panoramas, dioramas, and sketches of the flaneur – is a self-validating system, created for commercial purposes, with only a highly mediated relation to the experience it is supposed to represent. The understanding of the city as a place of intolerable menace does not reflect, as Benjamin believes it does, the fear and horror of those who first saw the urban crowd. It reflects a specific change in the relation of the bourgeoisie to the experience of the crowd that took place, for commercial journalistic reasons, at a time when the crowds that had existed for some time were actually becoming in many respects less menacing.

This view of the city as a horrifying place, where the most spectacular anomalies are imagined to constitute or at least emblematize "everyday life in the city," is such a successful basis for a commercial culture of urban images that it makes any other conception of the city seem naive and inaccurate. The negative quality of this image, the ease with which it can attach itself to a specious moral component, obscures the fact that as much as the flaneur, it is geared toward the process of consumption. It cynically takes advantage of and revels in the fact that if one lives within reasonable proximity to ten or even twenty million people, something atrocious is likely to happen within that space with reasonable frequency. This sells a lot of newspapers and makes a lot of people watch the local news. Projected onto the national culture, this conception of metropolitan life is the premise of the cop shows, crime movies, and crime novels that form a substantial part of American popular culture. At the same time it is the foundation for "serious" literature addressed to an audience that is conditioned by its education to expect its juicy and interesting urban images to be placed in a "responsible," morally disapproving framework that defines the city as a locus of rot, corruption, alienation, violation, paralysis, incoherence, discontinuity, selfishness, cupidity, and so on. The product of these parallel cultures is a distressingly common conception of cities (and particularly New York, the city that has the greatest claim to being considered America's metropolis) as demon worlds of alienated otherness, as places where no "sane" person can manage a coherent life, be moral, courteous, or happy.

It is difficult for the flaneur, or any other form of urbanism to take root in such a climate. Any kind of equanimity or accommodation to the conditions of urban life is immediately suspect, as a form of "deadened" sensibility or moral callousness. In the modernist tradition of American urban writing, extending from Eliot, Dreiser, and Dos Passos to Bellow and McInerney, the city is not something you're supposed to reach an accommodation with. It makes you worse. It's what's bad about modern life. Within this framework, the modern idea of the menacing city is united with ancient archetypal ways of thinking about cities. In so much modern American discourse, the city is represented as if it had a mythic life, identity, and self-determination of its own, as if it were in some way responsible for the violence, suffering, and immorality that can be encountered within it, as if its problems were not the result of complex social forces but part of the intrinsic nature of the "metropolis," the just deserts of an ancient and un-American blight upon a pristine American landscape. A distressingly large proportion of well-educated Americans, in the nineteenth and twentieth centuries, have given credence to the idea that peace of mind can only be attained in the modern world by fleeing the city, by abandoning any responsibility toward it, as if America really could function just as well as a Jeffersonian network of happy little farms and villages. If we had a viable tradition of urbanism, if we had a tradition of believing that the health and stability of our commercial, industrial, and cultural centers were a serious matter of national concern, as serious as the issue of the health of our natural environment, it is possible that we would have healthier cities, cities that would not, in their worst moments, lend credence to a paralyzing pastoralist nostalgia.

Paradoxically and tragically, American antiurbanism has helped to produce a society that depends upon the existence of the metropolis, and yet is conceptually unprepared to encompass the experience of it. Although few people in modern America would willingly dispense with the advantages of modernity, the fundamental assumptions of our culture remain hostile to even the most unavoidable conditions of modernity. Just as we are still dealing with the conception of cities that provoked Poe's invention of the detective story, we are still encumbered by the aesthetic and phenomenological expectations that inhibited Whitman's revolutionary embrace of urban life. Accommodation to urban conditions is not only represented as morally unacceptable, but phenomenologically impossible. In the dominant discourses of our literature, journalism, and conversation, it is still assumed that human beings can only handle a limited and relatively uniform amount of discontinuity and dissonance, that unity and order must somehow be imposed upon multiplicity so that consciousness can remain in control. Cities are still condemned for their lack of coherence, harmony, and intimacy, as if it were ever possible or desirable for complex and diverse cities of several million to be distinguished for these qualities. They are described as unmanageable and alienating, as if everyone managed or connected to their environment in the same way. In the literature that arises out of these expectations, the vital and inevitable diversity and incongruity of the modern city are routinely made to serve as metaphors of social chaos and decay. Physical ugliness and dirt are similarly used as metaphors for moral disarray. Thus the glory of a city like New York, its ethnic, social, and cultural diversity, becomes a symbol of a society that no longer shares certain values and assumptions. Poorly funded garbage pickup is read like a tea leaf revelation of a city's soul. The social problems of a city are read not as social problems worthy of the attention of an entire society but as signifiers of the archetypal wickedness of the metropolis. By means of these solemnly presented metaphoric substitutions, authors who are not sufficiently cognizant of their presuppositions persuade us to feel things we might not otherwise feel: a nostalgia for cultural homogeneity, a fastidious distaste for otherness or for anything that doesn't satisfy one's expectations, a rejection of the very possibility of metropolitan life.

If our ability to accommodate the experience of modern urban life is still inhibited by the same images and assumptions about urban life that influenced Poe and Whitman, it is also inhibited by the persistence of the moral and epistemological prejudices against urban spectatorship that made Hawthorne so diffident about representing cities. It is not only cities that are unacceptable. The very process of looking at them is suspect. In our culture, the sheer pleasure of urban spectatorship, or any approach to the city that is more generous or enthusiastic than the prevailing one, is often dismissed as a serious position on the grounds that it is epistemologically specious and morally callous. Epistemological speciousness and moral callousness were certainly among the traditional features of flaneur's sketches. This does not, however, establish what is often assumed: that the pleasure of watching strangers, permitting their signifying surfaces to serve as the basis for imaginative speculation, is somehow incompatible with a compassionate concern for the real human life that crosses the field of vision.

To assume that urban spectatorship is callous is not only to deny people an experience that has been one of the great pleasures of urban social life in every period in history. It is to deny them access to a form of spectatorship that, in spite of its detachment, is capable of stimulating a socially constructive interest in the diversity of the urban population. To find such interaction intrinsically inadequate is to suggest that the only legitimate forms of human interaction are those between people who know each other. To believe this is to automatically rule out the possibility of a decent society of millions of people. In a city of millions, we can't all be neighbors, family, and friends. It is impossible to be anything but an interested and extremely limited spectator to the lives of all but a small number of the people one encounters. In such a society we need a new, admittedly more abstract understanding of community and moral obligation, one that accepts a world of strangers and accepts the inevitability of what is frequently decried as "urban impersonality." I recognize the difficulty of this. I recognize how easily the inevitable conditions of impersonality can justify or produce moral indifference. I suggest, however, that the development of such a sense of involvement with and obligation toward a world of strangers is more likely to be fostered by the experience of seeing and watching them than it is by ways of life that involve avoiding the sight of them. Just as our commitment to cities may become stronger if we divest ourselves of images of the city formed by ancient archetypes and recent journalistic distortions, our ability to construct a modern urban concept of community will be enhanced if we can divest ourselves of assumptions about community that are only relevant to smaller, simpler societies. In order to do this, however, we need to develop a different perspective on urban spectatorship as a social activity.

Taken together, all of these prejudices and assumptions prevent what the flaneur may have once provided. As silly and superficial as he may have been, the flaneur at least suggested the possibility of a bourgeois accommodation to urban life. He offered the example of a posture of curiosity and tolerance that, even if it was merely spectatorial, was nevertheless superior, as a constructive social attitude, to the irresponsible fearmongering and demonization of the other that to a large extent succeeded him. Although he glossed over the problem of their mystery and to a certain degree of their otherness, he was at least reconciled to the inevitability of living in a world of strangers. If the flaneur was not equipped to explore the full dimensions and complexity of otherness, his benign tolerance at least permitted him to entertain the possibility of its legitimacy and its interest. Though it may be shallow, complacent, and even stupid to look at a crowd of strangers as a collection of harmless and interesting types, it is nevertheless better and I would even argue more accurate to look at them in this way than to look at them as an alienating swarm of indescribable menace. Though both of these bourgeois responses are limited, the former has much more potential than the latter to contribute to the actual health of modern cities. It is even conceivable, and Whitman's poetic project begins to demonstrate the possibility of this, that the flaneur's genial tolerance might become the basis, in ways that Romantic antiurban disgust never could have, of a sympathetic and generous involvement in the life of an urban community.

It seems to me, at this point, that we should either accept the experience of spectatorship as an intrinsic part of life in the modern world or else explicitly accept the consequences of a return to a world where it is not a prominent feature. We should either develop an aesthetic and a posture of modernity that can accept and even celebrate incoherence, dissonance, discontinuity, and the freedoms of impersonality or we should explicitly accept the consequences of a return to a world in which these qualities are not encountered. A world in which we know and know about everyone we see, a world in which we have clearly defined reciprocal bonds with everyone we meet, is a village world, or a feudal world, a world few of us would sincerely want except in moments of nostalgic fancy, a world that is not only incompatible with the processes and benefits of industrial society, but which would, practically speaking, involve a return to a degree of homogeneity, fixity of values, and rigidity of social roles that most modern people would find intolerable. It is about time, I am suggesting, that we started openly valuing the cosmopolitan freedom and richness of experience that such a world would deprive us of. It is about time that we stopped sentimentalizing both the urban and rural past, neither of which was as harmonious, intimate, civil, or decent as our fantasies make them out to be. The modernist rejection of modernity, which forms such a substantial part of what is taken for granted in our discourse about the modern world, is not just an encumbrance, leading us into paradoxical situations. It is actually dangerous, and not only because it allows us to guarantine and abandon the social problems that are most evident in our cities. In its Spenglerian manifestations, this refusal to accept modernity was a crucial part of the anticosmopolitan ideology of fascism. Much of the twentieth century establishes, I believe, the actual danger of believing that the freedom and richness of modernity are an inadequate compensation for the loss of the order, coherence, and meaning that may or may not have been characteristic of the experience of earlier periods. I have no problem with individual and nonuniversal-izing efforts to restore these qualities to experience. I do not believe, however, that this goal can be accomplished in the modern world, on a large social scale, without a brutal repression of people and forms of experience that are perceived to threaten the harmony of a restored, antimodern, and anticosmopolitan order.

In light of this, I think it would be wise for us to accept and begin to accommodate the world we live in: to accept the fact that people want to be individuals, with as many real and imagined options as possible, that people enjoy being spectators and consumers and that this does not necessarily dehumanize them or deprive them of their autonomy, that people enjoy collecting and fondling a broad range of experiences, and that their need for order and meaning within experience may have been overestimated. To say this is not necessarily to acquiesce, as the flaneur does, in the cultural and economic milieu that has created the possibility of this form of experience. The particular pleasures and freedoms of modern existence can still be integrated with an ideal of social justice. An acceptance of a world created by capitalism does not involve a pledge to accept capitalism as it is.

While it may seem quaint or bizarre for a book of literary criticism to end with a prescription, I want to say that there seems to me to be no intrinsic reason why there can't be a perspective on modernity that preserves the flaneur's tolerance, curiosity, and love of spectacle, while adding a deeper social, cultural, and moral awareness. There seems to me to be no reason why we can't enjoy the spectatorial pleasures of the flaneur, while expanding the scope of those pleasures to include pleasure in various forms of dissonance and discontinuity that were excluded when the flaneur crowded out his more subversive, carnivalesque rivals. There also seems to me to be no good reason why there can't be a perspective on modern urban life that understands the terrible things that can be seen or experienced in a city in the context of society as a whole, and not as a sign of the inevitable depravity of cities or the inevitable squalor of modern life. It is not so much that the modern world is incoherent, impersonal, and immoral compared with earlier periods as that we have failed to develop effective and accurate ways of perceiving, imagining, and representing it. We will only develop a better way of imagining cities if we divest ourselves of our obsolete expectations and historically inaccurate nostalgia. With some flexibility, historical perspective, tolerance, and imagination, I see no reason why we can't develop an American urbanist literature. In spite of Wordsworth's complaint, it should not in the end matter that "the face of every one that passes is a mystery!" It cannot be otherwise. And it is not so bad.

Notes

1. THE FLANEUR AND MODERNITY

1 In formulating this conception of modernity, I am most indebted to recent discussions in the work of Berman, Buck-Morss, Frisby, Habermas, Kellner, and Rolleston.

2 Walter Benjamin's "Paris Arcades" project (*Passaqenarbeit*) was to have been an integrative materialist analysis of a connected series of nineteenth-century cultural phenomena (the arcades, the *flâneur*, panoramas, world expositions, etc.) in which Benjamin saw the image of the nineteenth-century culture of commodity capitalism. Some completed fragments of the work, as well as some outlines, have been collected and translated by Harry Zohn in a volume entitled *Charles Baudelaire: A Lyric Poet in the Era of High Capitalism*. [Throughout this book, all citations from the work of Walter Benjamin refer to this volume, unless otherwise specified.] Benjamin's folders of notes for the "Arcades" project (most of which are collected quotations from French and German sources) were published for the first time in 1982 as volume 5 of Benjamin's *Gesammelte Schriften*. The role of Benjamin's work, as source and template for the conception of modernity I am working with in this study, has been dealt with most extensively by Buck-Morss, Eagleton (*Walter Benjamin*), Frisby, Rolleston, and Wolin.

3 There has never been an exact English equivalent for the French word *flâneur*, particularly as it is used by Baudelaire and Benjamin. I will therefore use this word, throughout the discussion, to refer to the sensibility I define in this chapter. The *flâneur* exemplifies only one possible mode of urban spectatorship, so to use the English phrase "urban spectator" would be inexact. Dickens referred to the *flâneur* narrator of his *Sketches by Boz* as a "speculative pedestrian," but I have decided not to use this English phrase because it is cumbersome and little known. I have chosen to use the word *flâneur* because it is, through translations of Benjamin's work, increasingly familiar to English-speaking audiences, and because it is the term used by Baudelaire and Benjamin, from whose work my own understanding of the *flâneur* is derived.

The word *flâneur* is, in fact, slowly making its way into the English language. It can be found in the 1971 edition of the *Oxford English Dictionary*, with a circumflex, defined as "A lounger, or saunterer. An idle 'man about town.'" It appears, with a circumflex, in *Webster's New World Dictionary of the American Language–Second College Edition* (1980), defined as "a person who strolls about idly, as along the boulevards, idler." It appears, for the first time without a circumflex, in *Webster's Third New International Dictionary of the English Language* (1981), defined (inadequately) as "a) an aimless and usually self-centered and superficial person or b) an intellectual trifler." Because of the increasing acceptance of the *flâneur* as an English word, I have decided, in consultation with the editors at the Cambridge University Press, to treat it as if it is an English word. It will therefore be printed, from this point onward, without italicization or a circumflex.

Because Baudelaire also discusses the dandy as a modern type in "The Painter of Modern Life," and because several of the affectations of the two figures are similar, the dandy and the *flâneur* are often confused with each other, in criticism and in common reference. As the previous description makes clear, however, their sensibilities are radically different. The *flâneur* aspires to invisibility, rejoicing in his incognito. The dandy, on the other hand, wishes to attract the curious gazes of others. The *flâneur* is endlessly curious and responsive to what he sees, the dandy is blasé, affecting an attitude of insensibility. For Baudelaire, both are appropriate to urban civilizations at the same historical moment, but their responses to the environment that produces them are in no way similar. They are, if anything, inverted mirror images of each other.

4 Benjamin first discussed the flaneur in an essay entitled "The *Flaneur*," which was originally intended to be the second of three essays in a work entitled "The Paris of the Second Empire in Baudelaire," which was itself intended to be the second of three parts of a work on Charles Baudelaire that Benjamin decided, in the late 1930s, to produce from the materials he had collected for the "Paris Arcades" project. In response to Adorno's critique of his work, Benjamin wrote "Some Motifs in Baudelaire" to replace "The *Flaneur*" as the second essay of "The Paris of the Second Empire in Baudelaire." This more complex and ambitious essay also deals at some length with the flaneur as part of the Parisian cultural context of Baudelaire's poetry. Both essays have been published in *Charles Baudelaire*, trans. Zohn.

5 When referring to the flaneur, I will use masculine pronouns, because I think that the flaneur is an explicitly male figure. His freedom from social attachments and responsibilities, his invisibility and inaccessibility within a crowd, and his freedom to explore, stare at, and observe everything within a city would have been understood by his audience as exclusively male privileges. In the period covered by this book (up to the middle of the nineteenth century), I have not been able to find any examples of works written by women that fit the definition I have assembled of the genre. Considering that many of the most enthusiastic spectators of the urban crowd and urban commercial life in

the nineteenth century must have been women, the absence of *flaneries* written by women is undoubtedly significant, and presumably reflects a sense in the culture that there is something inappropriate about women enjoying the degree of access to the consciousness and character of others that the flaneur traditionally claims for himself, or expressing the unselfconscious love of spectacle and luxury that he traditionally expresses. Another aspect of this sense that the flaneur cannot be a woman undoubtedly has to do with the specific social meaning of a solitary woman, walking the streets without any apparent purpose, looking into the faces of passers-by. Although it is possible that some of the voluminous anonymous literature of journalistic flaneurs may have been written by women, it is significant that in all of that literature, the persona of the flaneur is invariably male.

6 The correspondence between T. W. Adorno and Walter Benjamin on "Paris – Capital of the Nineteenth Century" and on Benjamin's plans for the "Paris Arcades" project has been collected and translated in Theodor Adorno, Walter Benjamin, et al., *Aesthetics and Politics*, ed. Fredric Jameson, pp. 100–41.

7 This phrase is used throughout the correspondence.

8 In his notes for the "Paris Arcades" project, Benjamin collected a large folder of quotations referring to efforts to "interiorize" city life.

9 "Die Erfahrung ist der Ertrag der Arbeit, das Erlebnis ist die Phantasmagorie des Mussiggangers" (*Gesammelte Schriften*, 5:962). The translation I have provided in the body of the text is from Rolleston, 24. In Benjamin's implications about the historical dimensions of these terms, and in a certain tradition of Marxist interpretation of bourgeois culture beginning with Marx and extending from William Morris to Benjamin, I find what I feel is a historically dubious and potentially reactionary glorification of the kind of experience that is imagined to have existed in preindustrial societies. Much of what can be designated as *Erlebnis*, in my view, are valuable forms of pleasure that can be found to some degree in all historical periods, and among all classes of society, and much of what can be designated as *Erfahrung* refers to rigid, simplistic, and traditional interpretations of experience that limit freedom as completely or more completely than anything bourgeois industrial society has been able to come up with. Although I wish to dissociate myself from these implications, I think that Benjamin's terms are still useful. Whatever experience may have been like before capitalism and industrialization, what Benjamin refers to as *Erlebnis* certainly seems to be the dominant and characteristic mode of experience in the kind of culture in which the flaneur plays an important role.

10 Benjamin was familiar with "The Man of the Crowd," as was, of course, Baudelaire. Though both wrote about Poe's story in relation to the phenomenon of the flaneur, neither was familiar with its American context. For a fuller account of Baudelaire and Benjamin's treatment of "The Man of the Crowd," see Chapter 5. Unless otherwise specified, all citations from Poe are from the *Collected Works*, ed. Mabbot. Parenthetical citations in the text refer to volume and page number in this edition.

11 Unless otherwise specified, all citations from Hawthorne are from the Centenary edition. Parenthetical citations in the text refer to volume and page number in this edition.

12 Unless otherwise specified, all citations from Whitman are from *Leaves of Grass: Comprehensive Reader's Edition*, ed. Blodgett and Bradley. Parenthetical citations in the text refer to page number in this edition.

13 The few discussions of Poe's treatment of the city in "The Man of the Crowd" have, it seems to me, been excessively preoccupied with the often conventional hellish qualities of the narrator's description of London, paying little attention to his curious composure or to the fascinating and frustrating structure of the story. See Mazurek and Levine.

14 The most notable efforts to consider Hawthorne's treatment of urban themes are Levy and Gatta. For a fuller account of these, see Chapters 6 and 7.

15 Most of the efforts to consider Whitman's use of the city, while at points useful, are disappointingly vague, restricting themselves to a paraphrase of Whitman's apparent celebrations of the aspect of Broadway, etc. Machor and Weimer are exceptions to this. There have been a number of excellent readings of Whitman's finest urban poem, "Crossing Brooklyn Ferry," but many of the remarks about the representation of the city in that poem appear to me to demonstrate the excessive influence of the antiurban models. The difficulty of characterizing Whitman's response to the city is undeniable and it has been noted. Observing that Whitman's poetic apprehension of New York is very hard to pin down, Weimer has written: "Having introduced the city to American poetry, Whitman displayed considerable uncertainty as to what to do with it" (33). For a fuller treatment of this issue, see Chapter 8.

16 In their correspondence, Adorno criticized Benjamin for what he felt was his ahistorical privileging of the nineteenth century throughout "Paris – The Capital of the Nineteenth Century." Adorno wrote: "The specific commodity character of the nineteenth century, in other words, the industrial production of commodities, would have to be worked out much more clearly and materially. After all, commodities and alienation have existed since the beginning of capitalism – i.e. the age of manufactures, which is also that of baroque art; while the unity of the modern age has since then lain precisely in the commodity character" (*Aesthetics and Politics*, 114). As I hope to demonstrate, much of what would contribute to the production of the consciousness of the flaneur simply requires the existence of a culture of commodities, not necessarily industrially produced commodities. It should not therefore be surprising that the flaneur begins to develop long before the nineteenth century. The recent studies of Rolleston and Saisselin offer particularly clear examples of historically sophisticated studies that are handicapped by their acceptance of Benjamin's ahistorical claim that the flaneur originates in response to innovations and conditions that were exclusive to the nineteenth century.

2. THE DEVELOPMENT OF THE FLANEUR IN ENGLAND

1 For the historical information in this chapter about the demographics and economy of sixteenth- and seventeenth-century London, I am primarily indebted to Rasmussen; Beier and Finlay; Finlay; Finlay and Shearer; and Ashton.

2 According to Beier and Finlay, there is a developing consensus, among commercial historians, that "the economic and social configurations of consumer society predated the industrial revolution" (5). They suggest that the manufacturing capability of Europe and particularly England before the late eighteenth century was sufficient to provide for the consumer economy referred to here, so that when the factory system of production was developed, it did not create consumer society so much as it made possible an intensification and diffusion of a consumer culture that had already existed in some form for centuries.

3 Though the Royal Exchange was based upon a marketplace in Antwerp, both of these northern European markets were undoubtedly based upon arcaded shopping spaces in Italy (some of which still exist, like the Straw Market and the arcaded shopping gallery of the Uffizi in Florence), which themselves probably owe something to the greatest continuously operating enclosed marketplace, the Grand Bazaar of Constantinople. The style also had precedents in the arcaded shopping spaces of antiquity, for example in the agoras of Athens and Delos. Although the arcades which Benjamin considered to be the natural habitat of the flaneur could only be built with nineteenth-century metalworking and glass-working technology, sheltered and traffic-free promenades for strolling, shopping, and the display of goods and people have been a part of urban life in the West for at least twenty-five hundred years. No doubt some of the features of urban spectatorship with which this discussion is concerned have therefore been around as long as well.

4 For discussions and descriptions of the Royal Exchange and the New Exchange, see Dorothy Davis and Adburgham.

5 Stow's survey was updated in 1618 by Anthony Munday and in 1633 by Henry Dyson. Notable successors to Stow's survey include Donald Lupton's *London and the Countrey Carbonadoed* (1634), *A New View of London; or an Ample Account of That City* (1708); and Daniel Defoe's *A Tour Thro' London about the year 1725*.

6 For an account of the role that has been played by metropolitan life as a space for personal experimentation, a realm in which the limits of bourgeois life are tested by well-heeled postadolescents, see Seigel. Though the "gilded vagabonds" referred to by Routh differ in several significant respects from the nineteenth-century bohemians dealt with in Seigel's study, they do, I think, anticipate them in the way I suggest here.

7 For an account of the development and history of the English Theophrastian character, see Boyce. According to Boyce, English interest in the *Characters*

of Theophrastus developed after the publication of Isaac Casaubon's Latin translation in 1592. Joseph Hall's *Characters of Vertues and Vices*, a Theophrastian imitation, appeared in 1608, but according to Boyce the real beginning of the vogue of the character begins in 1614 with the publication of the first edition of Thomas Overbury's *Characters* (these were, in fact, written by a group of which Overbury was the principal member). From 1614 until the Puritan revolution, the Theophrastian character enjoyed a constant and substantial popularity in England and assumed a variety of forms. Among the most notable character books were Nicholas Breton, *The Good and the Badde, or Descriptions of the Worthies, and Unworthies of this Age*; John Earle, *Microcosmographie*; R.M., *Micrologia*; Francis Lenton, *Characterismi*; Richard Brathwaite, *Whimzies: Or, A New Cast of Characters*; and Wye Saltonstall, *Picturae Loguentes. Or Pictures Drawne forth in Characters*. Several of the most popular character books, notably Overbury's and Earle's, were often reprinted in this period. Though characters were still written during the Puritan period, they were universally satirical and written in isolation, not in character books (315–17). After the Restoration, according to Boyce, the character was never restored to its original form. As I will consider later in this chapter, however, many of its functions were taken over by other genres.

8 Like the urban genres that had preceded them, the Theophrastian characters were geared toward a metropolitan readership living in a world of strangers, potentially threatening but fascinating to observe. Like these earlier genres, the English character enjoyed by far its greatest popularity in the city of London, and an overwhelming proportion of the types represented in the English character would be more likely to be encountered in London than in the countryside. In those rare instances in which a distinctly rural figure is typed, particular emphasis is given to the way in which such a figure looks and behaves when he comes to London. Overbury's country gentleman is chiefly notable as easy "prey of every cutpurse" (65) and for his inappropriate dress and manners at court. Earle's "Plain country fellow" is distinguished by the way his feet "stink so unbecomingly . . . when he trots after a lawyer in Westminster hall" (51). Even if the typed individual is not urban, the perspective and the setting generally are.

9 As linguistically structured encyclopedias of human typology, the Theophrastian character books anticipate the eighteenth-century gallery of physiognomical types like that found in Lavater, or the twentieth-century photographic anthologies of types like Sander.

10 More than other forms of economic organization, capitalism depends upon the division of the crowd into types, since successful commercial activity depends upon the ability to identify types of individuals who have a need for a specific commodity. Commercial society also creates a situation in which individuals may wish to identify themselves with a specific type, through the purchase of commodities associated with it.

11 For an account of La Bruyère's debt to the English Theophrastians, see Knox, 22ff.

12 Barthes writes: "What is the world for someone who speaks? An initially formless field of objects, beings, phenomena which must be organized, i.e. divided up and distributed. La Bruyère does not fail this obligation, he divides up the society he lives in into great regions, among which he will distribute his 'characters'" ("La Bruyère" in *Critical Essays*, 223).

13 For a general overview of the development of periodical publication in England in the seventeenth century, see Richmond Bond, *Studies in the Early English Periodical*, 1–48.

14 Conant credits Giovanni Paolo Marana with having invented this genre in his *L'Espion Turc* (1684). The two most important examples of this kind of work, in terms of their influence upon Addison and Steele, were Charles Riviere Dufresny's *Amusements serieux et comiques* (1699) and Thomas Brown's *Amusements Serious and Comical* (1700). Brown's *Amusements*, much of which was plagiarized from Dufresny and transposed from Paris to London, was extremely popular in England and was certainly read by Addison and Steele (Graham, "Some Predecessors of the *Tatler*").

15 The fullest description of this obscure but crucially important genre can be found in Graham, 50–3. Besides the works discussed here, other examples of serials in this genre were, according to Graham, Dunton's *Night Walker* (1696), the *Weekly Comedy* (1699), the *Infallible Astrologer* (1700), *Merry Mercury, or a Farce of Fools* (1700), and the *Secret Mercury* (1702).

16 Though what I have designated as the carnivalesque urban spectator seems to disappear in England in the eighteenth century, he appears to have survived in the more tolerant cultural environment of France, most notably in *Les nuits de Paris* by Nicolas-Edmé Restif de la Bretonne.

17 For typical invocations of the frame story of "The Limping Devil," see Egan, 46, and Hunt, "A Walk in the City" in *The Wishing-Cap Papers*. I will also refer, in later chapters of this discussion, to other invocations of "The Limping Devil" in the works of various English and American flaneurs. Although he does not directly cite Le Sage, Sir Arthur Conan Doyle used this image to define the conception of the city implicit in the urban detective story. In the opening pages of "A Case of Identity," Holmes observes to Watson: "If we could fly out of that window hand in hand, hover over this great city, gently remove the roofs, and peep in at the queer things which are going on, the strange coincidences, the plannings, the cross-purposes, the wonderful chain of events, working through generations, and leading to the most outré results, it would make all fiction with its conventionalities and foreseen conclusions most stale and unprofitable" (191). The particular suitability of this image to represent the consumption of the city as spectacle is indicated by the fact that one of the first Parisian department stores was called "Le Diable Boiteux" (Clark, 55)

18 This description seems to owe a great deal to the description that Democritus Junior, the Cynic philosopher who is the putative narrator of Robert Burton's *Anatomy of Melancholy*, offers of himself at the beginning of that work: "Though I live still a collegiate student, as Democritus in his garden, and lead a monastic life... in some high place above you all... I hear and see

what is done abroad, how others run, ride, turmoil, and macerate themselves
in court and country. . . . I laugh at all. . . . I have no wife nor children good
or bad to provide for . . . a mere spectator of other men's fortunes and adventures, and how they act their parts, which methinks are diversely presented
unto me, as from a common theatre or scene" (18).

19 *Speculation* is the word most frequently used by English flaneurs to describe
their activity. The mirrorlike quality of the flaneur's empathy is vividly expressed in Leigh Hunt's assertion, in his essay "A Human Being and a Crowd":
"A crowd is but the reduplication of ourselves, of our faces, fears, hopes,
wants, and relations . . . our own strengths, weaknesses, formidable power,
pitiable tears. . . . All hearts beating in those bosoms are palpitations of our
own" (*The Seer*, 86).

20 Although they had existed since 1660 as a public garden, Vauxhall Gardens
was opened as the first pleasure garden, in the sense in which the term was
understood in the eighteenth and nineteenth centuries, in 1732 by Jonathan
Tyers. Ranelagh opened in 1741. These pleasure gardens were clearly inspired
by such Renaissance gardens as the Boboli Gardens, attached to the Pitti Palace
in Florence and the gardens of the Villa d'Este at Tivoli. They anticipate the
more elaborate pleasure gardens of the nineteenth century, as well as the
amusement parks of the late nineteenth and twentieth centuries. The Tivoli
Gardens in Copenhagen is the only remaining pleasure garden, the only place
where it is still possible to approximate the experience of eighteenth-century
visitors to Vauxhall or Ranelagh. For discussions and descriptions of the
English pleasure gardens of the eighteenth century, see Altick, 93–8.

21 In the context of his discussion of French Impressionist painting, T. J. Clark
offers a particularly interesting and sophisticated account of how Baron Haussman's redesign of Paris during the Second Empire altered the perception and
the functioning of the city. See, in particular, pp. 54–66.

22 For an account of this tradition, see Graham, chap. 3, "Imitators of the *Tatler*
and *Spectator* before 1750." Bateson (132) counts 314 imitations of the spectatorial framework of the *Tatler* and the *Spectator* in the eighteenth century
alone.

23 Eliza Haywood's *Female Spectator* (1745) is, significantly, nothing more than
a conduct book. In it, only the prescriptive aspects of the Addisonian tradition
are evident. There is no consumption, no panoramic encompassment, no
presumptuous analysis. There is not even the obligatory presentation of a
detached philosophical reader of social life in the opening number that one
finds in even the most moralistic of the periodical series written by men. This
suggests, I think, the degree to which the attitudes and presumptions of the
flaneur would not have been considered suitable for a woman. There was also
a *Female Tatler* (1709–10), written by Thomas Baker, which was the putative
product of a "Mrs. Crackenthorpe, a Lady that knows everything." This
antifeminist satire also suggests the degree to which the traditional panoramic
omniscience of the flaneur was something that would only have been considered absurd, amusing, and, if seriously asserted, intolerable in a woman.

3. THE FLANEUR IN THE NINETEENTH
CENTURY

1 This would be immediately evident, I think, to anyone who either leafs through the old volumes or grinds their way through the microfilm. Klancher also observes this (83).

2 For an account of this tradition, see Schwarzbach, 35–7.

3 For an account of this revival, see Law.

4 This project of voluntary marginalization, for the purpose of enjoying the spectacle of urban life, is analogous to the project of social distancing characteristic of the urban types defined in Georg Simmel's essay "The Stranger" and Robert Park's "Human Migration and the Marginal Man."

5 Debord writes: "The spectacle presents itself simultaneously as society itself, as a part of society, and as instrument of unification. . . . The spectacle presents itself as an enormous unutterable and inaccesible actuality. It says nothing more than 'that which appears is good, that which is good appears.' The attitude which it demands in principle is this passive acceptance, which in fact it has already obtained by its manner of appearing without reply, by its monopoly of appearance" (3, 12).

6 Most of the pieces collected under the general title *Sketches by Boz* were originally published as serial essays in two newspapers, the *Morning Chronicle* and the *Evening Chronicle* or in a magazine known as *Bell's Life in London*. For a general account of their publishing history, see Butt and Tillotson, 38–50. In the following discussion I will be primarily concerned with those sketches that have been, since 1839, classified under the headings "Scenes" and "Characters." Most of these were originally published as "Street Sketches" in the *Morning Chronicle* or as "London Sketches" in the *Evening Chronicle*.

7 The *Tatler* and the *Spectator* were among the few books in the Dickens family library at Chatham, which Forster has referred to as the "birthplace of [Dickens's] fancy" (15).

8 In creating Boz, Dickens was undoubtedly influenced by the essays of Lamb, Hunt, and Irving. For an account of Dickens's debts to these urban essayists, see Baker, 3:243. See also *The Letters of Charles Dickens*, ed. House, Storey, et al., 1:485; 2:250, 267. Dickens is also likely to have been influenced by the urban sketches of John Poole (Butt and Tillotson, 37n), and as a widely read and practicing journalist, he was no doubt familiar with many other examples of this genre in the London journalism of his time.

9 Cited in Butt and Tillotson, 44. Dickens eliminated this passage in the version published in *Sketches by Boz*, possibly because he may have retrospectively considered it callous, but more probably because there are so many such passages in the *Sketches* that he may have wanted to eliminate redundancy.

10 See especially "Greenwich Fair" and the nostalgic reveries in "Hackney-Coach Stands" and "Scotland Yard."

11 As Altick describes, static and clockwork models were exhibited in London as early as the seventeenth century. Transparencies (paintings illuminated from

behind), magic lanterns, camerae obscurae, and other forms of representation that depended upon images, lenses, and light sources were extremely popular after they were developed in the eighteenth century. So too were eidophusikons, developed in 1771 by Phillipe Jacques de Loutherbourg. The eidophusikon synthesized principles of the clockwork mechanism, the transparency, and the magic lantern into a moving and illuminated model show.

The word *panorama* was originally applied to cylindrical paintings which created a particularly convincing sense of reality by adapting the principles of perspective to a 360-degree surrounding surface. The panorama was invented in 1787 by Robert Barker, a Scottish portraitist who developed the principles of cylindrical painting in a mirrored observatory he had built for the purpose on a hilltop on the edge of Edinburgh. After the success of his panoramic painting of Edinburgh, Barker immediately painted one of London, which was exhibited there in 1792. Although panoramas were extremely popular in the first half of the nineteenth century, few of them have been preserved. Two that have, Vanderlyn's panorama of the palace and gardens of Versailles, in the Metropolitan Museum of Art in New York, and the panorama of Rome in the Victoria and Albert Museum in London, demonstrate the uncanny effect of schematic verisimilitude of which panoramas are capable. The word *panorama* was also later used to refer to a long canvas that would be gradually unrolled in front of an audience by the turning of a spool.

Dioramas were originally distinguished from panoramas in that they were flat paintings, or a series of interacting flat painted surfaces that were movable and that would reveal different features depending upon changes in lighting. The first "diorama" was invented in 1822 by a Frenchman named Louis Jacques Mande Daguerre, who was to contribute to the decline of the popularity of his invention by inventing daguerrotypy seventeen years later. As mechanical stagecraft developed in the early nineteenth century, these model shows became more elaborate and it became more difficult, and ultimately meaningless, to separate them into different types. All were considered to be among the main attractions of the metropolis (London, Paris, or New York), all offered schematic reductions of complex and generally urban environments, all were evaluated according to what was thought to be their fidelity to what they represented rather than their intrinsic beauty, all were used to figuratively represent the activity and the representations of the flaneur, and all, collectively, constituted a culture of representation that anticipated and was ultimately superseded by the culture of photographic representation.

12 Although he does not pursue the question at any length, Foucault, in a footnote in *Discipline and Punish* (317n), wonders if Bentham, developing the model of the Panopticon in 1791, was aware of its similarity to the panorama Barker began to construct in 1787.

13 Horner's panorama, forty times larger than any earlier panorama, was the largest and most ambitious of all of the panoramas that were ever exhibited in London. It was housed in the Colosseum from 1833 to 1863.

14 Lefebvre writes that "everyday life . . . crown(s) and conceal(s)" modernity,

"revealing and veiling it" (24). It is what is "taken for granted," what appears to be "humble and solid" (24). It is, as I am using the term here, the shared set of unacknowledged assumptions, determining images, and invisible constructions that create a sense of the reality and fixity of that which actually changes as a culture changes.

15 Murray describes how, observing the urban crowd, he cannot help but "recollect . . . that, in fifty years, these jostling crowds will, with few exceptions, be mingled with the silent dust" (1:33). This emotion is so commonly expressed in the literature of the flaneur, almost always at a moment of panoramic encompassment, that it had become a cliché, though the ability of a poet to reanimate such an observation is demonstrated by Whitman's great poem "Crossing Brooklyn Ferry," which has its sources in a flaneur's moment of panoramic encompassment. This paradoxical sense of urban plenitude and ephemerality may have been the impetus behind many efforts to panoramically represent great metropolises at a specific moment of their history. Benjamin quotes an account that Paul Bourget offered of the moment that inspired Maxime du Camp to write his six-volume panorama of Paris, *Paris, ses organes, ses fonctions, et sa vie dans la seconde moitié du XIXe siècle* (1886). Standing on the Pont Neuf, waiting for his eyeglasses to be repaired, du Camp's "visit to the optician," according to Bourget, "reminded him of the law of the inevitable infirmity of all human things. . . . It suddenly occurred to the man who had travelled widely in the Orient, who was acquainted with the deserts whose sand is the dust of the dead, that this city, too, whose bustle was all around him, would have to die some day, the way so many capitals had died. It occurred to him how extraordinarily interesting an accurate description of Athens at the time of Pericles, Carthage at the time of Barca, Alexandria at the time of the Ptolemies, and Rome at the time of the Caesars would be to us today. . . . In a flash of inspiration, of the kind that occasionally brings one an extraordinary subject, he resolved to write the kind of book about Paris that the historians of antiquity failed to write about their cities" (Benjamin, 86).

16 In 1846, while writing *Dombey and Son* at Lausanne, Dickens wrote to Forster that he was experiencing creative difficulties, which he supposed was "partly" due to "the absence of streets and numbers of figures. I can't express how much I want these. It seems as if they supplied something to my brain which it cannot bear, when busy, to lose. For a week or a fortnight I can write prodigiously in a retired place (as at Broadstairs) and a day in London sets me up again and starts me. But the toil and labour of writing day after day, without that magic lantern, is IMMENSE!" ("Letter to John Forster, 30 August 1846," in *The Letters of Charles Dickens*, ed. Tillotson, 4:612).

17 Harold Child, in *The Cambridge History of English Literature*, offers the following choice dismissal of *Life in London*: "[Egan's] book, with its leer and wink of knowing vice, its sickly affectation of warning young men from the haunts and pursuits that it lusciously describes, would have disgusted even Sterne in the moments when his physical weakness was most perverting his facile imagination" (14:223). Egan has suffered from the same sort of prudish

dismissal of his importance as Ward, Brown, and the English Lucian. Although there are other reasons not to value *Life in London* very highly, few modern readers would be bothered by what were felt, for over a century, to be its unpardonable lapses in taste.

18 In his *Crime and Industrial Society in the Nineteenth Century*, J. J. Tobias suggests that, contrary to what was "observed" by contemporary observers, the weight of evidence suggests that as a result of social reforms, greatly improved street lighting, and the development of "an improved machinery for enforcing the law" (39), the amount of crime and its degree of violence consistently decreased in London throughout the entire period 1700–1900.

19 As Nelson and Seccombe (100), Frank (17), and Mott (220–33) observe, detailed descriptions of crimes and executions were a staple of English journalism from the seventeenth century onward. In addition to being published in the early newspapers and magazines, they were often published and sold independently.

4. THE FLANEUR IN AMERICA

1 Turner proposed his thesis in a speech entitled "The Significance of the Frontier in American History," delivered to a meeting of the American Historical Association at the Chicago World's Columbian Exposition in 1893. For the fullest history and analysis of the phenomenon identified by Turner, see Henry Nash Smith.

2 For a discussion of the archetypal nature of popular urban literature in nineteenth-century America, see Stout and Siegal.

3 In addition to Bridenbaugh, Glaab, and Brown, other historians and cultural critics who have, in contrast to prevailing assumptions, emphasized the urbanism of early nineteenth-century American society, are Warner, Wade, Green, Barth, Bender, and Machor.

4 For accounts of the nature and pace of American urbanization, see Glaab and Brown, Warner, and Green. For the growth of New York in particular, see Spann and Still.

5 For a lucid account of the varied and complex reasons why New York became America's metropolis, see Spann, especially 1–22.

6 For an account of the urbanity of the early American magazines, see Mott.

7 The fullest account of the aggressive urbanism of the intellectuals who formed the Young America movement has been given by Perry Miller, who deals with it as part of the intellectual context of Melville's literary career. As Miller points out, this tradition of New York urbanism was a self-conscious reaction against the dominant antiurbanism in New England literary culture at this time. In formulating their ideal of cosmopolitan journalism, Miller suggests that the editors and writers of the *Knickerbocker* were particularly influenced by the *London Quarterly*, the *Edinburgh Review*, the *North British Review*, and *Blackwood's* (12) all of which were widely read in the United States, and all of which frequently published flaneur's sketches.

8 For brief considerations of this early American tradition, see the introduction to Granger and Hartzog; see also Granger.

9 All citations from Willis are from *Prose Works*, unless otherwise specified.

10 All three of the authors treated in this study had an extensive familiarity with the British periodical and essay tradition in which the English-speaking flaneur had his origins. Their familiarity, and their participation in this tradition, is considered in detail in the chapters of this discussion concerned with their work.

11 Poe writes: "London, how shall I describe it? how convey to the reader any idea of its vastness and magnificence – its interminable winding of streets and lanes – its public squares, its gardens and palaces, the residences of the nobility, the populousness of its streets. . . . It beggars all description. . . . I dare not hope for success. Take Boston for instance – multiply three-quarters of its population, taken indiscriminately, by twenty – a certain fat gentleman therein, who serves good dinners, by ten thousand – one dozen inimitable looking boys . . . that sell newspapers in State Street by five thousand – all the pastry-cooks, coal beavers, scissor grinders by five hundred, and you have the population of London. Take the shop on the corner of Ann and Union Sts., the Old State House, the Governor Phipps's house, all the Harris' Folly and Uncle Sam's Madness, the towns of Salem, Newburyport, and Hull, multiply them by fifteen, then shake them well together and drop them anywhere between East Boston and Dedham . . . bring all the omnibuses in the United States, multiply them by three and put them in motion in the streets – draw an immense canopy of black crape over the whole at a suitable distance above the chimneys, and you have London itself. Poe, *English Notes by Quarles Quickens* (Boston: Daily Mail Office, 1842).

12 Willis, in the first issue of his *Home Journal*, promises that his aggressively cosmopolitan New York magazine will offer its readers a "phototype . . . [of] the passing scene" (*Rag Bag*, 14). Willis also gave the name of "Daguerrotypes of the Present" to a series of urban essays he wrote for the *New York Mirror*. A flaneur named Walter Whitman, writing in the *New York Leader*, called one of his essay series "City Photographs."

13 Neither Foster nor any other American flaneur who uses the metaphor ever feels the need to explain who Asmodeus is. The currency of the frame story of Le Sage's "Limping Devil" in American culture is suggested by the fact that Asmodeus is even used in advertisements. An advertisement for Foster's *Fifteen Minutes around New York* proclaimed of its author: "Like Asmodeus he is omnipresent – here, there, and everywhere."

14 For examples of similar treatments of New York's profusion of dandies, see: Green, 79–83; Foster, *Fifteen Minutes around New-York*, 40; *New York in Slices*, 9 and 76–9; Willis, *The Rag Bag*, 28–31.

5. FROM THE FLANEUR TO THE DETECTIVE:
INTERPRETING THE CITY OF POE

1 See Poe, "Review of 'Watkins Tottle and Other Sketches, Illustrative of Every-

Day Life and Every-Day People. By Boz,'" in *The Complete Works*, ed. Harrison, 9:45–8. In his "Introduction" and notes to "The Man of the Crowd" in the *Collected Works*, Mabbot suggests that Poe is indebted to the *Sketches by Boz* for some of the details of his description of London. Mabbot does not, however, note the resemblance between the narrator and Boz himself.

2 See Poe, "Review of 'Twice-told Tales,'" in Harrison, 9:105. Evaluating Hawthorne's essays in his review of "Twice-Told Tales," Poe compares them with those of Addison, Steele, Lamb, Hunt, and Irving. Campbell (183–4) documents Poe's extensive familiarity with each of these authors, a familiarity that would hardly have been surprising for an English-speaking man of letters of the early nineteenth century. Poe's epigraph to "The Man of the Crowd" suggests that he was probably familiar with La Bruyère.

3 Allen documents Poe's extensive familiarity with the British magazine tradition.

4 See "Cabs" in *Collected Works*, ed. Mabbot, 2:493–4 and "Omnibuses," in the appendix of Poe, *Doings of Gotham*, ed. Mabbot.

5 For an account of Poe's familiarity with and changing opinions of Willis, see Benton, "N. P. Willis as a Catalyst."

6 I agree with J. Gerald Kennedy's suggestion that the "real conflict in the tale" is not the pursuit, or even the narrator's futile effort to read the old man, but "the psychological tension between the narrator's detached, analytical view of human experience and his mounting subjective fascination with 'the man of the crowd'" (186). This fascination is necessarily irrational. I therefore take issue with Patrick Quinn and others who have faulted this story for the apparent implausibility of the narrator's quest. In my view, the implausibility of a convalescent pursuing a man for twenty-four hours in the rain, far from weakening the story, simply illustrates the extraordinary intensity of his obsession.

7 Several other critics have used the concepts of repression and self-recognition to explain the narrator's obsession. Patrick Quinn sees the old man as "a prophetic image of [the narrator's] future self" (230). Davidson suggests that, "in 'The Man of the Crowd,' we are pursuing the narrator himself, who is so terrified of admitting who or what he is that he projects himself into this desperate and wholly imagined fugitive" (190). Bonaparte tries to explain the intensity of the narrator's quest by suggesting that the old man is a representation of Poe's foster father, John Allan (418).

8 In "The *Flaneur*," Benjamin did refer to the old man in "The Man of the Crowd" as a flaneur, but in "On Some Motifs in Baudelaire," which was written to replace "The *Flaneur*" as the central section of *The Paris of the Second Empire in Baudelaire*, he revised this mistaken identification. Benjamin writes: "Baudelaire saw fit to equate the man of the crowd, whom Poe's narrator follows through the length and breadth of nocturnal London, with the flaneur. It is hard to accept this view. The man of the crowd is no flaneur. In him, composure has given way to manic behavior" (128). I am not sure that Benjamin is correct to assert that Baudelaire equates the old man with the flaneur. Nowhere in the essay to which Benjamin is referring ("The Painter of Modern

Life") does Baudelaire directly identify the old man as a flaneur. In fact, Baudelaire identifies the convalescent sensibility of the narrator of the story with that of Constantin Guys, whom he refers to as the classic flaneur. Benjamin's original confusion may have derived from the fact that Baudelaire's definition of the flaneur in "The Painter of Modern Life" seems to combine aspects of the sensibilities of both the narrator and the man he pursues. This probably reflects the fact that Baudelaire's own urban sensibility is a hybrid of that of the flaneur and that of the old man.

Although Benjamin, in "On Some Motifs in Baudelaire," does acknowledge the existence of an English-speaking flaneur by identifying the narrator of "The Man of the Crowd" as a representative of the type, he does not attempt to account for Poe's familiarity with the flaneur. He even implies that Poe may have independently invented him.

9 For an account of the great popularity of the Wandering Jew as a character and image in the first half of the nineteenth century, see Anderson.

10 Kennedy has also drawn attention to the fact that the narrator's conviction of the old man's criminality is not supported by anything he learns or sees in the story.

11 For an account of the controversy over the changes that may or may not have taken place in the character and quantity of urban crime, see Tobias, 122–47.

12 For accounts of the popularity and nature of crime journalism in this period, see Walsh and David Reynolds, 171–81.

13 The American "mysteries" genre developed in the 1840s after the publication of American versions of Sue (1842) and Reynolds (1844). It appears, however, that this genre was less exclusively metropolitan than the flaneur's sketch. Although there was a very popular series entitled *Mysteries of New York* by Edward Zane Carroll Judson, there were also mysteries of such comparatively innocuous towns as Salem, Fitchburg, and Troy. For a discussion of the "mysteries" genre in America, see David Reynolds, chap. 2, and particularly 82–4.

14 Often a well-publicized murder could spawn a whole series of representations, exploiting different aspects or different understandings of the crime. Edward Zane Carroll Judson's *Mysteries of New York* includes an episode involving the discovery, on the New Jersey banks of the Hudson, of the body of a "pretty cigar girl" named Mary Sheffield. This version of the story of Mary Rogers is able to make use of the discovery, made shortly after Poe had written his story, that Rogers had actually died of complications from an abortion, her body having been thrown in the Hudson by the abortionists.

15 For an account of Vidocq and his importance for the development of detective fiction, see Symons, 17–35.

16 For a history of the development of police and detective forces, see Tobias.

17 It seems to me that it is only in this sense that Dupin can be thought of as a double of the narrator. I therefore disagree with Lemay's suggestion that Dupin is the narrator's *Doppelgänger*.

18 For examples of this acceptance of the narrator's account of Dupin's method, see Bandy, Walsh, and Lemay.

19 Stauffer has perceived this discrepancy and attributes it to the notion that "Dupin's problem-solving genius is derived from intuition" (121), rather than the "analysis" described by the narrator at the opening of these stories. Irwin also calls attention to the intuitive nature of Dupin's method, as do Davidson and Hoffman (*Poe, Poe*), who suggest that Dupin uses the preconscious mind in his ratiocination. Like Harrowitz, who compares Dupin's method to Peirce's conception of "abduction," I think that Dupin uses intuition within the context of a method, and that it can only be brought into play after a systematic elimination of the assumptions that inhibit it. In any case, whatever Dupin does, it seems to me to have little to do with what the narrator says that he does.

6. THE URBAN SPECTATOR IN HAWTHORNE'S SKETCHES

1 Hawthorne's first literary venture was a family newspaper he entitled the *Spectator* (Martin, 4).
2 Machor, the only critic who appears to have found something disturbing in this sketch, suggests that in it, the "charming medley of cityscape and landscape is rendered discordant by a violent thunderstorm, which destroys the placidity of the scene, washes away its beauty, and causes the narrator to admit that he is part of a 'tumult which I am powerless to direct or quell'" ("Pastoralism and the American Ideal," 342). As I have argued, what I see as discordant in the sketch is the inadequacy of the spectacle in relation to the ambition of the spectator. In my view, the thunderstorm and the rainbow represent feeble efforts by the narrator to restore his sense of power.
3 For a recent example of this kind of reading, in an otherwise excellent treatment of the sketch, see Dryden.
4 The old man, Nina Baym suggests, is someone who so "lacks inner life" that "there is nothing in the surface he presents that an author can use as an index of the person" (Baym, *Hawthorne's Career*, 104).
5 See the sketch entitled "Thoughts about People."
6 In his review of "Twice-Told Tales," Poe had singled out "Wakefield" for particular praise."

7. THE BLITHEDALE ROMANCE AND THE CULTURE OF MODERNITY

1 For an account of the vogue of panoramas in England and America in this period, see Altick, Zarobila, and Dondore.
2 This confusion is embedded in Clifford's use of the term *electricity*. Adherents of mesmerism believed that mesmeric electricity and physical electricity were related phenomena. For a discussion of the development of mesmerism and its career in the United States, see Tatar.
3 Among those who have faulted *The Blithedale Romance* for this reason are Elliot and Waggoner.

4 Among those who have seen the subjectivity of Coverdale as the central focus of the romance are Matthiessen, Male, Crews, Hedges, Baym, and Griffith. For a useful summary of the two traditions of reading *The Blithedale Romance*, see Griffith, 15.

5 Treating the *The Blithedale Romance* in light of its urban theme, Levy has also drawn attention to the way in which Coverdale is "damaged" by his exposure to his culture. In the best essay to date to deal with *The Blithedale Romance* as a "willfully present-minded book" (71), James McIntosh draws attention to the specifically modern quality of Coverdale's consciousness and experience. In McIntosh's words, Coverdale is "a key representative of the disintegration he reveals" (81). His fluid selfhood, and cosmopolitan tendency to avoid commitments makes him "the self-erasing center of a chaotic world" (81). Though McIntosh places less emphasis on the urban aspect of Coverdale's subjectivity, what he observes about Coverdale's modernity also relates to Levy's emphasis on the way in which Coverdale's consciousness represents an especially urban fragmentation.

6 By identifying Coverdale with the culturally displaced urbanite and the alienated artist, Levy and Bell lay the groundwork for what I am suggesting by seeing Coverdale as the archetypal cosmopolitan personality. I also agree with Poirier that Coverdale can be identified with the cosmopolitan spectatorial figures in James's novels (115). However, I do not agree with Poirier's assertion that in his representation of Coverdale, Hawthorne can be credited "with seeing in the dandy much that Baudelaire was to see in him" (121). This is an example, I think, of the confusion I discuss in note 3 of Chapter 1. Although Coverdale, like many flaneurs, shares some of the foppish qualities of the dandy, he corresponds to Baudelaire's description of the "perfect *flaneur*," "the passionate spectator," and not to his description of the dandy. According to Baudelaire, the dandy is historically related to the spectator, but his strategy of response to modernity is fundamentally different. The dandy, unlike Coverdale, affects an attitude of blasé indifference, and is not interested in seeing so much as being seen.

7 Bell considers how Coverdale is so transparently a voyeur that he is gradually excluded from everyone's confidence.

8 I agree with Baym's assertion (in "a Radical Reading") that, contrary to the way in which Coverdale had been spoken of, at least up to 1968, he is not coldly and indifferently curious. There is no intrinsic reason, it seems to me, why someone who aspires to spectatorial invisibility cannot be deeply emotionally involved in what he is watching and in fact wish for a more active role in it.

9 Crews has written that, in *The Blithedale Romance*, the city "comes to stand for the restrictions and also the comforts of conventional life" (159). I would expand this to suggest that the city also represents the possibilities for spectatorial freedom and license, which is more important to Coverdale than anything else. It is not merely the comforts of his bachelor chambers that he misses at Blithedale.

10 Hirsch also argues that Hawthorne has an ironic distance from Coverdale's

assumption about the sameness of people, as inferred from the architecture of their houses.

11 See *The American Notebooks*, 8:496–508.

12 As Minter points out (158), Coverdale always seems to arrive too late to observe the conversations and encounters that are most relevant to what he is trying to discover.

13 David Minter has offered the most thorough description of the structure of the romance as a series of questionable interpretations of veiled and confusing mysteries. In this way it is, Minter argues, a representation of the problem of the observing and interpreting consciousness, particularly in an American context, in which Hawthorne presents Coverdale as "an obvious surrogate for the American writer as failed poet," whose "failure points beyond itself . . . to Hawthorne's limited achievement" (159).

14 See, for example, the Blind Beggar passage in the seventh book of Wordsworth's *Prelude*.

15 Stoehr discusses the connections between mesmerism and utopian reform (139–46), a connection that, he suggests, would have been clear to Hawthorne's audience, even if it appears obscure to us.

16 See Crews's discussion of the analogies between "Westervelt's debased art and Coverdale's." See also Baym, *Hawthorne's Career*, and Stoehr.

17 Baym writes: "As a seamstress Priscilla represents the whole range of exploited female roles in society" (*Hawthorne's Career*, 196).

18 The Lefcowitzes have found, in the text of *Blithedale*, what they consider to be several suggestions that Priscilla may have been a prostitute who was to have been reformed by the Blithedale community.

19 For some reason – and, of course, particularly in the past – critics have taken Coverdale's account of the female characters in the book more at face value than they have taken his view of anything else. Other critics who feel, as I do, that Coverdale's view of the characters of the two women are represented within the narration to be different from the way in which Coverdale perceives them include Baym and Strychacz. In her article "Thwarted Nature: Nathaniel Hawthorne as Feminist," Baym offers (58–63) an excellent summary of the way in which Hawthorne's women characters have been read through various ideological prisms, which are, as she suggests, even more reductive than any of the opera glasses Coverdale uses to view his women.

20 In attributing this degree of strength and independence to Priscilla, I am in disagreement with what appears to be a dominant critical tradition (Porte is a notable exception) of viewing Priscilla as a sweet, subservient, fair-haired lady, or as someone, in Hoffman's words, "so concealed behind her veil that she has no character at all but only a presumptive innocence" (*Form and Fable*, 215). Although I am arguing here that Priscilla has more character than she is usually given credit for, I wish to make clear that this does not mean that I disagree with Baym's contention that "Priscilla is the woman in history, distorted by her social role and misrepresented by the ideals derived from her" (*Hawthorne's Career*, 196). The strength and independence I am calling attention to in Priscilla are not indications that she has transcended this con-

dition. Rather, it seems to me that Priscilla represents the intransigence of the misrepresented and the way in which their efforts to gain independence and power are distorted in a society that offers them no meaningful form of independence or power. Priscilla, it must be remembered, desires and achieves nothing more than guardianship over a broken Hollingsworth.

8. "IMMENSE PHANTOM CONCOURSE": WHITMAN AND THE URBAN CROWD

1 See Matthiessen, 543; Chaffin, 114; Freedman, 103; White, 2; and Weimer, 33.

2 For discussions of the similarity between Whitman's poetry and Impressionist painting, see Daiches and St. Armand.

3 For brief considerations of Whitman's familiarity with the English magazines, see G. W. Allen, 130–1 and Stovall, 143.

4 As Stovall (34) has suggested, these sketches are very reminiscent of those of Willis. Among the pieces Whitman wrote that could be classified within the tradition of the flaneur are "Our City," "Life in New York," "Life in a New York Market," "New York Boarding Houses," "An Hour in a Balcony," "Yesterday," "A Peep at the Israelites," "A Peep in at Hudson's Rooms," "Centre Market Festival," "Sentiment and a Saunter," and "Broadway Yesterday," in *Walt Whitman of the "New York Aurora"*; "The Little Sleighers: A Sketch of a Winter Morning on the Battery," "A City Fire," "Philosophy of Ferries," "A Walk about Town," and "Matters which Were Seen and Done in an Afternoon's Ramble," in *Uncollected Poetry and Prose*; "Saturday Night–'Items' Makes a Tour," in *I Sit and Look Out*; and several of the "Letters From a Travelling Bachelor," from the New York *Sunday Dispatch*, reprinted in Rubin.

5 The *Aurora* was one of the most expensive and exclusive newspapers of the time. It characterized itself as "the acknowledged journal of the beau monde, the Court Journal of our democratic aristocracy" (cited in the introduction of *Walt Whitman of the "New York Aurora," * 2). Perhaps in order to identify himself with his audience, Whitman describes, in a sketch, his extremely dandyish attire.

6 See, for example, such early journalistic pieces as "Morbid Appetite for Money" (*Uncollected Poetry and Prose* [*UPP*], 1:123–5), "The City of Dirt" (*The Gathering of the Forces*, 2:52–3), "Working Women" (*UPP*, 1:137), "Cutting Down Those Wages" (*The Gathering of the Forces*, 1:156), and "On Vice" (*UPP*, 2:5–8).

Thomas reads the contrasting passages from *Democratic Vistas* as an indication that Whitman, after the war, and after he had ceased to be resident in New York, had become disillusioned with it and could no longer summon the enthusiasm evident in the poetry he had written before the war. I do not agree with this because Whitman, in the articles cited here (as well as many others), appears to have been fully aware, before the war, of the shortcomings of New York life that he catalogs in the passage from *Democratic Vistas*. In of New York life that he catalogs in the passage from *Democratic Vistas*. In several postwar texts and utterances, most notably *Specimen Days*, Whitman expresses the same unqualified embrace of New York evident in his poems. I think that the difference is not due to change or disillusionment but to the fact that throughout his life, Whitman appears to have had several different "telescopes" with which he viewed the city and his "moral telescope" never showed him the same city as he saw with "spiritual" or "poetic" ones.

7 For an account of the relationship between Whitman's interest in phrenology and his conception of himself as a poet, see Kaplan, 146–53 and Stovall, 154–6. For an account of the panoramas and dioramas Whitman is likely to have seen, see Zarobila.

8 For an excellent recent treatment of Whitman's interest in photography, see Orvell.

9 This dynamic and vocabulary is also evident in some lines, virtually automatic writing, which Whitman composed in Pfaff's cellar in 1861 or 1862. Entitled "The Two Vaults," the unpublished poem is a remarkably condensed expression of the interaction with crowds represented in "Crossing Brooklyn Ferry" and in several later poems. Whitman writes:

> The thick crowds, well-dressed –
>   the continual crowds as if they
>   would never end,
> The curious appearance of the
>   faces – the glimpse just caught
>   of the eyes and expressions, as
>   they flit along,
> You phantoms! oft I pause,
>   yearning, to arrest some one of
>   you!
> Oft I doubt your reality – whether
>   you are real – I suspect all is but
>   a pageant. (661)

The formulaic quality of these lines suggests how completely Whitman's consciousness of crowds was determined by the paradigms they contain.

10 Aspiz, 143–5, suggests a resemblance between mesmerism and the way in which Whitman claims to contact the consciousness of others. Stovall, 154–6, draws attention to Whitman's indebtedness to Andrew Jackson Davis's *The Great Harmonia*, one of the most influential mesmeric treatises, for many of the ideas in "Crossing Brooklyn Ferry."

11 Beside a mention of Wordsworth in an article in his scrapbook of clippings, Whitman wrote: "Wordsworth lacks sympathy with men and women – that does not pervade him enough by a long shot"

(Stovall, 128). In another annotation cited by Price, he says much the same thing, asserting that "The egotism of Wordsworth colors all his writings" (554).

12 Matthiessen has commented on the resemblance between Whitman's prefaces to *Leaves of Grass* and Wordsworth's preface to the second edition of *Lyrical Ballads*. In a letter to Whitman, Thomas William Rolleston called Wordsworth "the true predecessor of the *Leaves of Grass*" and asserted that Edward Dowden shared this opinion (Whitman and Rolleston, ed. Frenz, 78). For the fullest discussion of Whitman's familiarity with Wordsworth, see Asselineau, "Whitman et Wordsworth." Asselineau considers that Whitman did not own a copy of Wordsworth's poetry and he may have only been familiar with a few poems in anthologies. He points out, however, that Whitman's heavy and involved annotation of clippings of articles about Wordsworth suggests that he was much more interested in Wordsworth than his professed personal disdain would suggest. Whitman, to judge from the date of most of these annotations, appears to have been particularly interested in Wordsworth around the time he began to conceive of himself as the poet the age and nation had been waiting for.

13 I do not agree with Coffman's assertion that "there is no question but that the last objects in the list are presented as alien and forbidding" (229). Hoople elaborates upon this, suggesting that the foundries of the final lines of the catalog in the third section are "representations of the city as hell" with "foundries belching fire into an inchoate darkness, the streets becoming chasms in some fiery vision of night" (47). The fact that such objects as foundries and dark city streets were perceived as forbidding by the Romantic antiurban orthodoxies of the 1850s (and the 1950s or late 1960s for that matter) is part of Whitman's point. In Whitman's descriptions of them, both in the third and the ninth sections, I do not see any sign that he is any less impressed by their beauty and power than anything else in his list.

14 I disagree here with Ziff, who associates the "questionings" with the "dark patches" (241). It seems to me that the latter refer to the imperfections of human existence, while the former refer to metaphysical speculations that are welcomed by the poet as the beginning of a process that leads to a conviction of unity.

15 Because they are syntactically confusing, these lines have been interpreted in a variety of ways. Often, "being" is understood to be a mysterious noun. I read it, however, as a participle referring to the "cities."

16 "Crossing Brooklyn Ferry" was first published in the second (1856) edition of *Leaves of Grass*. At that time, Whitman gave it the title of

"Sun-Down Poem," though he changed the title to "Crossing Brooklyn Ferry" in the 1860, and in all subsequent editions. Like most Whitman critics, I have used the 1860 (and final) version of the poem in this discussion, a version that differs only in minor ways (and in no ways that are significant for my argument) from the 1856 version. The "Calamus" poems were first published in 1860, and the best available evidence, according to Blodgett, suggests that Whitman began to write them a few months after the publication of the second edition in August 1856. Thirteen were written by the summer of 1857 and the remaining thirty-one were written between 1857 and 1860. The "Drum-Taps" poems were first published in the fourth edition of 1865.

17 Waskow (76) has also pointed out this neglect of Whitman's ideas about the ideal nature of Calamus love in the twentieth century, with James Miller being the chief exception to this pattern (201).

18 The "Calamus" poems are often read as a rejection of the possibilities of urban life. Edwin Miller sees in it an ideal of "a pastoral society, a new–old Eden, where a loosely knit fraternal organization replaces political institutions, and where the bonds between men are affectional, not mechanical" (150). Zweig asserts that, in the sequence, "Whitman renounces his promiscuous love affair with the present age and becomes absorbed in a private love" (301). Waskow agrees, suggesting that "the Calamus lover avoids the pageants, spectacles, and feasts of the 'city of orgies,' . . . retreats from 'shifting tableaus,' the 'coming and going,' into the sure, permanent love of comradeship" (79). Ziff suggests that "the 'Calamus' poems withdraw from the streets of cities into secret places in nature: 'paths untrodden / In the growth by margins of pond waters,' or 'back of a rock,' or 'solitary, in a wide flat space' " (242). As what follows will make clear, I disagree with these interpretations. In my view, only Hoople has given sufficient emphasis to the necessarily urban origins of "Calamus" love and to Whitman's apparent belief that "adhesiveness is supreme and that the city best promotes its fruition" (48).

19 Although this particular poem is in the "Children of Adam" series, it was originally a "Drum-Taps" poem. Dealing with a separation that leads to a conviction of an oceanic unity, and concerned with a kind of love that involves looking and then parting, it fits the pattern of the "Calamus" poems, as does the other anomalous poem in the "Children of Adam" series, "Once I Pass'd through a Populous City," which originally described an encounter with a male lover.

Works Cited

Adburgham, Alison. *Shopping in Style: London from the Restoration to Edwardian Elegance*. London: Thames and Hudson, 1979.

Addison, Joseph, and Richard Steele. *The Spectator*, ed. Donald Bond. Oxford: Oxford University Press, 1965.

Adorno, Theodor and Walter Benjamin, et al. *Aesthetics and Politics*, ed. Fredric Jameson. New York: Verso, 1988.

Allan, Mozelle. "Poe's Debt to Voltaire." *University of Texas Studies in English* 15 (1935): 63–75.

Allen, Gay Wilson. *The Solitary Singer: A Critical Biography of Walt Whitman*. New York: Macmillan, 1955.

Allen, Michael. *Poe and the British Magazine Tradition*. New York: Oxford University Press, 1968.

Altick, Richard D. *The Shows of London*. Cambridge: Harvard University Press, 1978.

Anderson, George K. *The Legend of the Wandering Jew*. Providence, R.I.: Brown University Press, 1965.

Anonymous. "Unpublished Passages in the Life of Vidocq, the French Minister of Police." *Burton's The Gentleman's Magazine*, September to December, 1838.

Arcturus. New York: December 1840–May 1842.

Ashton, Robert. *The City and the Court, 1603–1643*. Cambridge: Cambridge University Press, 1979.

Aspiz, Harold. *Whitman and the Body Beautiful*. Urbana: University of Illinois Press, 1980.

Asselineau, Roger. "Whitman et Wordsworth: Etude d'une influence indirecte." *Revue de Literature Comparée* 29 (1955): 505–12.

Auser, Cortland P. *Nathaniel Parker Willis*. New York: Twayne, 1969.

Baker, Ernest A. *The History of the English Novel*, vol. 3. New York: Barnes and Noble, 1966.

Baker, Thomas. *The Female Tatler by Mrs. Crackenthorpe*. London, 1709–10.

Bakhtin, Mikhail. *Rabelais and His World*, trans. Helene Iswolsky. Bloomington Indiana University Press, 1984.

Bandy, W. T. "Who Was Monsieur Dupin?" *PMLA* 79 (1964): 509–10.

Barth, Gunther. *City People: The Rise of Modern City Culture in Nineteenth-Century America*. New York: Oxford University Press, 1980.

Barthes, Roland. "La Bruyère." In *Critical Essays*, trans. Richard Howard. Evanston, Ill.: Northwestern University Press, 1972.

Camera Lucida: Reflections on Photography, trans. Richard Howard. New York: Hill and Wang, 1981.

Sade, Fourier, Loyola, trans. Richard Miller. New York: Hill and Wang, 1976.

Bateson, F. W. "Addison, Steele, and the Periodical Essay." In *The New History of Literature*, ed. Roger Lonsdale, 4:117–36. New York: Peter Bedrick Books, 1987.

Baudelaire, Charles. "New Notes on Edgar Poe." In *Baudelaire on Poe*, trans. and ed. Lois Hyslop and Francis E. Hyslop, Jr. State College, Penn.: Bald Eagle Press, 1952.

"The Painter of Modern Life." In *The Painter of Modern Life and Other Essays*, trans. and ed. Jonathan Mayne, London: Phaidon Publishers, 1964.

Paris Spleen, trans. Louise Varese. New York: New Directions, 1970.

Baym, Nina. "*The Blithedale Romance*: A Radical Reading." *Journal of English and Germanic Philology* 67 (1968): 545–69.

Novels, Readers and Reviewers: Responses to Fiction in Antebellum America. Ithaca, N.Y.: Cornell University Press, 1984.

The Shape of Hawthorne's Career. Ithaca, N.Y.: Cornell University Press, 1976.

"Thwarted Nature: Nathaniel Hawthorne as Feminist." In *American Novelists Revisited: Essays in Feminist Criticism*, 58–77. Boston: G. K. Hall and Co., 1982.

Beier, A. L., and Finlay, Roger, eds. *The Making of the Metropolis: London 1500–1700*. New York: Longman Group, 1986.

Belden, E. Porter. *New York: Past, Present, and Future*. New York: G. Putnam, 1849.

Bell, Millicent. *Hawthorne's View of the Artist*. Albany: State University of New York Press, 1962.

Bender, Thomas. *New York Intellect: A History of Intellectual Life in New York City from 1750 to the Beginnings of Our Own Time*. New York: Alfred A. Knopf, 1987.

Toward an Urban Vision: Ideas and Institutions in Nineteenth-Century America. Baltimore: Johns Hopkins University Press, 1975.

Benjamin, Walter. *Charles Baudelaire: Lyric Poet in the Era of High Capitalism*, trans. Harry Zohn. London: New Left Books, 1973.

One-Way Street and Other Writings, trans. Edmund Jephcott and Kingsley Shorter. London: Verso, 1985.

"Das Passagen-Werk," ed. Rolk Tiedemann. In *Gesammelte Schriften*, vol. 5. Frankfurt-am-Main: Suhrkamp Verlag, 1982.

Benton, Richard P. "Poe's 'Lionizing': A Quiz on Willis and Lady Blessington." *Studies in Short Fiction* 5 (1968): 239–44.

"The Works of N. P. Willis as a Catalyst of Poe's Criticism." *American Literature* 39 (1967): 315–24.

Bergmann, H. "Panoramas of New York: 1845–1860." *Prospects: An Annual of American Cultural Studies* no. 10, ed. Jack Salzman, 119–38. New York: Cambridge University Press, 1985.

Berman, Marshall. *All That Is Solid Melts into Air*. New York: Simon and Schuster, 1981.

Blake, William. *The Poetry and Prose*, ed. David Erdman. Garden City, N.Y.: Doubleday, 1970.

Blodgett, Harold, ed. *An 1855–56 Notebook toward the Second Edition of "Leaves of Grass."* Carbondale: University of Southern Illinois Press, 1959.

Bonaparte, Marie. *The Life and Works of Edgar Poe: A Psycho-Analytic Interpretation*. London: Imago, 1949.

Bond, Richmond P., ed. *Contemporaries of the Tatler and Spectator*. Los Angeles: The Augustan Reprint Society, William Andrews Clark Memorial Library of the University of California, 1954.

Studies in the Early English Periodical. Chapel Hill: University of North Carolina Press, 1957.

Boyce, Benjamin. *The Theophrastian Character in England to 1642*. Cambridge: Harvard University Press, 1964.

Bridenbaugh, Carl. *Cities in Revolt: Urban Life in America, 1743–1776*. New York: Alfred A. Knopf, 1965.

Briggs, Asa. *The Age of Great Cities*. London: Odham's Press, 1963.

Brown, Thomas. *Amusements Serious and Comical and Other Works*, ed. Arthur L. Hayward. New York: Dodd, Mead, and Company, 1927.

Bucke, R. M. *Notes and Fragments*. New York: G. P. Putnam's Sons, 1902.

Buck-Morss, Susan. "Benjamin's *Passagen-Werk*: Redeeming Mass Culture for the Revolution." *New German Critique* 29 (1983): 211–40.

"The *Flâneur*, the Sandwichman and the Whore: The Politics of Loitering." *New German Critique* 39 (1986): 99–141.

Butt, John, and Kathleen Tillotson. *Dickens at Work*. London: Methuen, 1963.

Byer, Robert H. "Mysteries of the City: A Reading of Poe's 'The Man of the Crowd.'" In *Ideology and Classic American Literature*, ed. Sacvan Bercovitch and Myra Jehlen, 221–46. New York: Cambridge University Press, 1986.

Cameron, Sharon. *The Corporeal Self: Allegories of the Body in Melville and Hawthorne*. Baltimore: Johns Hopkins University Press, 1981.

Campbell, Killis. "Poe's Reading." *University of Texas Studies in English* 5 (1925): 183–4.

Chaffin, J. Thomas, Jr. "Give Me Faces and Streets: Walt Whitman and the City." *Walt Whitman Review* 23 (1977): 109–20.

Child, Harold. "Caricature and the Literature of Sport." In *The Cambridge History of English Literature*, ed. A. W. Ward and A. R. Waller, 14:212–39. Cambridge: Cambridge University Press, 1950.

Clark, T. J. *The Painting of Modern Life: Paris in the Art of Manet and His Followers*. London: Thames and Hudson, 1985.

Coffman, Stanley K., Jr. "'Crossing Brooklyn Ferry': A Note on the Catalogue Technique in Whitman's Poetry." *Modern Philology* 51 (1954): 225–32.

Colman, George, and Bonnel Thornton. "The Connoisseur." In *The British Essayists*, vols. 18–19, ed. Robert Lynam. London: J. F. Dove, 1827.

Conan Doyle, Arthur. *The Complete Sherlock Holmes*. Garden City, N.Y.: Doubleday, 1930.

Conant, Martha. *The Oriental Tale in England*. New York: Columbia University Press, 1908.

Crews, Frederick C. "A New Reading of *The Blithedale Romance*." *American Literature* 29 (1957): 147–70.

Daiches, David. "Walt Whitman: Impressionist Prophet." In *Two Studies*. N. p.: Folcroft Library Editions, 1970.

Daughrity, Kenneth L. "Poe's 'Quiz on Willis.' " *American Literature* 5 (1933): 55–62.

Davidson, Edward H. *Poe: A Critical Study*. Cambridge: Harvard University Press, 1957.

Davis, Andrew Jackson. *The Great Harmonia*. Boston: Bela Marsh, 1867.

Davis, Dorothy. *A History of Shopping*. London: Routledge and Kegan Paul, 1966.

Debord, Guy. *Society of the Spectacle*. Detroit: Black and Red, 1970.

Defoe, Daniel. *A Tour Thro' London about the year 1725*, ed. Mayson M. Beeton and E. Beresford Chancellor. London: B. T. Batsford, 1929.

Dekker, Thomas. *English villanies six severall times prest to death, now the seventh time discovered*. London: A. Matthewes, 1632.

  Lanthorne and Candlelight or The Bell-Man's Second Nights-Walke. London: John Busby, 1609.

de Man, Paul. *Blindness and Insight: Essays in the Rhetoric of Contemporary Criticism*. Minneapolis: University of Minnesota Press, 1983.

Dickens, Charles. *The Letters of Charles Dickens*, ed. Madeleine House, Graham Storey, et al. Oxford: Oxford University Press, 1965–.

  The Letters of Charles Dickens, ed. Kathleen Tillotson. Oxford: Clarendon Press, 1977.

  The Sketches by Boz. In *The New Oxford Illustrated Dickens*. London: Oxford University Press, 1957–.

Dondore, Dorothy Anne. "Banvard's Panorama and the Flowering of New England." *New England Quarterly* 11 (1938): 817–26.

Dryden, Edgar A. *Nathaniel Hawthorne: The Poetics of Enchantment*. Ithaca, N.Y.: Cornell University Press, 1977.

Eagleton, Terry. *The Function of Criticism: From "The Spectator" to Post-Structuralism*. London: Verso, 1984.

  Walter Benjamin or towards a Revolutionary Criticism. London: New Left Books, 1981.

Earle, John. *Microcosmography or, A Piece of the World Discovered in Essays and Characters*, ed. L. L. Williams. Albany, N.Y.: Joel Munsell, 1867.

Egan, Pierce. *Life in London, or The Day and Night Scenes of Jerry Hawthorne, Esq. and His Elegant Friend Corinthian Tom in Their Rambles and Sprees through the Metropolis*. London: Chatto and Windus, 1900.

Elliot, Robert E. *"The Blithedale Romance."* In *Hawthorne Centenary Essays*, ed. Roy Harvey Pearce. Columbus: Ohio State University Press, 1964.

The English Lucian; or Weekly discoveries of the witty intrigue, comical passages and remarkable transactions in town and country. With reflections on the vices and vanities of the times, nos. 1–15. London: January 7, 1698–April 18, 1698.

Fanger, Donald. *Dostoievsky and Romantic Realism*. Chicago: University of Chicago Press, 1965.

Finlay, Roger. *Population and Metropolis: The Demography of London 1580–1650*. Cambridge: Cambridge University Press, 1981.

Finlay, Roger, and Beatrice Shearer. "Population Growth and Suburban Expansion." In *The Making of the Metropolis, London, 1500–1700*. New York: Longman Group, 1986.

Forster, John. *The Life of Charles Dickens*. Garden City, N.Y.: Doubleday, Doran, and Company, 1928.

Foster, George G. *Celio: or New York Above-Ground and Under-Ground*. New York: Robert M. DeWitt, 1850.

Fifteen Minutes around New York. New York: De Witt and Davenport, 1854.

New York by Gaslight with Here and There a Streak of Sunshine. New York: DeWitt and Davenport, 1850.

New York in Slices: By an Experienced Carver: Being the Original Slices Published in the "New York Tribune," Revised, Enlarged, and Corrected by the Author. New York: W. F. Burgess, 1849.

New York Naked. New York: no date.

Foucault, Michel. *Discipline and Punish*, trans. Alan Sheridan. New York: Pantheon, 1977.

Fourier, Charles. *Design for Utopia: Selected Writings of Charles Fourier*, trans. Julia Franklin. New York: Schocken Books, 1971.

Frank, Joseph. *The Beginnings of the English Newspaper: 1620–1660*. Cambridge: Harvard University Press, 1961.

Freedman, Florence B. "A Sociologist Views a Poet: Robert Ezra Park on Walt Whitman." *Walt Whitman Review* 16 (1970): 99–104.

Frisby, David. *Fragments of Modernity: Theories of Modernity in the Work of Simmel, Kracauer, and Benjamin*. Cambridge: MIT Press, 1986.

Gatta, John. "'Busy and Selfish London': The Urban Figure in Hawthorne's 'Wakefield.'" *ESQ* 23 (1977): 164–72.

Gay, John. "Trivia: Or, the Art of Walking the Streets of London." In *Poetry and Prose*, ed. Vinton A. Dearing, 1:134–80. Oxford: Oxford University Press, 1974.

Glaab, Charles N., and A. Theodore Brown. *A History of Urban America*. New York: Macmillan, 1967.

Godwin, William. *Caleb Williams*. London: Oxford University Press, 1970.

Graham, Walter. *English Literary Periodicals*. New York: Thomas Nelson and Sons, 1930.

"Some Predecessors of the *Tatler*." *Journal of English and Germanic Philology* 24 (1925): 548–54.

Granger, Bruce. "The Whim-Whamsical Bachelors in Salmagundi." *Costerus* 2 (1972): 63–69.

Granger, Bruce I., and Martha Hartzog. Introduction to Washington Irving, *Letters of Jonathan Oldstyle, Gent. and Salmagundi: Or the Whim-whams and Opinions of Launcelot Langstaff, Esq. and Others*, ed. Bruce I. Granger and Martha Hartzog. Boston: Twayne Publishers, 1977.

Grant, James. *The Great Metropolis*. 2 vols. New York. Saunders and Otley, 1837.

Green, Constance McLaughlin. *The Rise of Urban America*. New York: Harper and Row, 1965.

Greene, A. *A Glance At New York*. New York: Craighead and Allen, 1837.

Greene, Robert. *A Notable Discovery of Coosnage* and *The Second Part of Conny-Catching*. London: John Lane, Bodley Head Limited, 1923.

Griffith, Kelley. "Form in *The Blithedale Romance*." *American Literature* 40 (1968): 15–26.

Habermas, Jurgen. *The Philosophical Discourse of Modernity: Twelve Lectures*, trans. Frederick Lawrence. Cambridge: MIT Press, 1987.

Harrowitz, Nancy. "The Body of the Detective Model: Charles S. Peirce and Edgar Allan Poe." In *The Sign of the Three*, ed. Umberto Eco and Thomas Sebeok, 179–97. Bloomington: Indiana University Press, 1983.

Hawthorne, Julian. *Nathaniel Hawthorne and His Wife: A Biography*. 2 vols. Boston: J. R. Osgood, 1884.

Hawthorne, Nathaniel. *The Centenary Edition of the Works of Nathaniel Hawthorne*. Columbus: Ohio State University Press, 1962–.

Haywood, Eliza. *The Female Spectator*. London: T. Gardner, 1745.

Hedges, William L. "Hawthorne's *Blithedale*: The Function of the Narrator." *Nineteenth-Century Fiction* 14 (1960): 303–16.

Hirsh, John C. "The Politics of Blithedale: The Dilemma of the Self." *Studies in Romanticism* 11 (1972): 138–46.

Hoffman, Daniel. *Form and Fable in American Fiction*. New York: Oxford University Press, 1961.

  Poe Poe Poe Poe Poe. Garden City, N.Y: Doubleday, 1972.

Hohendahl, Peter. *The Institution of Criticism*. Ithaca, N.Y.: Cornell University Press, 1982.

Hoople, Robin. "Walt Whitman and the City of Friends." *American Transcendental Quarterly* 18 (1973): 43–51.

Hunt, Leigh. "A Human Being and a Crowd." In *The Seer, the Indicator, and The Companion*. London: Edward Moxon, 1840.

  The Seer, the Indicator, and the Companion. London: Edward Moxon, 1840.

Irving, Washington. *The Sketchbook of Geoffrey Crayon*. Boston: Ginn, 1901.

Irwin, John T. *American Hieroglyphics: The Symbol of the Egyptian Hieroglyphics in the American Renaissance*. New Haven: Yale University Press, 1980.

James, Henry. *Hawthorne*. New York: Harper and Brothers, 1879.

James, William. "On a Certain Blindness in Human Beings." In *Essays on Faith and Morals*. New York: Longmans, Green, 1943.

Janin, M. Jules. *The American in Paris, or Heath's Picturesque Annual for 1843*, trans. John Sanderson. London: Longman, Brown, Green, and Longmans, 1843.

Jefferson, Thomas. *The Writings of Thomas Jefferson*, ed. Merrill D. Peterson. New York: The Library of America, 1984.

Joyce, James. *Ulysses*. New York: Random House, 1961.

Judson, Edward Zane Carroll. *The Mysteries and Miseries of New York: A Story of Real Life by Ned Buntline [pseud.]*. Dublin: James M'Glasham, 1849.

Juvenal. *The Sixteen Satires*, trans. P. Green. Harmondsworth: Penguin, 1967.

Kaplan, Justin. *Walt Whitman: A Life*. New York: Simon and Schuster, 1980.

Kellner, Douglas. *Critical Theory, Marxism and Modernity*. Baltimore: Johns Hopkins University Press, 1989.

Kennedy, J. Gerald. "The Limits of Reason: Poe's Deluded Detectives." *American Literature* 47 (1975): 184–96.

Kesselring, Marion. *Hawthorne's Reading 1828–1850: A Transcription and Identification of Titles Recorded in the Charge-Books of the Salem Atheneum*. New York: New York Public Library, 1949.

Klancher, Jon P. *The Making of English Reading Audiences, 1790–1832*. Madison: University of Wisconsin Press, 1987.

Knox, Edward C. *Jean de La Bruyère*. New York: Twayne, 1973.

La Bruyère, Jean de. *The Characters*, trans. Henri van Laun. London: George Routledge, 1929.

Lalor, Gene. "Walt Whitman among the New York Literary Bohemians: 1859–1862." *Walt Whitman Review* 25 (1979): 131–45.

Lamb, Charles. *The Complete Works in Prose and Verse* ed. R.H. Shepherd. London: Chatto and Windus, 1875.

Lavater, Johann Caspar. *Essays on Physiognomy*, trans. Thomas Holcroft. London, 1804.

Law, Marie Hamilton. *The English Familiar Essay in the Early Nineteenth Century*. Philadelphia: University of Pennsylvania, 1934.

Lefcowitz, Allan, and Barbara Lefcowitz. "Some Rents in the Veil: New Light on Priscilla and Zenobia in *The Blithedale Romance*." *Nineteenth-Century Fiction* 21 (1966): 263–76.

Lefebvre, Henri. *Everyday Life in the Modern World*, trans. by Sacha Rabinovitch. New York: Harper and Row, 1971.

Lemay, J. A. Leo. "The Psychology of 'The Murders in the Rue Morgue.'" *American Literature* 54 (1982): 165–88.

Le Sage, Alain René. *The Devil Upon Two Sticks*, trans. Tobias Smollett. In *The Novelist's Magazine* 2 (1780).

Levine, Stuart. *Edgar Poe: Seer and Craftsman*. N. p. Everett Edwards, 1972.

Levy, Leo B. "*The Blithedale Romance*: Hawthorne's Voyage through Chaos." *Studies in Romanticism* 8 (1968): 1–15.

Lindner, Burkhardt. "The *Passagen-Werk*, the *Berliner Kindheit*, and the Archaeology of the Recent Past." *New German Critique* 39 (1986): 25–48.

Lippard, George. *The Quaker City, or The Monks of Monk Hall. A Romance of Philadelphia Life, Mystery, and Crime*. Philadelphia: Leary, Stuart, and Co., 1876.

Lowe, Donald. *A History of Bourgeois Perception*. Chicago: University of Chicago Press, 1982.

Lupton, Donald. *London and the Countrey Carbonadoed and Quartred into Severall Characters*. Edinburgh: Aungerville Society Reprints, Second Series, 1884.

M., R. *Micrologia, Characters, Or Essays, Of Persons, Trades, and Places, Offered to the City and Countrey*. London: 1629.

Machor, James L. *Pastoral Cities: Urban Ideals and the Symbolic Landscape of America*. Madison: University of Wisconsin Press, 1987.

"Pastoralism and the American Urban Ideal: Hawthorne, Whitman, and the Literary Pattern." *American Literature* 54 (1982): 329–53.

Male, Roy, R. *Hawthorne's Tragic Vision*. Austin: University of Texas Press, 1957.

Martin, Terence. *Nathaniel Hawthorne*. Boston: Twayne Publishers, 1983.

Marx, Leo. *The Machine in the Garden*. New York: Oxford University Press, 1964.

Mathews, Cornelius. *A Pen-and-Ink Panorama of New York City*. New York: John S. Taylor, 1853.

Matthiessen, F. O. *American Renaissance*. New York: Oxford University Press, 1972.

Mazurek, Ray. "Art, Ambiguity, and the Artist in Poe's 'The Man of the Crowd.'" *Poe Studies* 12 (1979): 25–8.

McIntosh, James. "The Instability of Belief in *The Blithedale Romance*." *Prospects* 9 (1984): 71–114.

McKendrick, Neil, John Brewer, and J. H. Plumb. *The Birth of a Consumer Society: The Commercialization of Eighteenth-Century England*. London: Europa Publications, 1982.

Messac, Roger. *Le detective novel et l'influence de la pensée scientifique*. Paris: Honoré Champion, 1929.

Miller, Edwin H. *Walt Whitman's Poetry: A Psychological Journey*. New York: New York University Press, 1968.

Miller, J. Hillis. "The Fiction of Realism: *Sketches by Boz, Oliver Twist*, and Cruikshank's Illustrations." In *Charles Dickens and George Cruikshank*, 1–69. Los Angeles: William Andrews Clark Memorial Library, University of California, 1971.

Miller, James E. *A Critical Guide to "Leaves of Grass."* Chicago: University of Chicago Press, 1957.

Miller, Michael B. *The Bon Marche: Bourgeois Culture and the Department Store*. Princeton: Princeton University Press, 1981.

Miller, Perry. *The Raven and the Whale: The War of Words and Wits in the Era of Poe and Melville*. New York: Harcourt, Brace, and Company, 1956.

Minter, David. *The Interpreted Design as a Structural Principle in American Prose*. New Haven: Yale University Press, 1969.

Mott, Frank Luther. *A History of American Magazines*, vol. 1. New York: D. Appleton, 1930.

Murray, John Fisher. *The World of London*. 2 vols. London: William Blackwood and Sons, 1843.

Nelson, C., and M. Seccombe. *Periodical Publications 1641–1700: A Survey with Illustrations*. London: Bibliographical Society, 1986.

A New View of London; or an Ample Account of That City. London, 1708.

Nicklaus, Robert. *The Eighteenth Century, 1715–1789*. In *A Literary History of France*, ed. P. E. Charvet. London: Ernest Benn, 1970.

Orvell, Miles. "Reproducing Walt Whitman: The Camera, the Omnibus, and *Leaves of Grass*." *Prospects: An Annual of American Cultural Studies* 12 (1987): 321–46.

Overbury, Thomas. *The Miscellaneous Works in Prose and Verse of Thomas Overbury*, ed. Edward F. Rimbault. London: John Russell Smith, 1856.

The Oxford English Dictionary. New York: Oxford University Press, 1971.

Park, Robert. "Human Migration and the Marginal Man." In *Classic Essays in the Culture of Cities*, ed. Richard Sennett. 131–42. Englewood Cliffs, N.J.: Prentice-Hall, 1969.

Perluck, Herbert. "The Artist as Crafty Nincompoop: Hawthorne's 'Indescribable Obliquity of Gait' in 'Wakefield.'" *Nathaniel Hawthorne Journal* (1978): 181–94.

Poe, Edgar Allan. *Collected Works of Edgar Allan Poe*, ed. Thomas Ollive Mabbot. Cambridge: Harvard University Press, 1978.

   The Complete Works of Edgar Allan Poe, ed. James A. Harrison. New York: AMS Press, 1979.

   Doings of Gotham, ed. Thomas Ollive Mabbot. Pottsville, Penn.: Jacob E. Spannuth, 1929.

   English Notes by Quarles Quickens. Boston: Daily Mail Office, 1842.

   Essays and Reviews, ed. G. R. Thompson. New York: Library of America, 1984.

   The Letters of Edgar Allan Poe, ed. John Ward Ostrom. Cambridge: Harvard University Press, 1948.

Poirier, Richard. *A World Elsewhere: The Place of Style in American Literature*. New York: Oxford University Press, 1966.

Pollin, Burton R. "Poe's 'Murders in the Rue Morgue': The Ingenious Web Unravelled." In *Studies in the American Renaissance*, ed. Joel Myerson, 235–59. Boston: Twayne, 1978.

Porte, Joel. *The Romance in America: Studies in Cooper, Poe, Hawthorne, Melville, and James*. Middletown, Conn.: Wesleyan University Press, 1969.

Quinn, Arthur Hobson. *Edgar Allan Poe: A Critical Biography*. New York: Cooper Square, 1969.

Quinn, Patrick F. *The French Face of Edgar Poe*. Carbondale: Southern Illinois University Press, 1957.

Rasmussen, Steen Eiler. *London: The Unique City*. London: Jonathan Cape, 1948.

Restif de la Bretonne, Nicolas-Edmé. *Les nuits de Paris; or The Nocturnal Spectator: A Selection*, trans. Linda Asher and Ellen Fertig. New York: Random House, 1964.

Reynolds, David S. *Beneath the American Renaissance: The Subversive Imagination in the Age of Emerson and Melville*. New York: Alfred A. Knopf, 1988.

Reynolds, G. W. M. *The Mysteries of London*. 4 vols. London: George Vickers, 1846.

Richards, Jeffrey H. "Hawthorne's Posturing Observer: The Case of 'Sights from a Steeple.'" *ATQ* 59 (1986): 35–41.

Rolleston, James L. "The Politics of Quotation: Walter Benjamin's Arcades Project." *PMLA* 104 (1986): 13–27.

Ross, Joel H. *What I Saw in New-York; or a Bird's Eye View of City Life*. Auburn, N.Y.: Derby and Miller, 1851.

Routh, H. V. "London and the Development of Popular Literature, Character Writing, Satire, and the Essay." In *The Cambridge History of English Literature*, ed. A. W. Ward and A. R. Waller, 16:316–51. Cambridge: Cambridge University Press, 1950.

Rowlands, S. *Greenes ghost haunting conie-catchers*. London: F. Williams, 1626.

Rubin, Joseph Jay. *The Historic Whitman*. University Park: Pennsylvania State University Press, 1973.

St. Armand, Barton Levi. "Transcendence through Technique: Whitman's 'Crossing Brooklyn Ferry' and Impressionist Painting." *Bucknell Review* 24 (1978): 56–74.

Saisselin, Remy G. *The Bourgeois and the Bibelot*. New Brunswick, N.J.: Rutgers University Press, 1984.

Sander, August. *Men without Masks: Faces of Germany, 1910–1938*. New York: New York Graphic Society, 1973.

Schwarzbach, F. O. *Dickens and the City*. London: Athlone Press, 1979.

Seigel, Jerrold. *Bohemian Paris: Culture, Politics, and the Boundaries of Bourgeois Life, 1830–1930*. New York: Viking Penguin, 1987.

Sennett, Richard. *The Fall of Public Man: On the Social Psychology of Capitalism*. New York: Random House, 1976.

Shelley, Percy Bysshe. *Poetical Works*, ed. Thomas Hutchinson. Oxford: Oxford University Press, 1970.

Siegal, Adrienne. *The Image of the American City in Popular Literature, 1820–1870*. Port Washington, N.Y.: Kennikat Press, 1981.

Simmel, Georg. "The Metropolis and Mental Life." trans. H. H. Gerth and C. Wright Mills. In *The Sociology of Georg Simmel*, ed. Kurt Wolff, 409–24. Glencoe, Ill.: Free Press, 1950.

"The Stranger." In *The Sociology of Georg Simmel*, ed. Kurt Wolff, 402–8. Glencoe, Ill.: Free Press, 1950.

Smith, Henry Nash. *Virgin Land: The American West as Symbol and Myth*. Cambridge: Harvard University Press, 1970.

Sontag, Susan. *On Photography*. New York: Farrar, Straus, and Giroux, 1977.

Spann, Edward K. *The New Metropolis: New York City, 1840–1857*. New York: Columbia University Press, 1981.

Stallybrass, Peter, and Allon White. *The Politics and Poetics of Transgression*. Ithaca, N.Y.: Cornell University Press, 1986.

Stauffer, Donald Barlow. "Poe as Phrenologist: The Example of Monsieur Dupin." In *Papers on Poe*, ed. Richard P. Veler, 113–25. Springfield, Ohio: Chantry Music Press, 1972.

Steele, Richard, et al. *The Tatler,* ed. George A. Aitken. London: Duckworth, 1898–9.

Still, Bayard. *Mirror for Gotham.* New York: New York University Press, 1956.

Stoehr, Taylor. *Hawthorne's Mad Scientists.* Hamden, Conn.: Archon Books, 1978.

Stout, Janis P. *Sodoms in Eden: The City in American Fiction before 1860.* Westport, Conn.: Greenwood Press, 1976.

Stovall, Floyd. *The Foreground of "Leaves of Grass."* Charlottesville: University Press of Virginia, 1974.

Stow, John. *Survey of London.* London: J. M. Dent and Sons, 1965.

Strychacz, Thomas F. "Coverdale and Women: Feverish Fantasies in *The Blithedale Romance.*" *American Transcendental Quarterly* 62 (1986): 29–46.

Sue, Eugene. *The Mysteries of Paris.* New York: Century Company, 1903.

Symons, Julian. *Mortal Consequences: A History from the Detective Story to the Crime Novel.* New York: Harper and Row, 1972.

Tatar, Maria. *Spellbound: Studies on Mesmerism and Literature.* Princeton: Princeton University Press, 1978.

Theophrastus. *The Characters,* ed. and trans. J. M. Edmonds. New York: G. P. Putnam's Sons, 1929.

Thomas, M. Wynn. "Walt Whitman and Mannahatta – New York." *American Quarterly* 34 (1982): 362–78.

Thompson, G. R. *Poe's Fiction: Romantic Irony in the Gothic Tales.* Madison: University of Wisconsin Press, 1973.

Tobias, J. J. *Crime and Industrial Society in the Nineteenth Century.* New York: Schocken Books, 1968.

Troyer, Howard William. *Ned Ward of Grub Street: A Study of Sub-Literary London in the Eighteenth Century.* Cambridge: Harvard University Press, 1946.

Wade, Richard C. *The Urban Frontier: The Rise of Western Cities, 1790–1830.* Cambridge: Harvard University Press, 1959.

Waggoner, Hyatt. *Hawthorne: A Critical Study.* Cambridge: Harvard University Press, 1955.

Walsh, John. *Poe the Detective: The Curious Circumstances behind "The Mystery of Marie Roget."* New Brunswick, N.J.: Rutgers University Press, 1968.

Ward, Edward. *The London Spy,* ed. Kenneth Fenwick. London: Folio Society, 1955.

The London Spy Compleat, in Eighteen Parts. London: Casanova Society, 1924.

Warner, Sam Bass, Jr. *The Urban Wilderness: A History of the American City.* New York: Harper and Row, 1972.

Waskow, Howard. *Walt Whitman: Explorations in Form.* Chicago: University of Chicago Press, 1966.

Watson, Melvin R. *Magazine Serials and the Essay Tradition, 1746–1820.* Baton Rouge: Louisiana State University Press, 1956.

Webster's New World Dictionary of the American Language – Second College Edition, ed. David B. Guralnik. New York: Simon and Schuster, 1980.

Webster's Third New International Dictionary of the English Language, ed. Philip Babcock Gove. Springfield, Mass.: G. and C. Merriam, 1981.

Weimer, David. *The City as Metaphor*. New York: Random House, 1966.

White, Morton and Lucia. *The Intellectual versus the City*. Cambridge: Harvard University Press, 1962.

Whitman, Walt. *The Collected Writings of Walt Whitman*, ed. Gay Wilson Allen and Scully Bradley. New York: New York University Press, 1963–.

The Gathering of the Forces, ed. Cleveland Rodgers and John Black. 2 vols. New York: G. P. Putnam's Sons, 1920.

I Sit and Look Out: Editorials from the Brooklyn Daily Times by Walt Whitman, ed. Emory Holloway and Vernolian Schwarz. New York: Columbia University Press, 1932.

Leaves of Grass, "Comprehensive Reader's Edition," ed. Harold W. Blodgett and Sculley Bradley. In *The Collected Writings of Walt Whitman,* ed. Gay Wilson Allan and Scully Bradley. New York: New York University Press, 1965.

Prose Works, 2 vols., ed. Floyd Stovall. In *The Collected Writings of Walt Whitman*, ed. Gay Wilson Allan and Scully Bradley. New York: New York University Press, 1964.

The Uncollected Poetry and Prose of Walt Whitman, ed. Emory Holloway. 2 vols. New York: Peter Smith, 1932.

Walt Whitman of the "New York Aurora," ed. Joseph Jay Rubin and Charles H. Brown. State College, Penn.: Bald Eagle Press, 1950.

Whitman, Walt, and Thomas Rolleston. *Whitman and Rolleston: A Correspondence*, ed. Horst Frenz. Humanities Series, no. 26. Bloomington: Indiana University Publications, 1951.

Willis, Nathaniel Parker. *The Prose Works*. Philadelphia: Henry C. Baird, 1852.

The Rag Bag: A Collection of Ephemera. New York: Charles Scribner, 1855.

Wolin, Richard. *Walter Benjamin: An Aesthetic of Redemption*. New York: Columbia University Press, 1982.

Wordsworth, William. *The Poetical Works of William Wordsworth*, ed. E. de Selincourt and Helen Darbishire, vol. 4. Oxford: Oxford University Press.

The Prelude or Growth of a Poet's Mind, ed. E. de Selincourt, rev. Helen Darbishire. Oxford: Oxford University Press, 1959.

The Prose Works of William Wordsworth, ed. W. J. B. Owen and Jane Worthington Smyser. Oxford: Oxford University Press, 1974.

The World. In *The British Essayists*, ed. Robert Lynam, vols. 16 and 17. London: J. F. Dove, 1827.

Yarrow, P. J. *The Seventeenth Century*. In *A Literary History of France*, ed. P. E. Charvet. London: Ernest Benn, 1967.

Zarobila, Charles. "Walt Whitman and the Panorama." *Walt Whitman Review* 25 (1979): 51–9.

Ziff, Larzer. *Literary Democracy*. New York: Viking Press, 1981.

Zweig, Paul. *Walt Whitman's Poetry*. New York: Basic Books, 1984.

Index

Addison, Joseph, 26, 86, 128, 204 n14,
204–5 n18, 205 n22, 211 n2
  contribution to development of the flaneur, 31–40
  Dickens's familiarity with, 46, 206 n7
  Hawthorne's familiarity with, 107
  moralism of, 32–3, 40, 43
  Poe's familiarity with, 79, 211 n2
  popularity in America, 66
  see also England, historical development
  of the flaneur in; journalism; Steele,
  Richard
Adburgham, Alison, 15, 202 n4
Adorno, T. W., 7, 199 n4, 200 n6, 201
  n16
aestheticism, 8
Allen, Gay Wilson, 163, 216 n3
Allen, Michael, 211 n3
Altick, Richard, 51, 53, 206–7 n11, 213 n1
  (ch7)
Anderson, George K., 212 n9
arcades, 8, 12, 13, 15, 68, 74, 138–9, 186
  predecessors of, 15–16, 28–30, 35–6, 75,
  202 n3, 202 n4
  see also Burlington Arcade, consumer
  society, department stores, Royal
  Exchange
Ashton, Robert, 202 n1
Aspiz, Harold, 217 n10
Asselineau, Roger, 218 n12

badaud, the, 84–5
Bakhtin, Mikhail, 29–31
Balzac, Honoré de, 42, 155, 187, 190
Bandy, W. T., 94, 212 n18
Barker, Robert, 206–7 n11, 207 n12

Barnum's (P. T.) American Museum,
  75–6, 160
Barth, Gunther, 209 n3
Barthes, Roland, 26, 117–18, 167–70, 177,
  204 n12
Baudelaire, Charles, 30, 35, 73, 87, 116,
  166, 187, 190
  conception of the flaneur, 5–6, 10, 186,
  198–9 n3
  conception of modernity, 2, 4–6, 186
  on Poe, 93, 200 n10, 211–12 n8, 214 n6
Baudelaire, Charles: works
  "The Painter of Modern Life," 3–6, 45,
  198–9 n3
  Paris Spleen, 35
Baym, Nina, 108, 148, 213 n4, 214 n4,
  214 n8, 215 n16, 215 n17, 215 n19,
  215 n20
Beier, A. L., 15, 202 n1, 202 n2
Belden, E. Porter, 74–5
Bell, Millicent, 121, 214 n6, 214 n7
Bellow, Saul, 192
Bender, Thomas, 65, 209 n3
Benjamin, Walter
  conception of the flaneur, 6–9, 10, 12–
  13, 14, 24, 31, 33, 39, 40, 43, 186,
  198–9 n3, 201 n16
  conception of modernity, 2, 7–9, 12–13,
  14, 37, 186–7, 200 n9
  on the detective story, 79, 90
  on experience of the urban crowd, 44,
  63, 84, 208 n15
  on Poe's "The Man of the Crowd," 79,
  200 n10, 211–12 n8
Benjamin, Walter: works
  "The Flaneur," 45, 79, 199 n4